Instructional Practices for Students with Behavioral Disorders

WHAT WORKS FOR SPECIAL-NEEDS LEARNERS

Karen R. Harris and Steve Graham
Editors

Strategy Instruction for Students with Learning Disabilities
Robert Reid and Torri Ortiz Lienemann

Teaching Mathematics to Middle School Students
with Learning Difficulties
Marjorie Montague and Asha K. Jitendra, Editors

Teaching Word Recognition:
Effective Strategies for Students with Learning Difficulties
Rollanda E. O'Connor

Teaching Reading Comprehension to Students with Learning Difficulties
Janette K. Klingner, Sharon Vaughn, and Alison Boardman

Promoting Self-Determination in Students
with Developmental Disabilities
*Michael L. Wehmeyer with Martin Agran, Carolyn Hughes, James E. Martin,
Dennis E. Mithaug, and Susan B. Palmer*

Instructional Practices for Students with Behavioral Disorders:
Strategies for Reading, Writing, and Math
J. Ron Nelson, Gregory J. Benner, and Paul Mooney

Instructional Practices for Students with Behavioral Disorders

Strategies for Reading, Writing, and Math

J. Ron Nelson
Gregory J. Benner
Paul Mooney

Series Editors' Note by Steve Graham and Karen R. Harris

THE GUILFORD PRESS
New York   London

© 2008 The Guilford Press
A Division of Guilford Publications, Inc.
72 Spring Street, New York, NY 10012
www.guilford.com

Printed in the United States of America

This book is printed on acid-free paper.

Last digit is print number: 9 8 7 6 5 4 3 2 1

Library of Congress Cataloging-in-Publication Data

Nelson, J. Ron.
   Instructional practices for students with behavioral disorders : strategies
for reading, writing, and math / J. Ron Nelson, Gregory J. Benner, Paul
Mooney.
       p. cm. — (What works for special-needs learners)
   Includes bibliographical references and index.
   ISBN 978-1-59385-672-4 (pbk.: alk. paper)
   ISBN 978-1-59385-673-1 (hardcover: alk. paper)
   1. Problem children—Education—United States.   2. Mentally ill
children—Education—United States.   3. Emotional problems of children—United
States.   4. Behavior disorders in children—United States.   I. Benner, Gregory
J.   II. Mooney, Paul.   III. Title.
   LC4802.N45 2008
   371.94—dc22
                                                                                      2007049598

About the Authors

J. Ron Nelson, PhD, is Associate Professor and Co-Director of the Center for At-Risk Children's Services at the University of Nebraska–Lincoln. Dr. Nelson has over 20 years' experience in the field of special education as a teacher, technical assistance provider, and professor. He has a national reputation as an effective researcher and received the 2000 Distinguished Initial Career Research Award from the Council for Exceptional Children. Dr. Nelson's research career includes over 18 million dollars in external funding and the publication of more than 100 articles, book chapters, and books that focus on research issues and on serving children at risk of school failure. He has developed a number of behavior and literacy interventions that have been recognized by the U.S. Department of Education.

Gregory J. Benner, PhD, is Associate Professor in the Education Program at the University of Washington–Tacoma. Dr. Benner specializes in preventive and systematic approaches to building the academic skills of students, particularly those with emotional and behavioral disorders (EBD). As a secondary special education teacher, he was awarded the Apple Excellence in Education Award for improving the academic outcomes of students with EBD. As Reading Assessment Coordinator at the University of Nebraska Center for At-Risk Children's Services, Dr. Benner implemented effective systems for improving the responsiveness of students with EBD to scientifically based instruction. In 2002, he was awarded the Wesley Becker Award for Outstanding Research from the Association for Direct Instruction. Dr. Benner has worked on over 90 presentations and publications that reflect his ability to disseminate research findings and best practices to the field.

Paul Mooney, PhD, is Assistant Professor in the Special Education Programs at Louisiana State University. Dr. Mooney's teaching and research interests are presently directed at assessment- and intervention-related issues for children and youth at risk for or verified with academic and behavioral disabilities. Recent publications have been aimed at increasing the relationship between general outcomes assessment and progress monitoring to reading intervention at the elementary and secondary school levels. With his special education colleagues, Dr. Mooney has also devoted time to increasing both the number and quality of special education practitioners. Prior to completing his doctoral study at the University of Nebraska, Dr. Mooney worked as a school psychologist and newspaper reporter.

Series Editors' Note

Recently, a friend sent us a list obtained from the Internet titled "Why English Teachers Have Higher Stress Levels: Examples of Creative High School Writing." All told, there were 28 examples of students' writing. Below is a selective sample of a few of these:

> "It hurt the way your tongue hurts after you accidentally staple it to the wall."
> "It was an American tradition, like fathers chasing kids around with a power tool."
> "The hailstones leaped from the pavement, just like maggots when you fry them in hot grease."

Fortunately, only a few of the writing examples were this twisted, but it did make us wonder about the mental health of the youngsters who wrote them! These writing samples also reminded us that students who experience emotional and behavioral difficulties often experience academic difficulties as well. This includes academic difficulties learning basic skills, such as reading, writing, and math. *Instructional Practices for Students with Behavioral Disorders* tackles this problem directly by providing teachers and other practitioners with validated instructional techniques for teaching academic skills to students with emotional and behavioral difficulties and disorders.

This book is part of the series "What Works for Special-Needs Learners," which addresses a significant need in the education of learners with special needs—students who are at risk, those with disabilities, and all children and adolescents who struggle with learning or behavior. Researchers in special education, educational psychology, curriculum and instruction, and other fields have made great progress in understanding what works for struggling learners, yet the practical application of this research base remains limited. This is due in part to the lack of appropriate materials for teachers, teacher educators, and in-service teacher development programs. Books in this series present assessment, instructional, and classroom management methods with a strong research base and provide specific "how-to" instructions and examples of the use of proven procedures in schools.

Instructional Practices for Students with Behavioral Disorders presents instructional techniques and activities that are scientifically validated. The volume begins by examining the characteristics of students with emotional and behavioral difficulties; moves on to an exploration of fundamental instructional principles for assessing and teaching academic skills to these youngsters; presents specific validated practices for teaching reading, writing, and math; and ends with specific recommendations on how to manage the instructional environment so that learning is maximized. The evidence-based practices included in this book provide teachers with the tools they need to make sure students with emotional and behavioral difficulties and disorders learn basic academic skills. An invaluable resource for practitioners, this book is also suitable for use in special and regular education methods courses.

STEVE GRAHAM
KAREN R. HARRIS

Preface

Our schools have been challenged to respond to societal pressure and recent legislation promoting fundamental changes in the approach schools use to ensure that all students achieve positive academic and social outcomes. The No Child Left Behind (NCLB) Act of 2001 and the Individuals with Disabilities Education Act (IDEA) of 2004 require that all students, including those with behavioral disorders (BD), achieve established learning outcomes. This book is intended to guide educators and others in helping students with BD meet established learning outcomes; it is designed to serve as a text for undergraduate, graduate, and in-service courses for teachers, support personnel, and administrators interested in improving the academic achievement of students with BD. Because of its focus on scientifically based early instruction practices for these students, the book can also serve as a supplemental text for a methods course on BD.

APPROACH

Our approach in this book is based on seven core principles. The first principle centers on the belief that students with BD *can* learn. This principle requires educators to shift their thinking from the student as the problem to the instructional programs and procedures provided to them. We believe that all students, including those with BD, will experience success once the correct set of instructional programs and procedures have been identified and resources are used to deliver them in a manner that is directly proportional to their needs.

The use of scientifically based instructional programs and procedures, which is the focal point of the second principle, is especially important in the case of students with BD because they experience the worst social, academic, and vocational outcomes relative to all other disability groups. Scientifically based instructional programs and procedures are based on research that applies rigorous, systematic, and objective methods to obtain valid knowledge applicable to instructional and academic performance. This approach creates instructional programs and procedures that have a high probability of success. The use of scientifically based instructional programs and procedures allows schools to use time and resources efficiently as well as protect students from ineffective practices.

The third principle focuses on the need for universal screening of students. Screening all students on a regular basis (typically three times per year) provides an objective measure of an individual student's performance and progress compared to that of his or her peer group. Educators use the screening data to identify students early who have, or are at risk of, academic deficits. The screening data can also be used to determine group patterns in specific academic skills (e.g., identifying letter names). The instruction provided to students can then be adjusted to address these core patterns. The detection of academic deficits should occur *early* in students' education experience. It is this notion that undergirds our emphasis on early reading, mathematics, and written language skills.

The use of multitiered models of service delivery, in which each tier represents an increasingly intensive level of services associated with increasing levels of learner needs, is the focal point of the fourth principle. The response-to-intervention (RTI) model described in this book reflects a three-tiered design. All multitiered systems, regardless of the number of levels, are designed to yield the same practical effects and outcomes. Multitiered models reflect the fact that the instructional needs of students vary. Thus, the nature (e.g., skills, intensity) of the instruction changes at each tier, becoming more strategic and intensive as students move through the tiers. In a three-tiered model all students receive instruction in the core curriculum (Tier 1), supported by strategic and intensive interventions at Tiers 2 and 3 when needed. Thus, all students, including those with BD, are found in Tiers 1, 2, and 3. Important features, such as universal screening, progress monitoring, and fidelity of implementation and problem solving, occur within each tier. Here we focus on instructional programs and procedures for Tiers 2 and 3.

The fifth principle centers on data-based decisions using a problem-solving approach. Decisions within RTI models are made by teams using individual and/ or standard protocol problem-solving approaches. The individualized model results in instruction or interventions specially designed for the student (sometimes referred to as a "big" problem-solving model). Alternately, the standard protocol model involves using standardized instruction and interventions that have proven effective for students with similar difficulties (e.g., problems with fluency) (sometimes referred to as a "little" problem-solving model). The overall purpose of problem solving is to identify the best instructional approach for a student with a problem (e.g., academic, social). Individual and standard protocol problem-solving approaches provide a structure for using data to monitor student learning so that good decisions, with a high probability of success, can be made at each tier. When using problem-solving approaches, teams answer five interrelated questions:

1. Is there a discrepancy between current and expected performance?
2. Why is there a discrepancy between current and expected performance?
3. How much growth is required for students to meet the expected academic and social outcomes?
4. What changes in instruction and interventions will be implemented to ensure that students meet the performance benchmark goals?
5. Are the changes made in instruction and interventions working?

Individual and standard protocol problem-solving approaches ensure that decisions about a student's needs are driven by his or her responses to scientifically based interventions.

The sixth principle centers on monitoring student progress frequently. Problem-solving teams must establish and implement progress monitoring procedures. Progress monitoring involves assessments that can be collected frequently and are sensitive to small changes in student performance. Data collected through progress monitoring are used to inform the team's decision making regarding whether changes in the instructional program or procedures are necessary. Fortunately, a full range of reliable and valid curriculum-based measurements are available for monitoring student progress frequently.

The final principle centers on the importance of ensuring that students with BD achieve fluent performance in early reading, mathematics, and written language skills. Fluent performance is operationalized to include efficient visual processing, working memory, long-term memory, and executive functioning—which are all required to produce correct responses to early or rudimentary reading, mathematical, and written language tasks. Fluent performance involves high levels of accuracy (mastery) and speed. Fluency in early skills also is termed *overlearning* or *automaticity*. Basic early reading, mathematics, and writing skills are critical to high-order academic tasks (e.g., reading comprehension) and are best taught using a mastery-to-fluency instructional model. Thus, we focus on mastery (i.e., designed to teach students to perform early skills accurately/correctly) and fluency (i.e., designed to produce speedy/automatic performance) instructional programs and procedures in early reading, mathematics, and writing skills.

CONTENT AND ORGANIZATION

Chapter 1 introduces you to those background characteristics of students with BD that influence their academic achievement. The chapter describes the most common types of externalizing and internalizing BD as well as the problems associated with the underidentification of girls and overidentification of African Americans with BD to receive special education services under IDEA. The chapter also high-lights the fact that students with BD are likely to have statistically and education-ally significant academic achievement difficulties in all areas and that these diffi-culties are often compounded by significant language deficits. Additionally, we detail the risk factors for students with BD, indicating that they often are living in less than therapeutic environments.

Chapter 2 covers the three-tiered RTI model that provides the framework with which to situate the skills and concepts as well as instructional procedures detailed in the book. This chapter also discusses the principles of mastery and fluency in-struction. These principles provide the foundation for the early reading, writing, and math instructional procedures described in Chapters 5, 6, and 7, respectively. Furthermore, Chapter 3 highlights the progress monitoring procedures used to evaluate the effectiveness of the instructional procedures.

Chapter 4 provides information on commercially available Direct Instruction programs, which are well-designed instructional programs that have been proven to be effective with students with BD. These programs are used in a standard pro-tocol RTI problem-solving approach. We not only point out the design and presen-tation features of these programs, but also provide a general description of the cor-responding instructional goals, level of intervention (Tier 1, 2, or 3), number of lessons, teacher materials, and student materials. Additionally, we provide the pri-mary level of intervention and age level for each program.

Chapters 5, 6, and 7 present information on early reading, mathematics, and written language mastery and fluency instruction procedures, respectively. The corresponding skills, concepts, and instructional procedures are used in an indi-vidual protocol RTI problem-solving approach. Each chapter highlights the respec-tive intervention research conducted to date with students with BD and associated theoretical frameworks for supplemental instruction. Examples of instructional procedures used to teach students the skills and concepts described in each chapter are then presented.

The final chapter (Chapter 8) introduces fundamental instructional manage-ment concepts, including the placement of students during group instruction, teacher awareness skills, self-control skills, and interpersonal interaction skills. The bulk of the chapter describes self-management procedures and the Teacher–Student Learning Game, each of which can be used across all instructional situa-tions (e.g., large and small group, independent seatwork).

Each chapter follows a consistent format that includes a brief introduction to the concepts and practices, followed by a detailed presentation of the concepts and practices. Headings are used to clearly mark each of the primary concepts and practices being described. A summary designed to review the main points con-cludes each chapter.

ACKNOWLEDGMENTS

This book is the result of the collaborative efforts of our colleagues, friends, and families, and is an outgrowth from our research and direct experiences with students with BD. We thank all of the scholars from whom we have learned over the years. We want to acknowledge Kathleen Lane, Joseph Wehby, Hill Walker, Michael Epstein, Michael Nelson, George Sugai, Rob Horner, Phil Gunter, Ken Denny, and James Kaufmann (and others) for their work in the field of emotional and behavioral disorders, by which we have been inspired and from which we have drawn. We especially want to thank series editors Karen R. Harris and Steve Graham for their guidance; this book would not have been possible without their efforts and skills. We also thank all of the educators over the years who have provided us with insights into the need for the instructional programs and procedures described in this book. Finally, we dedicate this book to all students with BD who require specialized instructional programs and procedures to become successful in school.

Contents

Instructional Practices for Students with Behavioral Disorders

Behavioral, Demographic, and Functional Characteristics of Students with Behavioral Disorders

Within the general population, it is estimated that 6–9 million children and adolescents suffer from behavioral disorders (BD), an approximation representing 9–13% of all youths living in the United States (U.S. Department of Health and Human Services, 1999). Students with BD are categorized as having an emotional disturbance under the Individuals with Disabilities Education Act (IDEA; U.S. Department of Education, 2004), and during the past 10 years, there has been a 20% increase in the number of children identified (U.S. Department of Education, 2002). Public schools provide special education and related services to nearly half a million students labeled with emotional disturbance (U.S. Department of Education, 2002).

The No Child Left Behind Act (NCLB) of 2001 (U.S. Department of Education, Office of the Under Secretary, 2002) and the Individuals with Disabilities Education Improvement Act (2004) require that all students, including those receiving special education services for BD, have access to the general education curriculum, participate in state and district assessment programs, and meet the rising achievement standard for adequate yearly progress. These provisions have heightened educators' concerns regarding the academic outcomes of all students, including those with BD. Meeting these provisions is particularly challenging in the case of students with BD because they are likely to have significant academic difficulties that are challenging to remediate (Nelson, Benner, Lane, & Smith, 2004). The purpose of this chapter is to provide background information on the behavioral, demographic, and functional (including cognitive, language, and academic skills) characteristics that influence the academic achievement of students with BD.

BEHAVIORAL CHARACTERISTICS

Eligibility Criteria

BD and associated disorders, such as emotional disturbance and emotional and behavioral disorders, resist easy and precise definition. BD is an umbrella term for a group of disorders involving social and emotional dysfunctions that limit students' social, academic, and vocational success. As previously noted, students with such disorders are categorized as having an emotional disturbance under IDEA. The U.S. Department of Education defines emotional disturbance as at least one social or emotional characteristic exhibited over an extended period of time that adversely affects school performance, including: (1) problems with learning or interpersonal relationships; (2) inappropriate behavior under normal circumstances; (3) disorders of affect, such as depression or pervasive unhappiness; or (4) fears or physical symptoms in response to school or personal problems. The specific eligibility criteria for services under IDEA (U.S. Department of Education, 2004) include:

(i) The term [emotional disturbance] means a condition exhibiting one or more of the following characteristics over a long period of time and to a marked degree that adversely affects a child's educational performance:
  (A) An inability to learn that cannot be explained by intellectual, sensory, or health factors.
  (B) An inability to build or maintain satisfactory interpersonal relationships with peers and teachers.
  (C) Inappropriate types of behavior or feelings under normal circumstances.
  (D) A general pervasive mood of unhappiness or depression.
  (E) A tendency to develop physical symptoms or fears associated with personal or school problems.
(ii) The term includes schizophrenia. The term does not apply to children who are socially maladjusted, unless it is determined they have an emotional disturbance.

As with all disability categories, states define emotional disturbance and specify the eligibility criteria to be used by local school districts in the identification of students with BD. Although the eligibility criteria must be consistent with the federal definition, many states have adopted their own terminology and eligibility criteria (Swartz, Mosley, & Koenig-Jerz, 1987). For example, some states have dropped the socially maladjusted exclusion criterion. This criterion was dropped for two reasons: (1) There are no valid theoretical or empirical grounds for differentiating between social maladjustment and other BD; and (2) there are no reliable or socially validated instruments for making a distinction between social maladjustment and emotional disturbance (Stein & Merrell, 1992).

Differences in terminology and eligibility criteria across states and school staff interpretation of the criteria have resulted in great variation in rates countrywide. For example, Minnesota and Vermont have the highest rate of identification (1.92% of the states' school populations), whereas Arkansas has the lowest rate (.10%).

Additionally, although most students with emotional disturbance exhibit problems at an early age (Knitzer, 1996), students with this disability, like those with learning disabilities, are usually identified and provided with special education services only *after* they have experienced failure (U.S. Department of Education, 2002).

Other federal agencies that serve students with BD use different eligibility criteria than IDEA. The eligibility criteria of the Center for Mental Health Services require the presence of a diagnosable mental, behavioral, or emotional disorder of sufficient duration to meet diagnostic criteria specified within the *Diagnostic and Statistical Manual of Mental Disorders—Text Revision* (DSM-TR; American Psychological Association, 2000). Further, the mental, behavioral, or emotional disorder must result in a functional impairment that substantially interferes with or limits the child's role or functioning in family, school, or community activities. The Social Security Administration's eligibility criteria for the Supplemental Security Income program for children require the presence of a mental condition that can be proven medically (Social Security Administration, 2006). In addition, the mental condition must result in marked, severe functional limitations of substantial duration. Given the differences in criteria, eligibility for services under the Center for Mental Health Services and Social Security Administration does not necessarily mean that children are eligible for services under IDEA.

Types of BD

Most forms of BD can be categorized under one of two broad bipolar dimensions: externalizing or internalizing (Achenbach, 2001). Each of these dimensions includes specific syndromes (e.g., oppositional defiant disorder as an externalizing condition). *Externalizing* refers to all BD that are directed outwardly by the student toward the social environment. Externalizing BD involve behavioral excesses considered inappropriate by parents, teachers, other professionals, and peers. These behavioral manifestations often result in difficulties with social, academic, and vocational functioning. Examples of externalizing behavioral problems include (Walker & Severson, 1990):

- Aggressive behavior toward objects or persons
- Arguing
- Forcing the submission of others
- Defying the teacher
- Being out of the seat
- Not complying with teacher instructions or directives
- Having tantrums
- Being hyperactive
- Disturbing others
- Stealing
- Refusing to follow teacher- or school-imposed rules

The most common externalizing syndromes include conduct disorder, oppositional defiant disorder, attention-deficit/hyperactivity disorder (ADHD), and adjustment disorder (American Psychiatric Association, 2000). The characteristics for each of these syndromes are presented in Table 1.1. Additionally, high comorbidity rates are reported for externalizing syndromes (McConaughy & Skiba, 1994).

Internalizing BD involve problems with self that are directed inwardly—that is, away from the external social environment. Internalizing BD are often self-imposed and frequently involve behavioral deficits and patterns of social avoidance. As with externalizing behavior, these behavioral manifestations often result in difficulties with social, academic, and vocational functioning. Examples of internalizing behavioral problems include (Walker & Severson, 1990):

- Low or restricted activity levels
- Not talking with other children
- Shyness
- Timidity or unassertiveness
- Avoidance or withdrawal from social situations
- Preference to play or spend time alone
- Fearful behavior
- Avoidance of games and activities
- Unresponsiveness to social initiations by others
- Not standing up for oneself

TABLE 1.1. Characteristics for Externalizing Syndromes

Syndrome	Qualifying characteristics
Conduct disorder	• A repetitive and persistent pattern of behavior in which the rights of others or age-appropriate societal norms or rules are violated. Youths with conduct disorder tend to show aggression toward people or animals, destroy property, steal, lie, and break rules.
Oppositional defiant disorder	• Ongoing patterns of uncooperative, defiant, and hostile behavior directed toward authority figures. Youths with oppositional defiant disorder tend to be argumentative with adults, often lose their temper, appear angry, are prone to spite and vindictiveness, and are easily annoyed by others.
Attention-deficit/ hyperactivity disorder (ADHD)	• Poor impulse control, overactivity, and distractibility. Youths with ADHD tend to be inattentive, hyperactive, and impulsive.
Adjustment disorder	• Clinically significant emotional or behavioral responses to identifiable stressors (e.g., move, death, natural disaster). Youths with adjustment disorder tend to break rules, violate the rights of others, fight, and be truant from school.

The most common internalizing syndromes include obsessive–compulsive disorder, generalized anxiety disorder, social anxiety, separation anxiety disorder, posttraumatic stress disorder, and child/adolescent depression (American Psychiatric Association, 2000). The characteristics for each of these syndromes are presented in Table 1.2. Additionally, high comorbidity rates are reported for internalizing syndromes (McConaughy & Skiba, 1994).

TABLE 1.2. Characteristics for Internalizing Syndromes

Syndrome	Qualifying characteristics
Obsessive–compulsive disorder	• Intrusive, recurrent, and time-consuming behavior (e.g., hand washing, counting, repeating words silently) that leads to elevated levels of distress. Youths with obsessive–compulsive disorder tend to show the behavior in private to avoid being ridiculed by their peers and adults.
Generalized anxiety disorder	• Unrealistic, excessive, and persistent worries about general performance in school social activities. Youths with generalized anxiety disorder tend to engage in approval-seeking behaviors, perfectionism, intolerance for substandard performance, and constantly seek reassurance on their performance. Additionally, they frequently complain of headaches, have difficulty sleeping and concentration problems, and are restless.
Social anxiety disorder	• Unrealistic, excessive, and persistent worries about peer evaluations of performance in school and social activities. Youths with social anxiety disorder tend to avoid situations in which they perceive that their peers are evaluating their performance.
Separation anxiety disorder	• Extremely unrealistic and developmentally inappropriate worries when separated from significant attachment figures (usually the mother). Youths with separation anxiety disorder tend to avoid any situation that takes them away from familiar surroundings, cling to attachment figures, cry uncontrollably when separated from loved ones, fear being abandoned or not reunited with attachment figures, and experience distress over the possibility that some catastrophe will befall loved ones. Additionally, they frequently have difficulty sleeping and complain of physical symptoms.
Posttraumatic stress disorder	• Intrusive recollections, flashbacks, thoughts, and dreams of a traumatic life event (e.g., physical abuse). Youths with posttraumatic stress disorder tend to avoid situations associated with the traumatic event; demonstrate extreme fear, helplessness, anger, melancholy, horror, and denial; and become hypervigilant, lose interest in preferred activities, show irritability, have difficulty in concentrating, act much younger than their chronological age, are easily startled, and have difficulty falling asleep.
Child/adolescent depression	• Clinically significant dysphoria or low spirits, despondency, melancholy, mournfulness, sadness, or generalized unhappiness. Youths with child/adolescent depression tend to be irritable, tired, moody, negative, hostile, angry, and aggressive. Additionally, they often have difficulty sleeping, low energy, appetite disturbances, attention problems, and memory lapses.

DEMOGRAPHIC CHARACTERISTICS

Boys are more likely to have BD than girls. In a national study, more than three-fourths of students with BD receiving special education services were male (Wagner, Kutash, Duchnowski, Epstein, & Sumi, 2005). This represented the highest proportion of males to females in any of the disability categories. Lower identification rates for females have been attributed to two factors. First, the assessment and identification process is largely subjective and influenced by schools' behavioral norms and standards (Wehby, Symons, & Hollo, 1997). Teachers may simply be less willing to refer girls for special education services for BD than they are boys because of the increased stigma of labeling a girl with BD. The stigma arises because the BD labeling of a girl deviates more dramatically from cultural norms for behavior than in the case of boys. Second, girls are more likely than boys to exhibit internalizing BD, which typically does not interfere directly with classroom management. Teachers are much more likely to identify students who exhibit externalizing BD than those with internalizing syndromes (Gresham, MacMillan, & Bocian, 1996).

Whereas females are underrepresented among students receiving special education services for BD, African Americans are overrepresented. Higher identification rates for African American students have been attributed to two factors. First, there may be a mismatch between the normative behavior of African American students and teacher expectations regarding such behavior (Horowitz, Bility, Plichta, Leaf, & Haynes, 1998). This mismatch may result in higher referrals for special education services. Second, the overidentification of African American students may be due to the limited availability of culturally sensitive assessment instruments (Harry, 1994). Current behavioral rating scales used to identify students with BD do not account for cultural differences in normative behavior.

Additionally, students with BD are more likely than the general population to have demographic characteristics related to poor school outcomes. For example, people in the lowest income strata are three times more likely to have a mental disorder than those in the highest income strata (U.S. Department of Health and Human Services, 1999). As such, it is not surprising that children and youths with BD receiving special education services are more likely to live in low socioeconomic homes than students in the general population and those with other disabilities (Lewit, Terman, & Behrman, 1997; Wagner et al., 2005). More than 32% of school-age students with BD live in poverty; among their general population peers, the figure is approximately 17%.

In addition to poverty, children and youths with BD are more likely to experience a host of other risk factors for poor social, academic, and vocational outcomes (Nelson, Stage, Duppong-Hurley, Synhorst, & Epstein, 2007). Risk factors are those variables or factors that, when present in a child, increase the likelihood that the child will subsequently evidence BD. A range of risk factors across life domains plays an important predictive role in the social, academic, and vocational outcomes of students with BD (Greenberg, Lengua, Cole, & Pinderhughes, 1999; Huffman,

Mehlinger, & Kerivan, 2000; McEvoy & Welker, 2000; Nelson et al., 2007). The major life domains and associated risk factors for BD include:

1. Prenatal—maternal medical problems, emotional psychological distress.
2. Natal—premature or unusual delivery.
3. Postnatal—medical problems (breathing problems, umbilical cord around neck, blue or yellow color), prolonged hospital stay.
4. Externalizing behavior pattern during early childhood—overactive, impulsive, stubborn, temper outbursts, aggressive, destructive (e.g., toys), fearless.
5. Internalizing behavior pattern during early childhood—shy or timid, fearful, preferred to be alone, socially withdrawn, cautious, difficulty sleeping.
6. Childhood maladjustment—psychiatric hospitalization, runaway, suicide attempt, substance abuse, physically abusive to others, abusive to animals.
7. Childhood maltreatment—sexually abused, physically abused.
8. Antisocial and psychiatric family history—domestic violence, mental illness, psychiatric hospitalization, substance abuse, substance abuse treatment, convicted of a crime.
9. Family structure—one-parent, no high school diploma—and socioeconomic status (i.e., reduced or free lunch).
10. Family functioning—parental distress, parent–child dysfunctional interaction, difficult child.
11. Maternal depression.

FUNCTIONAL CHARACTERISTICS

The functional characteristics of students with BD that play an important and predictive role in social, academic, and vocational outcomes include cognitive, language, and academic domains (Greenbaum et al., 1996). An overview of these characteristics follows.

Cognitive Domain

BD tend *not* to be associated with cognitive impairment (Kaufmann, 2006). Just more than 1% of children who receive special education services for emotional disturbance under IDEA are reported to have mental retardation as a secondary condition (Wagner et al., 2005). Further, approximately 3% of elementary and middle schools students with emotional disturbance participate in programs for the gifted and talented. Nelson and colleagues (Nelson, Benner, & Cheney, 2005) reported that the mean IQ of a randomly selected sample (n = 155) of K–12 students with BD receiving special education services under IDEA was 99.6 (SD = 14.8), which is consistent with the results from a national longitudinal study (Wagner et al., 2005). When asked about the cognitive functioning of their children, parents of children with emotional disturbance were more likely than those with other disabilities to rate the cognitive function of their child as high (63% vs. 47%). Similarly, parents of children with emotional disturbance were less likely to rate the cognitive functioning of their child as low relative to those of other disabilities (3% vs. 6%).

Language Domain

Youths with BD are likely to have language disorders that interfere with their academic achievement and ability to communicate (Nelson, Benner, & Cheney, 2005). Language disorders are of two main types: receptive and expressive. Receptive (i.e., listening) language disorders involve problems with understanding language. Expressive (i.e., speaking) language disorders involve problems with using language (Owens, 2001). In addition, pragmatic language disorders involve difficulties with the rules related to language use in social settings (e.g., speaker–listener relationship, turn taking, eye contact).

The concomitant prevalence of language disorders in children and youths with BD is 10 times that of the general population (Donahue, Cole, & Hartas, 1994; Warr-Leeper, Wright, & Mack, 1994). Psychopathological problems associated with language disorders tend to worsen over time (Baker & Cantwell, 1987). Additionally, language disorders have been associated with persistent depressed academic achievement, increased grade retention, demoralization, psychiatric problems, and greater rates of reading disabilities than exhibited by children with typical language skills (Beitchman et al., 2001; Toppelberg & Shapiro, 2000).

Children with pure language disorders, especially those that are comprehension related (i.e., receptive), are at substantially higher risk for externalizing BD than those with speech or speech and language disorders. For example, Cohen and colleagues (Cohen, Davine, Horodezsky, Lipsett, & Isaacson, 1993) found that children with receptive language disorders were rated as the most delinquent and depressed by parents, most aggressive by teachers, and demonstrated more severe BD, whereas children with expressive deficits were rated as more socially withdrawn and anxious. Additionally, children with pure language disorders, especially receptive disorders, are at substantially higher risk of reading difficulties (Catts, Fey, Xuyang, & Tomblin, 1999).

Language disorders appear to have a devastating effect on interpersonal relationships (e.g., those with family and peers) throughout the lifespan. Children who are aggressive, for example, use less verbal communication and more direct physical actions to solve interpersonal problems due to limited language skills (Gallagher, 1999). Children prone to noncompliance may have receptive language deficits that limit their ability to comprehend and comply to repeated warnings or verbal cues (Fujiki, Brinton, Morgan, & Hart, 1999). As a result, such children may misinterpret communications, become frustrated, and consequently develop chains of miscommunication and antisocial behavior patterns (Ruhl, Hughes, & Camarata, 1992).

Nelson, Benner, and Cheney (2005) assessed the contribution of externalizing and internalizing BD to the prediction of the language skills of a K–12 sample of students receiving special education services for BD under IDEA. They found that externalizing BD predicted the language skills, whereas the internalizing syndromes did not. These results suggest that students who exhibit externalizing BD are more likely to experience language disorders than students who evidence internalizing syndromes.

Academic Domain

Students with BD receiving special education services under IDEA have academic achievement problems (Coutinho, 1986; Epstein, Kinder, & Bursuck, 1989; Nelson et al., 2004; Scruggs & Mastropieri, 1986; Sullivan, 1927). Most of the studies regarding the academic achievement of students with BD have compared their performance with other populations (Anderson, Kutash, & Duchnowski, 2001; Scruggs & Mastropieri, 1986; Wagner et al., 2005). Students with BD consistently show moderate to severe academic achievement difficulties relative to normally achieving students (Greenbaum et al., 1996; Mattison, Spitznagel, & Felix, 1998; Meadows, Neel, Scott, & Parker, 1994; Wagner, 1995; Wagner et al., 2005). Wagner and colleagues (2005), for example, used data from the Special Education Elementary Longitudinal Study (SEELS) and the National Longitudinal Transition Study–2 (NLTS-2) first wave of the School Characteristics, Students' School Profile, and found that a sample of second-grade students with BD, receiving special education services under IDEA, performed one or more standard deviations below normally achieving peers in vocabulary, listening comprehension, spelling, social science, and science. Furthermore, students with BD have academic achievement problems in all content areas (i.e., reading, math, written language, science, and social studies: Brier, 1995; Gajar, 1979; Scruggs & Mastropieri, 1986; Wilson, Cone, Bradley, & Reese, 1986).

Comparative analyses of students with BD and those with learning disabilities (Epstein & Cullinan, 1983; Gajar, 1979; Scruggs & Mastropieri, 1986; Wagner, 1995; Wilson et al., 1986) and mental retardation (Gajar, 1979; Wagner, 1995; Wilson et al., 1986) have been conducted to identify the relative adverse effect of these disabilities on academic achievement. Students with BD were more likely to show academic achievement difficulties than students with learning disabilities (Gajar, 1979; Scruggs & Mastropieri, 1986) and those with mental retardation (Gajar, 1979).

Anderson and colleagues (2001) found that students with BD performed significantly better than those with learning disabilities on reading and mathematic measures in kindergarten and first grade, but not in fifth and sixth grades. Moreover, the reading achievement scores of students with BD did not improve over time, whereas the students with learning disabilities demonstrated statistically significant improvement in the 5 years from intake to follow-up. These findings suggest that BD may have a more adverse impact on academic achievement over time than do learning disabilities.

The prevalence of academic achievement difficulties among students with BD receiving special education services under IDEA also has been studied (Mattison, Hooper, & Glassberg, 2002; Mattison et al., 1998) and shown to range widely—from 25% to 97%. For example, Mattison and colleagues (2002) examined the outcomes of elementary and secondary students with BD; less than 60% of students with BD experienced academic achievement difficulties (i.e., reading, math, or written language). In contrast, Greenbaum and colleagues (1996) found that 97% of students, ages 12–14, performed below grade level in mathematics. Differences in the reported prevalence rates are most likely a function of differences in the sampling procedures, measures used, and criteria for determining academic achievement problems. In regard to the latter issue, a majority of researchers used grade-equivalent scores from grade-level, group-administered academic achievement tests as indices for determining academic achievement difficulties (Nelson et al., 2004). The ordinal nature of these scores makes it problematic to rely on them as indicators of absolute performance (Martella, Nelson, & Marchand-Martella, 1999). This issue is especially problematic in the case of grade-level, group-administered achievement tests.

The prevalence of academic achievement problems among students with BD also has been assessed over time (Greenbaum et al., 1996; Mattison et al., 2002). Greenbaum and colleagues (1996) sampled youths across six states and found that the percentage of students reading below grade level at intake (ages 8–11), 4 years later (ages 12–14), and 7 years after intake (ages 15–18) was 54%, 83%, and 85%, respectively. The percentage of children performing below grade level in math at intake, 4 years later, and 7 years after intake was 93%, 97%, and 94%, respectively. In a more current study, Mattison and colleagues (2002) reported that prevalence rates of academic achievement difficulties among students with BD were 64% at intake (mean age = 8.6) and 62% 3 years later (mean age = 11.5). The findings of these studies indicate the prevalence rates of academic achievement problems experienced by students with BD remain relatively stable or worsen over time.

There is growing interest in identifying the particular types of problem behavior exhibited by students with BD that are related to academic achievement (Barriga et al., 2002; Mattison et al., 1998; Nelson et al., 2004). For example, Mattison and colleagues (1998) used the *Diagnostic and Statistical Manual of Mental Disorders—Fourth Edition* (American Psychiatric Association, 1994) to examine the categories of problem behaviors related to the academic achievement of students with BD. Conduct and oppositional disorders were related to academic achievement of elementary- and secondary-age students with BD. Moreover, the presence of comorbid ADHD and disruptive behavior disorders appears to be more strongly related with academic achievement difficulties than other psychiatric disorders alone or in combination (Abikoff et al., 2002). Thus, consistent with language disorders, externalizing behavior appears to be related to academic achievement problems, whereas internalizing ones are not.

CONCLUSIONS

The following conclusions can be drawn from the diverse research conducted on the behavioral, demographic, and functional characteristics of students with BD.

First, there is a wide range of BD that can be grouped under the broad bipolar externalizing and internalizing dimensions. High comorbidity rates are reported between the internalizing and externalizing dimensions and among the specific syndromes that make up BD (McConaughy & Skiba, 1994). The subjective nature of the assessment and identification process as well as lack of access to appropriate evaluation tools has resulted in the underidentification of girls and overidentification of African Americans with BD receiving special education services under IDEA (Wehby et al., 1997).

Second, students with BD often are being raised in challenging, less than therapeutic environments. For example, more than 32% of school-age students with BD, receiving special education services under IDEA, live in poverty; among their general population peers, the figure is approximately 17%. People in the lowest income strata are three times more likely to have a mental disorder than those in the highest income strata (U.S. Department of Health and Human Services, 1999). These individuals also are more likely to experience academic achievement difficulties (National Academy of Sciences, 1998) and language disorders (Hart & Risley, 1995).

Third, it appears that BD of an externalizing nature is more likely to be related to academic achievement problems and language disorders than internalizing BD (e.g., Nelson et al., 2004; Nelson, Benner, & Cheney, 2005, respectively). The strength of the relationship between externalizing behavioral and academic achievement difficulties is relatively small, indicating that it may be mediated by other variables. Nelson and colleagues (Nelson, Benner, Neil, & Stage, 2006) used structural equation modeling to test the interrelationships among language skills, externalizing behavior, and academic fluency and their impact on the academic skills of students with BD. Results showed that language skills exerted a significant proximal effect *and* distal effect on academic skills. The effect of language skills was mediated through academic fluency, but also had a proximal effect on academic skills. However, externalizing behavior failed to have a statistically significant effect on language skills, academic fluency, or academic skills. These analyses indicate that the relationship among BD, academic achievement problems, and language disorders is complex and not well understood at this time.

Finally, it is clear why students with BD present one of the greatest challenges to teachers and schools: because they are likely to present both academic and behavioral deficits. Improving the social and academic outcomes of students with BD requires that teachers and schools use scientifically based behavioral and academic programs, interventions, and practices. Improving these outcomes also requires teachers and educators to focus on prevention of undesirable social and academic outcomes. Students with BD past the age of 8 are likely to have chronic social and academic difficulties (Kaufman, 2006). In this book we focus on scientifically based early reading, math, and written language instructional practices that teachers can use to ensure that students with BD achieve academic success.

CHAPTER 2

Response to Intervention and Fundamental Instructional Practices

Recent legislation is promoting fundamental changes in the approach schools use to ensure that all students achieve positive academic and social outcomes. As mentioned in the first chapter, NCLB of 2001 (U.S. Department of Education, Office of the Under Secretary, 2002) and of IDEA 2004 (U.S. Department of Education, 2004) require that all students, including those with BD, achieve established learning outcomes. The sweeping reforms of NCLB and IDEA are intended to refocus educators' efforts on proven, scientifically based instructional practices that help all students learn. Additionally, as of the 2005–2006 school year, NCLB requires: (1) annual testing of all public school students in reading and math for grades 3–12; (2) annual report cards on school performance for parents, voters, and taxpayers; (3) guarantees that every child reads by the third grade; and (4) the presence of a highly qualified teacher in every public school classroom.

Response to intervention (RTI) is referenced in NCLB and IDEA. RTI represents a systematic approach for evaluating student needs and fostering positive academic outcomes for all students, through the use of a continuum of carefully selected and implemented scientifically based instruction and interventions. A three-tiered RTI prevention model for providing students with instruction and interventions matched to their individual needs is embedded in the RTI approach. The focus on prevention in RTI is very important to the goal of improving the social and academic outcomes of students with BD because, as noted in Chapter 1, these students often experience periods of failure prior to receiving special education services. The purpose of this chapter is to provide background information in which to situate the instructional practices described in the remainder of this book. In this chapter we first provide a description of RTI for general and exceptional student populations; this overview includes a description of the three-tiered prevention model embedded in RTI. Next, we detail fundamental mastery and fluency instructional principles that underlie the assessment and instructional practices described in the remainder of this book. Finally, we summarize the chapter.

RESPONSE TO INTERVENTION

RTI is being used by schools as an alternative approach to the identification of learning disabilities and as a useful framework that guides instruction for all students (e.g., Batche et al., 2005; Gresham, 2003). We discuss the latter focus of RTI in this chapter.

RTI represents a significant change in how schools prevent, identify, and respond to academic and social difficulties because it turns attention from the students' academic and social difficulties toward evaluating the extent to which the instruction and interventions used by schools are matched to student needs (Gresham, 2003). The effect of this shift is to help educators focus on the type of instruction and number of interventions needed to ensure that all students achieve expected academic and social outcomes.

RTI includes five interrelated components (Batsche et al., 2005). The first component involves the high-quality implementation of scientifically based instructional practices matched to student need. Universal screening of all public school students comprises the second component. The third component features the use of a three-tiered prevention model for coordinating and integrating a continuum of scientifically based instruction and interventions. The fourth component consists of a problem-solving model to match student needs to the continuum of scientifically based instruction and interventions used within the three-tiered prevention model. The final component consists of frequent monitoring of student progress toward expected academic and social outcomes and the use of formal decision-making rules to make warranted changes in instruction and interventions.

Scientifically Based Research

NCLB defines scientifically based research (SBR) as research involving the application of rigorous, systematic, and objective procedures to obtain reliable and valid knowledge relevant to educational activities and programs. The defining characteristics of SBR have appeared across numerous sources since the enactment of NCLB (e.g., Coalition for Evidence-Based Policy, 2002; Comprehensive School Reform Program Office, 2002; National Research Council, 2002; Raudenbush, 2002). The four defining characteristics of SBR, identified across these sources, include:

1. *Empirical research.* Empirical research is based on, but not restricted to, measurement or observation experienced through the senses (National Research Council, 2002). Establishing scientifically based instruction and interventions requires empirical research based on such methods.

2. *Important research questions.* Important research questions build on, add to, fill a void in, or otherwise clarify what is known and practiced in schools (Comprehensive School Reform Program Office, 2002). The importance of a research question is determined by its relationship to prior research and theory and its relevance to policy and practice. SBR instruction and interventions are based on sound empirical and theoretical foundations and address important policy and practice issues facing schools nationwide, such as improving academic achievement for students whose education prospects are hindered by poverty, race, ethnicity, disability, or limited English proficiency.

3. *Appropriate methods.* Appropriate methods require the use of designs, procedures, and techniques that fit the nature of the question the study is attempting to answer (Raudenbush, 2002). Although no research design, method, or analytic technique, on its own, constitutes a program of research scientific, randomized experiments or quasi-experiments are the most appropriate methods for establishing scientifically based instruction and interventions (Coalition for Evidence-Based Policy, 2002; Raudenbush, 2002).

4. *Replicable and applicable results.* Consistent and meaningful findings indicate replicable and applicable results (National Research Council, 2002). The research is presented in sufficient detail to allow for replication and is conducted in such a manner as to ensure that educators can expect to see similar results when they apply the instruction and interventions.

Universal Screening

Schoolwide screening is an important component of RTI given the current focus on the performance of all students. Screening is conducted on a regular basis to determine whether students are performing as expected in response to schools' core curricula and the schoolwide positive behavioral support programs. Screening typically involves administering brief assessments to all students three times per year. Students' scores are compared to established performance standards or benchmarks. Students whose scores exceed the established performance benchmarks continue to receive general instruction in the core curriculum and schoolwide positive behavioral support program. Those students whose scores fall below the established performance standards are identified as being "at risk," and a change is made in the instruction and interventions they receive. Risk status varies depending upon the screening approach used and the benchmark standard set by schools (Jenkins & O'Connor, 2002)—which means that schools need to think carefully about the approach used and the benchmarks set.

Local or national norm groups are used to establish the performance benchmarks. Establishing local norms involves compiling all students' scores for a school or school district within a grade level or age group, grouping them by percentile ranks or quartiles, and then identifying students below an established level that represents an unacceptable level of risk (Shinn, 1989). National norm groups essentially use the same process to establish criterion benchmark scores that represent national samples of student performance. The Dynamic Indicators of Basic Early Literacy Skills (DIBELS) system includes empirically derived criterion benchmark scores in reading based on a national norm group (Good & Kaminski, 2002; a complete set of DIBELS benchmark levels is available at *dibels.uoregon.edu/benchmark.php*).

Although universal screening for basic reading, mathematics, and writing skills is relatively straightforward and efficient because there are well-established measures and benchmark standards for performance available to schools, this is not the case for social behavior. The *Systematic Screening for Behavior Disorders* (SSBD; Walker & Severson, 1992), one of the few available universal screening instruments for social behavior, involves three decision points consisting of four rating scales and classroom observations. Although the SSBD is psychometrically sound, it is lengthy and time consuming for teachers to complete, limiting its feasibility as a universal screener. Additionally, the SSBD is not designed to be administered several times per year. The lack of an efficient and valid universal screening approach represents a significant challenge to the implementation of an RTI approach in the area of social behavior.

Three-Tiered Prevention Model

Over the years schools have used instruction and interventions that involve many different levels of intensity—although not necessarily determined by SBR. Within RTI, these differing levels of scientifically based instruction and intervention are coordinated and integrated into a three-tiered prevention model at the primary (Tier 1), secondary (Tier 2), and tertiary (Tier 3) levels (Walker, Colvin, & Ramsey, 1995). This model is designed to help schools more directly link information about the school environment, instruction and interventions, administrative and management practices of the school, neighborhood and family characteristics, and characteristics of the student population to the development of a continuum of instruction and interventions that ensures that all students meet established academic and social outcomes. A three-tiered prevention model for facilitating student academic and social outcomes is depicted in Figure 2.1.

The three-tiered prevention model is based on the notion that in any school three types of students can be identified: (1) typical students not at risk for academic or social difficulties; (2) students at risk for developing academic or social difficulties; and (3) students who show significant academic and social difficulties (Walker et al., 1995). It has been estimated that 80–90% of students arrive at school with the prerequisite academic and social skills to be successful there (Sugai, Sprague, Horner, & Walker, 2000). Another 5–15% of students are at risk for developing academic and social difficulties and require supplementary instruction and interventions to prevent the development of chronic or intense academic and social

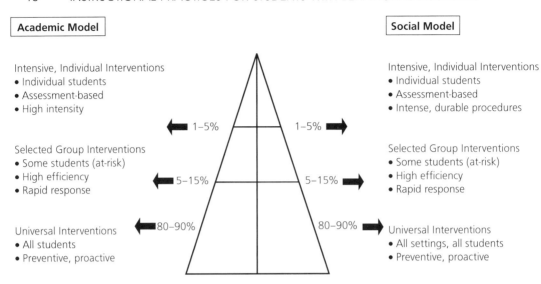

FIGURE 2.1. Three-tiered academic and social prevention models.

difficulties. Still another 1–5% of students experience severe academic and social difficulties and require intensive instruction and interventions. Members of each group are candidates for differing levels or types of instruction and interventions that represent greater specificity, comprehensiveness, expense, and intensity. Primary (Tier 1), secondary (Tier 2), and tertiary (Tier 3) levels of instruction and interventions are appropriate for each student group, respectively.

Primary (or Tier 1) instruction and interventions, provided to all students, consist of the core curriculum and schoolwide positive behavioral support program. Secondary (or Tier 2) instruction and interventions, which are relatively short-term and intensive, are provided to small groups of students in each classroom who do not respond to the primary instruction and interventions; these students are considered to be at risk for severe academic difficulties or BD if they do not receive supplemental instruction and interventions. This level of instruction and intervention is designed to supplement the core curriculum or schoolwide positive behavioral support program. Tertiary (or Tier 3) instruction and interventions, provided to students with severe academic difficulties or BD, are individualized, long-term and intensive, and may lead to special education services. This level of instruction and interventions can be designed to supplement the core curriculum or schoolwide positive behavioral support program, or it can be completely unique. Additionally, instruction and interventions at each tier are based on SBR.

Students are described as receiving Tier 1, 2, or 3 instruction and interventions. The three tiers are implemented in a flexible manner. A student may receive instruction and interventions within Tier 2 and then receive those in Tier 3 or Tier 1, depending upon progress. Or, a student could receive Tier 3 instruction and interventions immediately, based on his or her performance on the screening measure. Students' level of need dictates the tier of instruction and interventions provided to them. The length of time that instruction or interventions are provided to students at any given tier depends upon their responsiveness and realistic time periods required for the target skills to develop. Frequent monitoring of progress and data-based decision making are used to determine about how long and within which tier students will receive instruction and interventions. Additionally, it is likely that students at risk for, or with, academic difficulties or BD will receive instruction and interventions in more than one tier at any given time.

Problem-Solving Model

The well-established problem-solving model used by schools to develop pre-referral interventions for students as a part of the special education process provides the overarching framework for the implementation of RTI (Fuchs, Mock, Morgan, & Young, 2003). In RTI, however, the problem-solving model is conceptualized differently. The traditional prereferral problem-solving model tends to focus on teacher modifications of instruction and interventions and informal documentation of student outcomes before formal referral for special education services (Fuchs, Fuchs, Bahr, Fernstrom, & Stecker, 1990). In contrast, the RTI problem-solving model is conceptualized as having two major foci: (1) establishment of an educational environment conducive to student academic and social outcomes so problems do not occur in the first place; and (2) a problem-solving component, based on objective data, in which instruction and interventions matched to student needs are applied early in a student's educational experience to ensure that he or she meets expected academic and social outcomes.

Two types of RTI problem-solving models are used by schools: individualized and standard protocol. The individualized and standard protocol RTI problem-solving models include a series of steps in which objective data are used by educators to ensure that the instruction and interventions students receive are matched to individual need. In essence, the problem-solving steps reflect the scientific methods of defining and describing a problem and implementing, monitoring, and evaluating the effectiveness of a solution for the problem. As a general rule, the composition of the problem-solving team changes by adding additional specialists' expertise as students move from tier to tier. The interrelated problem-solving steps include the following:

1. *Problem identification.* The problem identification step focuses on addressing the question: "Is there a discrepancy between current and expected performance?" Systematic screening measures administered on a regular basis (typically three times per year) to all students are recommended to identify students who show a discrepancy between current and expected performance. The goal here is to derive a clear description of the problem or concern. The emphasis of this step is to break down a broad general concern, such as reading difficulties, into the specific behavior or skills related to the concern (e.g., phonemic awareness, decoding, fluency). The specific skills should be prioritized for intervention.

2. *Problem analysis.* The problem analysis step centers on addressing the question: "Why is there a discrepancy between current and expected performance?" Once the problem is defined, a hypothesis as to why the problem is occurring and continuing is identified. This step focuses on identifying the mismatch between the current instruction and interventions provided to students and those needed to ensure that he or she meets the expected academic and social outcomes. Attention is given to those variables that can be altered through instruction to create a potential solution. These variables include treatment fidelity (i.e., the degree to which the intervention is implemented as planned), missing skills, motivational factors, or lack of exposure to the general curriculum. The team should seek to identify explanations of the problem that can be addressed through instruction. In addition to the cause of the problem, the team needs to establish the student's rate of learning or baseline performance.

3. *Goal setting.* The goal-setting step focuses on addressing the question: "How much growth is required for the student to meet the expected academic and social outcomes?" Schools use local or national established benchmark performance standards to guide student goal setting. The established benchmark standards play a key role in evaluating whether students' rate of progress or growth is adequate. Students' beginning or current level of performance and the goal are used to establish a goal line. The goal line is used to gauge whether students are progressing at an adequate rate of growth necessary to meet the established benchmark. This estimation is accomplished by comparing student performance against the goal line. The slope, or trend, of this goal line displays the rate of progress throughout the year that students must exhibit in order to meet the expected goal (see instructional decision-making rules in the next section).

4. *Plan implementation.* The plan implementation step centers on addressing the question: "What changes in instruction and interventions will be done to ensure that students meet the benchmark performance goals?" An intervention approach is identified, including the relevant personnel who are responsible for carrying out the intervention and monitoring student progress. As noted above, schools can use either an individualized or a standard protocol problem-solving model. Regardless of the type of problem-solving model used, however, it is important to plan and monitor for high-quality implementation of the instruction and interventions.

5. *Plan evaluation.* The plan evaluation step focuses on addressing the question: "Are the changes made in instruction and interventions working?" Frequent monitoring of student progress is used to evaluate the effects of the changes in instruction and interventions. Student progress is typically monitored on a weekly or biweekly basis during the plan evaluation process. Systematic decision rules are used to evaluate the instruction and interventions (detailed in the next section). Student rate of progress, relative to the goal that was set, is analyzed. Additionally, in cases of failure, the evaluation should address treatment fidelity to determine whether an intervention, per se, failed or whether it was implemented incorrectly or inadequately.

Frequent Monitoring of Student Progress

Frequent monitoring of student academic or social progress is a critical component of RTI. Fortunately, well-established curriculum-based measurement (CBM) probes are available to assess students' mastery and fluency in basic reading, mathematics, and writing skills. These brief probes, which can be administered in 1–4 minutes, are used to screen all students to identify those in need of supplementary instruction and interventions and to provide an index of current performance levels and rates of growth over time. CBM has been found to be a reliable and valid indicator of basic reading, mathematics, and writing skills and is sensitive to changes in instruction and interventions. CBM also is useful for setting student benchmark goals and predicting future student performance (Deno, 2005).

The purpose of CBM is to document change in student performance over time to determine whether students are progressing appropriately in a particular instructional program. Teachers, then, must apply standard instructional decision-making rules to the graphed data (see Figure 2.2) to determine if and when an instructional change is warranted. The following instructional decision-making rules can be used by teachers to monitor student progress and make changes in instruction and interventions (when warranted):

1. Collect baseline performance (a minimum of 3 points) and set an end-of-year performance goal or benchmark. Connect baseline performance to the goal to show the goal line or students' anticipated rate of progress through the year in meeting the goal. The goal line provides an index with which to gauge the extent to which students' rate of progress is adequate to meet the established goal.

2. A dotted vertical line is drawn following the last baseline point to indicate the beginning of an instruction and interventions phase. Continue to monitor student performance on a frequent basis (one or two times per week). The scores are graphed to illustrate students' rate of growth relative to the goal line.

3. Four-point rule. After 3–6 weeks of implementing a change in instruction and interventions (at least 6 data points must be collected), examine the most recent 4 points. If all 4 points fall above the goal line, consider raising the goal. If the goal is changed, draw another dotted vertical line and reestablish a new goal line. If all 4 points fall below the goal line, draw a solid vertical line and implement a change in instruction and interventions.

4. Trend rule. In those cases in which the 4 points fall both above and below the goal line, keep collecting data. After collecting at least 8 data points, a trend line can be drawn that represents a line of best fit through the data. This trend line shows the relative rate of progress students are making during the most recent instructional phase. Compare the trend line to the goal line. If the trend line is steeper than the goal line, draw a dotted vertical line and raise the goal. If the trend line is less steep than the goal line, draw a solid vertical line and implement a change in instruction and interventions. It is important to note that the 4-point rule supersedes the trend rule.

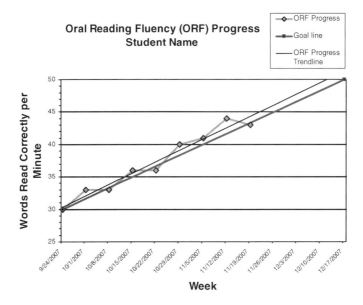

FIGURE 2.2. Curriculum-based measurement.

5. If either the 4-point rule or the trend rule indicates that students are not progressing at the anticipated rate, a change in instruction and interventions should be made. The teacher may be implementing instruction and interventions that are working well for other students but are not working well for a particular student. The teacher attempts to match the instruction and interventions to the needs of students who are not progressing as anticipated. The teacher may vary the type or content of instruction, instructional intensity in terms of opportunities to respond, the allocated time for instruction, the curriculum materials used, or the motivational strategies incorporated during instruction. After the teacher determines the nature of change in instruction and interventions, the new plan should be implemented for a minimum of 3 weeks prior to applying CBM decision-making rules to determine the success of the instruction and interventions.

6. Continue collecting CBM data on a frequent basis and apply these standard decision-making rules for each phase of instruction.

Well-established CBM-like probes are not available to monitor student social behavior. However, the same four measurement principles that underlie CBM probes can be applied for frequent monitoring of student social behavior. The first principle is that the problem must be defined in observable, discrete, and measurable terms. Second, the problem must be measured in terms of frequency, rate, duration, latency, or intensity. The third principle is that the measurement procedures must be sensitive to changes in instruction and interventions. The final principle is that the measurement procedures must produce reliable and valid results for describing the problem. A useful resource that can be used to guide teachers' implementation of these principles in the area of social behavior is *Conducting*

School-Based Assessments of Child and Adolescent Behavior (Shapiro & Kratochwill, 2000).

FUNDAMENTAL INSTRUCTIONAL PRINCIPLES

Basic reading, mathematics, and writing skills are best taught using a mastery-to-fluency instructional model. Mastery instruction involves the controlled presentation of unknown skills (low to moderate levels of accuracy) designed to teach students to master (apply accurately) basic reading, mathematics, and writing skills. Mastery instruction involves accuracy at 90% correct or above. Fluency instruction is the repeated presentation of known skills (high levels of accuracy) designed to produce fluent performance. Fluent performance involves high levels of accuracy and speed (i.e., at or near 100% accurate). Fluency in basic skills is also termed *overlearning* or *automaticity* (Meyer & Felton, 1999).

The admonition "Practice it until you get it correct, and then practice it four more times" characterizes well the mastery-to-fluency instructional model. Instruction initially emphasizes mastery of the basic skills being taught. Instruction then focuses on moving students beyond mastery or accuracy to building their fluency or speed with the skills they have mastered. The basic skills automatically "load" when students engage in high-order activities, such as reading a novel, solving an algebraic expression, or writing a story. Large amounts of cognitive resources are required by students when they are mastering basic skills, but only limited cognitive resources are needed by students once they become fluent with those skills (Logan, 1992). Differences in the cognitive resources (i.e., attention, cognitive load, effort, learning, memory retrieval, performance) used by students to master basic skills versus when they are fluent are noted in Table 2.1. Optimal learning occurs in students when instruction is carefully designed to help them master and then overlearn basic skills to the point that they can apply them fluently.

TABLE 2.1. Cognitive Resources Used to Master Basic Skills versus When Fluent

Cognitive resource	Master basic skills	Fluent with basic skills
Attention	• Highly focused on skills	• Little focus on or unaware of skills
Cognitive load	• Moderate to heavy	• Light
Effort	• Effortful and laborious at performing single skills	• Effortless at performing simultaneous skills
Learning	• Easy to adapt with instruction	• Difficult to adapt with instruction
Memory retrieval	• Inefficient and inaccurate	• Highly efficient and accurate
Performance	• Low to moderate accuracy and speed	• High accuracy and speed

Mastery Instruction

Two elements comprise mastery instruction—skills and procedures. The first element centers on the basic skills to be mastered by the student. The probability of a student mastering a set of basic reading, mathematics, and writing skills is increased if teachers use a well-defined scope and sequence that moves from simple to more complex. Such a method ensures that students experience both immediate and sustained success within and across lessons. In essence, determining a scope and sequence is much like a task analysis in which the teacher breaks down a complex skill into a logical sequence of subskills and strategies. A high-quality scope and sequence analysis will help students progress from skill acquisition to skill mastery in a natural and linear fashion. An example of a scope and sequence analysis for systematically teaching phonemic awareness skills across time is depicted in Figure 2.3. Students are initially introduced to the general structure of oral language through rhyming, sentence segmentation, syllable segmentation and blending, and onset–rime segmentation and blending instruction prior to developing an awareness of the smallest units of oral language (phonemes).

The second element of mastery instruction focuses on three interrelated procedures: (1) instructional format; (2) instructional presentation; and (3) error correction procedures. First, whether the teacher uses a small-group or one-to-one instructional format should be based on student need. Tier 2 instruction and interventions are typically conducted in a small-group format because these students typically do not have severe academic difficulties or BD. Tier 3 instruction and interventions may be conducted in a small-group or one-to-one instructional format, depending upon the severity of the students' academic difficulties or BD and the skills being taught. The one-to-one format is necessary to provide students with additional support (i.e., vary the level of task demands and support in response to the student's competence) and opportunities to respond, learn, and practice the skills being taught in each lesson. Furthermore, instructors can more easily adjust their pacing within (i.e., provide additional practice) and across lessons (i.e., repeat lessons) to ensure that students master the skills being taught.

Second, model–lead–test instructional presentation procedures should be used by teachers across all instructional activities. The instructor should begin each

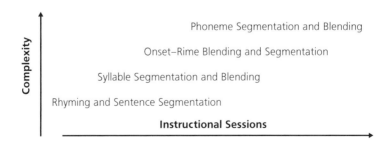

FIGURE 2.3. Scope and sequence for systematically teaching phonemic awareness.

activity by modeling the skill being taught and then immediately ask students to replicate the modeled example (lead). Using the content in Figure 2.4 as a guide, the teacher would say the words in the top boxes of each lesson and then ask students to say them. This instructional presentation procedure is designed to serve as a bridge between the skill modeled by the instructor to independent practice of the skill by students. Students then practice the new skill independently, using examples (e.g., practice sight words). Instructors should monitor whether students successfully progress from skill acquisition (i.e., they make many errors) to skill mastery (i.e., they make few errors). The progression from skill acquisition to mastery occurs naturally within and across instructional sessions if a well-defined and coherent scope and sequence are used to guide the introduction of basic skills. However, it may be necessary to give students more support by providing them with multiple models and by repeating lessons to ensure that they achieve skill mastery. Additionally, teachers' instructional presentation is more effective when the following conditions are met:

1. Teachers implement the instruction and interventions with integrity. For example, they do not improvise, leave out part of the lessons, or skip days.
2. Teachers are highly engaging and positive.
3. Teachers are well organized, use a brisk pace, and provide children with encouragement and feedback throughout the lessons.
4. Teachers get to know the instructional needs of students and adjust the level of scaffolding or support they give them (i.e., vary the level of task demands in response to students' competence) and provide opportunities to respond or practice the skills covered within each lesson. Furthermore, instructors adjust their pacing within and across lessons to ensure that students acquire the skills.
5. Teachers monitor students' strengths and weaknesses by carefully observing them and tracking their performance over time.

Finally, systematic error correction procedures should be used by teachers to ensure that students move efficiently from skill acquisition to mastery. Error correction procedures include two components: error detection and reteaching. It is critical that teachers detect errors immediately and reteach skills when appropriate. The teacher should prompt a student to "try again" when he or she makes a careless error or needs encouragement during the instructional activities. The instructor uses the model–lead–test instructional presentation procedures to reteach the skills when students are unable to respond independently.

Fluency Instruction

Six steps guide the process of developing students' skill fluency (these steps are fully described in Chapter 5). First, select observable, pivotal skills (e.g., sight

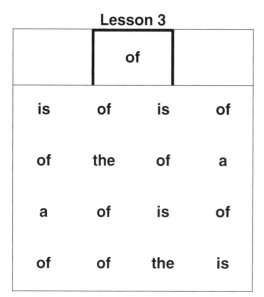

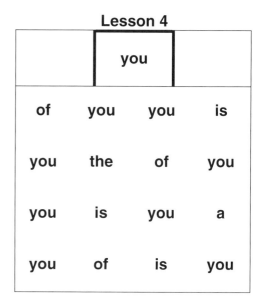

FIGURE 2.4. Sequential set of four mastery instruction lessons for sight words.

words) that are directly related to the content being taught (e.g., early reading skills). Second, select the range of skill practice items the student has mastered (i.e., has few or no errors). An example of a fluency practice sheet that would be introduced once students have mastered the sight words in Figure 2.4 (*the, a, is, of, you*) is presented in Figure 2.5. Third, develop fluency instruction sheets, which may be comprised of text or discrete items (e.g., letter names). Fourth, establish daily performance standards (number of correct responses in a specified time period). The performance standard during fluency instruction is continually reset through an interactive goal-setting process with students during fluency instruction. Fifth, conduct a series of short, timed (1–2 minutes) instructional trials. These trials can be conducted individually or in small groups of students who have similar competence levels. Finally, students chart the number of correct responses they achieved and are awarded a reinforcer if they met or exceeded the established performance standards.

CONCLUSIONS

The overall purpose of this chapter is to provide background information in which to situate the instructional practices described in this book. We provide information on the five interrelated components of the RTI approach used by schools to guide instruction and interventions for all students. Universal screening, frequent monitoring of student progress, and data-based decision making are the three components of the RTI approach. CBM assessment procedures, described more fully in Chapter 3, are being widely used by schools to screen all students on a regular basis. These procedures allow schools to identify students who need supplementary or unique instruction and interventions. These same CBM procedures also allow educators to monitor student progress and use established data-based decision rules about changes in instruction and interventions for individual students.

The high-quality implementation of scientifically based instruction and interventions is another important component of the RTI approach. The instructional practices detailed in this book are based on several reviews of the literature that have been conducted on academic instruction and interventions for students with BD (Mooney, Epstein, Reid, & Nelson, 2003; Mooney, Ryan, Uhing, Reid, & Epstein, 2005; Pierce, Reid, & Epstein, 2004; Ryan, Reid, & Epstein, 2004).

We also describe the three-tiered prevention model being used by schools to coordinate and integrate differing levels of scientifically based instruction and interventions at the primary (Tier 1), secondary (Tier 2), and tertiary (Tier 3) levels. Commercially available Tier 1, 2, and 3 early reading, written language, and mathematics direct instruction programs are discussed in Chapter 4. The instructional practices described in Chapters 5–7 are applied at Tiers 2 or 3 for students with BD.

Cumulative Number of Words	Sight Words				
5	is	you	the	a	of
10	a	the	you	of	is
15	you	of	is	a	the
20	is	you	the	a	of
25	you	of	is	a	the
30	a	the	you	of	is
35	a	the	you	of	is
40	you	of	is	a	the
45	is	you	the	a	of
50	a	the	you	of	is

FIGURE 2.5. Fluency practice sheet for the sight words presented in Figure 2.4.

Finally, we describe a mastery-to-fluency model for teaching basic reading, writing, and mathematics skills. Ensuring that students master basic skills involves careful attention to the instructional format, presentation, and error correction procedures. Teachers must then use a five-step process to develop students' skill fluency. Chapter 4 describes commercially available direct instruction programs that integrate mastery-to-fluency instructional practices. We highlight mastery and fluency instructional practices that can be applied to any published curriculum, academic skills, or content area in Chapters 5–7.

CHAPTER 3

Assessment for Effective Instruction

We now turn our attention to assessment. Salvia, Ysseldyke, and Bolt (2007) define assessment as "a process of collecting data for the purpose of making decisions about individuals and groups" (p. 4). Assessment processes are integral to the schooling of students with BD for a number of reasons; we highlight two of those reasons here. First, data gathering has historically been linked to instruction in special education because formal assessment is a precursor to placement in special education. Comprehensive assessment of current levels of performance and the determination of educational needs are critical to eligibility determination for all students, including those ultimately classified with emotional disturbance under IDEA. Moreover, educational teams are required to reassess student knowledge and skills periodically in order to determine if special education continues to be warranted.

Additionally, effective data gathering and analysis are essential to the effective implementation of RTI systems (detailed in Chapter 2). For example, periodic (usually three times yearly) assessment of all students (i.e., at the Tier 1 level) allows school officials to determine those students whose skills are developing within age- and/or grade-appropriate limits as well as those students whose skills are not developing at expected rates. In RTI systems, students deemed to be at risk for academic failure receive additional supports in Tier 2 and/or 3. Assessment results are the primary determinant of where students, such as those with BD, are placed (i.e., Tier 2 or 3). These results are also used to determine if changes in tier placement are warranted (e.g., improvement in a child's phonological awareness probe scores as a result of intervention indicates that he or she can move from Tier 3 to Tier 2 services). (Skill-based interventions for students with BD receiving Tier 2 and/or 3 supplemental academic services are addressed in Chapters 4–7.)

The second reason for assessment concerns the climate in which students with BD are likely to exhibit both academic and behavioral delays (along with the multitude of environmental risk factors outlined in Chapter 1) and schools are increasingly expected to demonstrate adequate yearly achievement growth. It is imperative that school professionals track the progress of the individualized programming instituted for this population of students. Such tracking is necessary to ascertain whether we are adequately addressing those needs identified during the eligibility assessment.

The purpose of this chapter is to demonstrate how teachers can consistently monitor the progress of academic skills development for primary school students with BD. We begin the chapter by highlighting the components of the eligibility determination and continuation processes for students with BD. We then provide (1) a rationale for ongoing progress monitoring within the context of an RTI framework; (2) directions for how to administer, score, and interpret CBM instruments across early reading, writing, and math skills instruction; and (3) an example of the implementation of progress monitoring in a school setting. Next we explore other considerations for data collection in school settings and conclude the chapter by summarizing its key points.

ASSESSMENT FOR ELIGIBILITY DETERMINATION AND CONTINUATION

In Chapter 1 we provided the federal definition of emotional disturbance as outlined in IDEA. In order to be verified as a student with emotional disturbance and served under IDEA, a student needs to demonstrate characteristics (e.g., learning or relational struggles, general unhappiness, inappropriate behaviors) that negatively impact educational performance over the long term and to a significantly greater degree than would be the case with the majority of same-age peers. School professionals engage in a host of related assessment activities as they attempt to gather data to determine if the listed characteristics exist and, if they do, to what degree they are evidenced. Often, school psychologists, speech–language pathologists, educational diagnosticians, and school social workers are included in the data-gathering process.

For example, school psychologists might administer intelligence tests to rule out significant cognitive delay as the reason for an inability to learn. School psychologists might also be involved in the assessment of achievement, classroom and school-based behavioral observations, and the administration and scoring of behavior rating scales completed by parents and teachers. In some states, educational diagnosticians might be charged with the assessment of achievement and conduct their own behavioral observations of students in school settings. Speech–language pathologists might use formal and informal language instruments, observations, and interviews to determine the extent to which expressive and receptive language delays are contributing factors to inappropriate behaviors. Social workers might serve as a liaison with parents, conduct formal or informal interviews, and administer measures of adaptive behavior. Additionally, some or all of these assessment personnel will contribute to the completion of a functional behavioral assessment designed to determine the reason(s) for the inappropriate behavior.

Once the gathering of intelligence, achievement, behavioral, and social data has been completed, members of the assessment team assemble to share their findings, identify student strengths and weaknesses, and make eligibility decisions. Parents, teachers, administrators, assessment specialists (such as those previously identified), and students, when appropriate, are charged with comparing the gathered data with state eligibility criteria to determine if a child is eligible and warrants special education. Once a decision is made to verify that a student has an emotional disturbance, then a similar team meets to create the educational program that will be implemented during the following year. These individualized education programs (IEPs) are reviewed at least annually. All IEPs must include annual goals and identify the mechanism for measuring goal attainment. At least once every 3 years, a comprehensive assessment, similar to the original assessment, is conducted to determine whether continued special education services are warranted.

RATIONALE FOR PROGRESS MONITORING

Once the planning team has delineated the annual IEP goals for students with BD, it is teachers who engage students in instructional interactions designed to provide success in meeting those goals. As we noted earlier, this is no easy proposition for teachers of students with BD. First, this population of students is likely to have coexisting behavioral and academic deficits in addition to a host of environmental risk factors. Such circumstances warrant effective use of time, including supplementary instruction in basic academic skills. Second, revisions in special education law mandate that students with BD not only access but profit from their least restrictive instructional programs. Other revisions in special education law allow educators to use special education funds to provide early—and hopefully preventive—instruction to children at risk of school failure (Fuchs & Fuchs, 2006). As detailed in Chapter 2, this RTI framework provides a useful structure for guiding core and supplemental educational programming for all students with its emphasis on (1) scientifically based instruction and intervention; (2) use of universal screening; (3) multitiered implementation models; (4) problem-solving processes; (5) and ongoing progress monitoring (Gresham, 2003). Given these factors, teachers of students with BD need to know that their students are making appropriate academic gains as a result of the instruction they are providing. Progress monitoring is a tool teachers can implement to ensure that their students are gaining necessary academic skill mastery and fluency.

According to the National Center on Student Progress Monitoring (2007; *www.studentprogressmonitoring.org*), progress monitoring is a scientifically based practice that has two functions: (1) to assess the academic performance of individuals or groups, and (2) to evaluate the effectiveness of instruction. Essentially, progress monitoring works because teachers are able to:

- Assess a student's current level of performance.
- Set measurable goals based on research indicating the performance level that predicts future success.
- Measure student academic performance in critical skill areas regularly.
- Determine whether or not students are on track to meet established measurable goals.
- Change instructional strategies quickly if data indicate that supplemental interventions are not having the desired effect.

An impressive body of progress monitoring research has demonstrated its efficacy and shaped its present appearance (Fuchs, 2004). Foremost in the literature is the systematic development and validation of CBM (Deno, 1985). CBM evolved out of the research program of Stanley Deno at the University of Minnesota. Deno's team was evaluating the effectiveness of an instructional model designed to gather data for special education teachers so that they could improve the quality of the interventions they were developing (Deno, 2003). Generic progress monitoring (i.e., CBM) procedures were developed and evaluated as part of the research program. Measures designed to be inexpensive, reliable, valid, and easy for teachers to administer and understand were developed and evaluated in reading, spelling, written expression, and math (Deno, 1985). Each measure also was designed to represent the skill-based performance desired at the end of the academic year (Fuchs, 2004). Multiple comparable forms were developed for each measure so that measurement could be frequent (e.g., weekly). In that way, the results of effective instruction could be demonstrated visually, across time, through appropriate gains in CBM scores (see Figure 3.1). Equally important, the results of ineffective instruction could be observed in real time (see Figure 3.2) so that instructional modifications could be made in an effort to increase student learning rates. Effective supplemental instruction is demonstrated in the graphs by noticing that progress monitoring performances are meeting and/or exceeding the goal lines laid out for students. Ineffective supplemental instruction, then, is demonstrated by progress monitoring data that continue to fall below the goal line. (See Chapter 2 for additional information on goal lines.)

In the early days of CBM, teachers were responsible for locating grade-level appropriate passages, word lists, or computation problems in order to evaluate fluency in reading, writing, and math. Moreover, teachers were responsible for creating their own data-based graphs with paper and pencil. In recent years, however, the technology has advanced to the point where both the skill probes and graphs are widely available. Today, teachers have access to free or commercially available

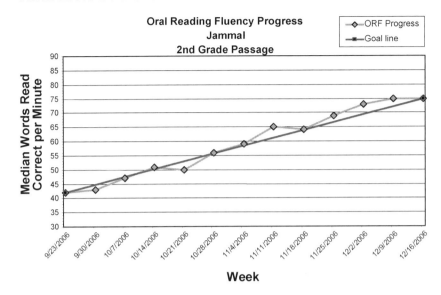

FIGURE 3.1. Example of progress monitoring graph when the student is responding to instruction.

measures of academic skill development in reading, writing, and math. These standardized measures (i.e., probes) of academic skill development can be administered easily and quickly to individuals or groups. Teachers of students with BD can use progress monitoring to identify areas of academic skill deficit, evaluate the effectiveness of a particular instructional strategy, and determine whether students are reaching the desired fluency levels in critical academic skill areas to help prepare them for success in the upper elementary, middle, and high school grades.

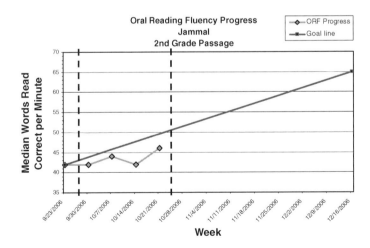

FIGURE 3.2. Example of progress monitoring graph when the student is not responding to instruction.

In addition to ease of administration, CBMs provide teachers with a clear way to communicate findings to students, parents, and teachers. Graphed data can (1) provide visual representations of data in a manner that encapsulates large amounts of information; (2) reflect important characteristics of academic skill performance; (3) provide informational and motivational feedback to students, parents, and school personnel; and (4) improve student performance (Gunter, Hummel, Denny, & Mooney, 2006). For example, Fuchs and Fuchs (1986) demonstrated that the performance of students whose achievement data were graphed was .8 standard deviation units better, on average, than a group of students whose achievement data were simply recorded. One of us (G.J.B.) has developed an Excel program that can be downloaded for use in ongoing progress monitoring efforts (*www.tacoma.washington.edu/education/docs/BAM_II.xls*). In the program, a teacher can, for example, enter a student's name and grade, the type of probe being administered, goal lines, the dates of periodic progress monitoring, and the progress monitoring data (see the figures in this chapter). Additionally, teachers can track when instructional or goal line changes are made. The program can be printed easily and serve as a communication tool for teachers as they share data with colleagues or conference with parents. And for teachers of upper elementary, middle, or high school students, the graphs can shape the discussion of individual conferences with students. Commercially available progress monitoring systems offer the possibility of class- and schoolwide graphs.

PROGRESS MONITORING OF ACADEMIC SKILLS

We devote the bulk of this chapter to identifying relevant measurement tools for academic skill development in reading, writing, and math and to describing how to administer, score, and interpret these measures. Table 3.1 provides a listing of skill-based probes available to school personnel for progress monitoring purposes. We begin this section with a discussion of early reading skill progress monitoring tools and follow with separate sections discussing early writing and math skill probes. (As previously mentioned, research-based intervention ideas are discussed in the coming chapters.)

TABLE 3.1. Measurement Tools for Academic Skills Development

Reading	Writing	Math
Initial Sound Fluency	Spelling	Oral Counting
Letter Naming Fluency	Written Expression	Number Identification
Phoneme Segmentation Fluency		Missing Number
Nonsense Word Fluency		Quantity Discrimination
Oral Reading Fluency		Single-Skill Math Computation
Retell Fluency		Multiple-Skill Math
Word Use Fluency		Computation

Reading

The last few decades have seen tremendous gains in our understanding of how to measure and positively impact early reading skill development in most public school students. The work of University of Oregon researchers Roland Good and Ruth Kaminski in the area of measurement has been especially beneficial. Good and Kaminski developed a progress monitoring system in early reading that has evolved to span the elementary school years (i.e., kindergarten through sixth grade). Dynamic Indicators of Basic Early Literacy Skills (DIBELS; Good & Kaminski, 2002) is an easily accessible set of standardized, individually administered measures of early reading development (*dibels.uoregon.edu/*). Alternate and comparable forms of seven fluency probes are designed to frequently measure individual student growth in the early reading skill areas of phonological awareness, alphabetic principle, and oral fluency. Individual scores in any of the seven probes can be compared against research-based norms to determine whether or not a student's skill development is emerging appropriately. Table 3.2 provides an example of DIBELS first-grade norms. Those students whose scores fall in an at-risk range for a given skill area (e.g., phonological awareness) can be given supplemental instruction and then monitored regularly to determine if the additional instruction results in meaningful skill development (i.e., gains that eventually move a child out of the at-risk range). Comprehensive administration and scoring guidelines can be downloaded from the DIBELS website. Following is a brief description of the purpose, administration procedures, and scoring procedures for the five DIBELS probes for which norms were available at the time of publication.

TABLE 3.2. First-Grade Benchmark Goals and Indicators of Risk for DIBELS Measures

DIBELS measure	Beginning of year: months 1–3		Middle of year: months 4–6		End of year: months 7–10	
	Scores	Status	Scores	Status	Scores	Status
Letter Naming Fluency (LNF)	LNF < 25 25 ≤ LNF < 37 LNF ≥ 37	At risk Some risk Low risk				
Phoneme Segmentation Fluency (PSF)	PSF < 10 10 ≤ PSF < 35 PSF ≥ 35	Deficit Emerging Established	PSF < 10 10 ≤ PSF < 35 PSF ≥ 35	Deficit Emerging Established	PSF < 10 10 ≤ PSF < 35 PSF ≥ 35	Deficit Emerging Established
Nonsense Word Fluency (NWF)	NWF < 13 13 ≤ NWF < 24 NWF ≥ 24	At risk Some risk Low risk	NWF < 30 30 ≤ NWF < 50 NWF ≥ 50	Deficit Emerging Established	NWF < 30 30 ≤ NWF < 50 NWF ≥ 50	Deficit Emerging Established
Oral Reading Fluency (ORF)			ORF < 8 8 ≤ ORF < 20 ORF ≥ 20	At risk Some risk Low risk	ORF < 8 8 ≤ ORF < 20 ORF ≥ 20	At risk Some risk Low risk

Initial Sound Fluency

Initial Sound Fluency (ISF; see Figure 3.3 for an example) measures development in phonological awareness by assessing a child's ability to recognize and produce the initial sound in an orally presented word. The probe is administered to kindergarten students. The benchmark goal is 25–35 correct sounds per minute by the middle of the kindergarten year (Good & Kaminski, 2002).

ISF ADMINISTRATION

The examiner presents four pictures to the child and asks him or her to identify (i.e., say or point) the picture that begins with the sound that the examiner orally

FIGURE 3.3. Dynamic Indicators of Basic Early Literacy Skills (DIBELS) Initial Sound Fluency (ISF) progress monitoring probe. Reprinted with permission from the University of Oregon.

produces. A model is provided initially. For example, using the probe shown in Figure 3.3, the assessor says, "This is mouse, flowers, pillow, letters. Mouse begins with the sound /m/. Listen, /m/, mouse. Which one begins with the sounds /fl/?" The examiner begins timing once each question has been asked and stops timing following the child's response or 5 seconds, whichever occurs first. The examiner continues in this fashion until all questions in the protocol have been asked and sufficient time allowed for a response (Good & Kaminski, 2002).

ISF SCORING

The examiner calculates the number of initial sounds correct in a minute. The number of initial sounds is calculated by (1) multiplying the number of correct sounds by 60; and (2) dividing the calculated sum by the number of seconds it takes the child to complete the task. For example, if a kindergarten student correctly identifies six initial sounds and it takes 23 seconds to finish the protocol, then the number of correct initial sounds in 1 minute would be 15 (i.e., $60 \times 6 = 360/23 = 15.6$) (Good & Kaminski, 2002).

Letter Naming Fluency

Letter Naming Fluency (LNF; see Figure 3.4 for an example) measures a child's ability to rapidly identify upper- and lower-case letters. Although it does not directly measure phonological awareness, alphabetic principle, or oral fluency, LNF is considered a measure of reading risk. That is, those students in the lowest 40% when compared to local norms can be considered at risk for reading delays. LNF is administered throughout kindergarten as well as at the beginning of first grade. Kindergarten students are considered at risk for reading delays if they identify less than 29 letter names in a minute by the end of the year (Good & Kaminski, 2002).

LNF ADMINISTRATION

The examiner presents the child with the protocol, which consists of randomly placed upper- and lower-case letters. The examiner says the following: "Here are some letters. Tell me the names of as many letters as you can." Students are asked to point to letters as they name them and are told that if they cannot name a letter, then the examiner will tell them the letter name. The examiner tells the student to begin and stops the student after 60 seconds (Good & Kaminski, 2002).

LNF SCORING

The examiner counts the number of correct letters identified by the student (Good & Kaminski, 2002).

FIGURE 3.4. Dynamic Indicators of Basic Early Literacy Skills (DIBELS) Letter Naming Fluency (LNF) progress monitoring probe. Reprinted with permission from the University of Oregon.

Phoneme Segmentation Fluency

Phoneme Segmentation Fluency (PSF; see Figure 3.5 for an example of an examiner scoring sheet) measures development in phonological awareness by assessing a student's ability to fluently segment three- and four-phoneme words into their individual phonemes. The probe is administered to kindergarten students beginning midway through the year, and to first-grade students. The benchmark goal is 35–45 correct phonemes in 1 minute in the spring of kindergarten and fall of first grade (Good & Kaminski, 2002).

PSF ADMINISTRATION

The examiner asks students to say the sounds in words that are presented orally. For example, the examiner says the following: "I am going to say a word. After

Progress Monitoring 1
Phoneme Segmentation Fluency
DIBELS

leaned /l/ /ea/ /n/ /d/	shine /sh/ /ie/ /n/	____/7
worm /w/ /ir/ /m/	smiled /s/ /m/ /ie/ /l/ /d/	____/8
porch /p/ /or/ /ch/	creek /k/ /r/ /ea/ /k/	____/7
grabbed /g/ /r/ /a/ /b/ /d/	bags /b/ /a/ /g/ /z/	____/9
lit /l/ /i/ /t/	kissed /k/ /i/ /s/ /t/	____/7
get /g/ /e/ /t/	pouch /p/ /ow/ /ch/	____/6
roared /r/ /or/ /d/	whale /w/ /ai/ /l/	____/6
broke /b/ /r/ /oa/ /k/	meet /m/ /ea/ /t/	____/7
raise /r/ /ai/ /z/	note /n/ /oa/ /t/	____/6
worth /w/ /ir/ /th/	points /p/ /oi/ /n/ /t/ /s/	____/8
that /TH/ /a/ /t/	cold /k/ /oa/ /l/ /d/	____/7
worked /w/ /ir/ /k/ /t/	fight /f/ /ie/ /t/	____/7

Error Pattern: Total: ____

FIGURE 3.5. Dynamic Indicators of Basic Early Literacy Skills (DIBELS) Phoneme Segmentation Fluency (PSF) progress monitoring probe. Reprinted with permission from the University of Oregon.

I say it, you tell me all the sounds in the word. So, if I say *sam*, you would say, '/s/ /a/ /m/.'" Following the model, the examiner tests the student's understanding and provides feedback. Then the examiner gives the student the first word on the protocol and starts timing. Words are presented immediately following a student's response or after 3 seconds of silence. The examiner stops timing after 60 seconds (Good & Kaminski, 2002).

PSF SCORING

The examiner counts the number of correct sounds in 60 seconds.

Nonsense Word Fluency

Nonsense Word Fluency (NWF; see Figure 3.6 for an example) measures development of the alphabetic principle by assessing a child's ability to demonstrate letter–sound correspondence and blending skills. The probe is administered in late kindergarten, first grade, and early second grade. The benchmark goal is 50 correct letter sounds in 1 minute by the middle of first grade (Good & Kaminski, 2002).

NWF ADMINISTRATION

The examiner asks students to view letter sequences that make up word forms and either sound out the word form or say the correct word form. For example,

um	jac	zoj	oc	kom
kic	raj	lon	zeb	ig
mes	juk	et	noj	vin
jic	wuj	om	hul	mid
bes	pek	moz	um	ut
pej	waj	rej	jul	nej
lat	puz	des	ud	nam
mid	tuf	num	yaz	dod
bok	feg	yud	haj	uv
huj	os	kel	rif	yuk

DIBELS™ Nonsense Word Fluency
© 2002 Dynamic Measurement Group, Inc.

Progress Monitoring 1
Revised: 06/24/02

FIGURE 3.6. Dynamic Indicators of Basic Early Literacy Skills (DIBELS) Nonsense Word Fluency (NWF) progress monitoring probe. Reprinted with permission from the University of Oregon.

the examiner places a piece of paper with the word *sim* in front of the child and says the following: "Look at this word. It's a make-believe word. Watch me read the word: '/s/ /i/ /m/,' *sim*. I can say the sounds of the letters, '/s/ /i/ /m/,' or I can read the whole word, *sim*." The examiner then tests the student's understanding by presenting another word and asking the student to complete the task. Feedback is then provided before the actual administration begins. The timing begins once a protocol has been placed in front of the student and the directions have been completed. If there is a 3-second silence during the task, then the examiner can present the next sound or word, depending upon how the student is responding to the task. The examiner stops timing after 60 seconds (Good & Kaminski, 2002).

NWF SCORING

The examiner counts the number of correct sounds in 60 seconds (Good & Kaminski, 2002).

Oral Reading Fluency

Oral Reading Fluency (ORF; see Figure 3.7 for an example) measures accuracy and fluency with connected text by assessing a child's ability to read written passages out loud. The probe is administered beginning midway through first grade and can continue to be administered throughout the elementary grades. The benchmark goals in the primary years are 40 words read correctly per minute by the end of

A Present from Me

I wanted to take my stepmother out to dinner for her birthday and pay for our dinner with my own money. I wanted it to be a surprise and I wanted it to be just from me. The problem was, I didn't have any money!

I went out to try to find ways to earn money. The lady who lives in the apartment upstairs said she wanted to get rid of all her empty soda cans and bottles. She said I could keep the money for the deposit if I took all of the cans and bottles back to the store. It took me five trips, but I got them all taken back to the store.

The man in the apartment downstairs said I could walk his dog after supper every night for two weeks. Our neighbor lady said she could use some help putting out the trash and getting rid of old newspapers. One lady in our building said she would like some help with her groceries, but she couldn't afford to pay me. I helped her anyway. She said she would give me some flowers to give to my stepmother.

The day before her birthday I asked Mom if she would go on a date with me for dinner. She was surprised when I paid for the dinner with the money I had earned. She made me tell her where I had gotten the money. Then she gave me a big hug and said it was the best birthday present ever. I think she liked the flowers the best of all.

DIBELS Oral Reading Fluency
© 2002 Dynamic Measurement Group, Inc.

Progress Monitoring 1
Revised 01/21/03

FIGURE 3.7. Dynamic Indicators of Basic Early Literacy Skills (DIBELS) Oral Reading Fluency (ORF) progress monitoring probe. Reprinted with permission from the University of Oregon.

first grade, 90 words per minute by the end of second grade, and 110 words per minute by the end of third grade (Good & Kaminski, 2002).

ORF ADMINISTRATION

The examiner asks the student to read a page of grade-level text, then presents a passage to the student and says the following: "Please read this out loud. If you get stuck, I will tell you the word so that you can keep reading." The examiner begins timing. If a student pauses for 3 seconds while reading, the examiner tells the student the word and encourages him or her to continue. The examiner stops timing after 60 seconds (Good & Kaminski, 2002).

ORF SCORING

The examiner counts the number of words read correctly in 60 seconds (Good & Kaminski, 2002).

Writing

Whereas DIBELS allows for free access to ready-to-use early reading skill measures and norms, access to writing progress monitoring tools involves adopting one of two possible approaches: (1) teachers can develop their own rate-based probes and incorporate local or other norming systems for comparison purposes; or (2) teachers can utilize ready-to-use, commercially available systems (e.g., AIMSweb). In terms of the former approach, teachers can use CBM technologies to create their own probes based on state or federal grade-level expectations and/or curricular materials used in their district. For example, in the area of reading, teachers can locate grade-appropriate texts, randomly select 50- to 200-word passages, and then create a student copy of the passage (which excludes pictures) and a teacher copy that includes a line-by-line word count (Mercer & Mercer, 2005).

In the area of writing, separate procedures have been developed for spelling and written composition. In spelling, words can be chosen from a number of sources, including all words at a given grade level in a curriculum series (Mercer & Mercer, 2005). In this manner, specific probes consist of words randomly selected from the curriculum's complete list. Spelling words might also be chosen from available lists. For example, Graham, Harris, and Loynachan (1993) developed a list of 850 spelling words for grades 1–5 (see Table 3.3 for a list of the first-grade words). The words were chosen because they were commonly used in children's writing, representative of a variety of genres, and universally used throughout the United States (Graham et al., 1993).

Spelling tasks can take the form of either student selection or response tasks. In selection formats, an incorrectly spelled word is underlined in a sentence, and students choose from four choices, one of which is correct. Scores are calculated based upon the number of words correctly identified. If a first-grade teacher was using

TABLE 3.3. Basic Spelling Vocabulary List for First Graders

a	fat	like	sat
all	for	look	see
am	fun	man	she
and	get	may	sit
at	go	me	six
ball	good	mom	so
be	got	my	stop
bed	had	no	sun
big	hat	not	ten
book	he	of	the
box	hen	oh	this
boy	her	old	to
but	him	on	top
came	his	one	toy
can	home	out	two
car	hot	pan	up
cat	I	pet	us
come	if	pig	was
cow	in	play	we
dad	into	ran	will
day	is	rat	yes
did	it	red	you
do	its	ride	
dog	let	run	

Note. Adapted from Graham, Harris, and Loynachan (1993). Published by Heldref Publications. Copyright 1993 by Heldref Publications. Adapted with permission from the Helen Dwight Reid Educational Foundation.

the list in Table 3.3 as a guide for developing selection format spelling tests, for example, she might show students the following selections:

1. He was a *gud* man.
   (a) gaed   (b) good   (c) goud   (d) gude
2. Jack and Jill went out to *pley.*
   (a) play   (b) plee   (c) playe   (d) plae

Each student would earn 1 point each for selecting *(b)* as the answer to the first sentence and *(a)* as the answer to the second. In response formats, students hear words dictated to them for 2 minutes at 7- or 10-second intervals, depending on grade level, and are expected to write down the correct spellings (see Figure 3.8 for an example of an AIMSweb third-grade spelling list). For response formats, scores are calculated based upon the number of correct words or letter sequences, whichever the teacher chooses.

Correct words are correctly spelled words. *Correct letter sequences* (CLS) are essentially correct patterns in words. In the word *cat,* for example, the space before the /c/ and the letter *c* together constitute a correct letter sequence. Other correct letter sequences in the example include /ca/, /at/, and /t (space afterward)/. Correct letter sequences are often represented with the use of the ^ symbol. Therefore, in the word *cat*, there are four correct letter sequences that can be scored (i.e., ^c^a^t^). Incorrect letter sequences are letter pairs that are wrongly ordered. Look at the selection format examples above. The word *good* has five correct letter sequences if spelled as it should be (i.e., ^g^o^o^d^). However, the written word *gud* has two correct letter sequences (i.e., ^g and d^). The written word *pley* has three correct letter sequences, (i.e., ^p^ley^), with the first, second, and fifth letter sequences correct and the third and fourth letter sequences incorrect. In Figure 3.8, one column on the right side of the page labeled *CLS* provides the total number of correct letter sequences per word. For *heel*, then, there are five correct letter sequences (i.e., ^h^e^e^l^). The column labeled *CCLS* contains the cumulative number of correct letter sequences. In Figure 3.8 there are 112 total correct letter sequences that could be scored if all of the spelling words on the list were administered. Norms for teacher-developed spelling CBM probes are generally based on

AIMSweb® Standard Spelling Benchmark Assessment List #1 (3rd Grade)

Given By: _____   Date Given: ___/___/___

ID	Word	CLS	CCLS
1	heel The heel of the shoe.	5	5
2	wise	5	10
3	face	5	15
4	speak	6	21
5	dinner	7	28
6	weren't Weren't there better things to do?	8	36
7	there It is over there!	6	42
8	river	6	48
9	nameless	9	57
10	able	5	62
11	tomorrow	9	71
12	highway	8	79
13	mess	5	84
14	headaches	10	94
15	wag	4	98
16	crown	6	104
17	scraped	8	112
		Total CLS	**112**

FIGURE 3.8. AIMSweb spelling progress monitoring probe. From AIMSweb. Copyright 2007 by Edformation, Inc. Patent pending. Reprinted by permission. All rights reserved.

researcher recommendations. In the area of spelling, Deno, Mirkin, and Wesson (1984) have suggested an instructional level of 20–39 correct letter sequences for first and second graders and 40–59 correct letter sequences for third through sixth graders.

In written expression, progress is determined through frequent assessment of timed writing samples based on story starters or topic sentences (Mercer & Mercer, 2005). In order to monitor writing performance, a series of story starters are developed for use over time. The student is instructed to listen to the story starter, think for 1 minute, and then write for 3 minutes on the topic. Examples of story starters include the following: "All of a sudden, the lights went out and . . . "; or "Mommy opened the door to my bedroom and. . . . " Multiple written expression scoring systems can be used, including the number of words written, the number of words spelled correctly, or the number of correct word sequences. Similar to the correct letter sequence, a *correct word sequence* is a correct pattern of words and punctuation marks. There are seven correct word sequences in the following sentence: "I drove to the grocery store" (i.e., ^I^drove^to^the^grocery^store.^). The first correct word sequence consists of the space before the *I* and the correctly capitalized word itself. The second letter sequence is between the correctly capitalized *I* and the word *drove.* The seventh correct sequence, then, follows the word *store,* with a correct sequence ensured by the fact that the final word in the sentence is followed by a period. Norms for teacher-developed written expression probes for primary-grade students have targeted the average number of words written. Deno et al. (1984) reported the following end-of-year benchmarks: 14.7 words for first graders, 27.8 words for second graders, and 36.6 words for third graders.

In terms of choosing commercially available systems, teachers generally log into systems purchased by their districts and have access to progress monitoring probes, administration and scoring procedures, norms, and graphing options at the individual and class level. Essentially, the CBM procedures we highlighted previously have been duplicated and made available for commercial application. We highlight administration and scoring procedures for the AIMSweb system spelling and written expression probes here (*www.aimsweb.com*). Administration and scoring guidelines, norms, and sample probes are readily downloadable from the AIMSweb website.

Spelling—CBM Administration

The examiner can administer the probes to individuals or groups of individuals. For first and second graders, the probe consists of 12 words that are administered at a pace of 1 every 10 seconds for 2 minutes. For third graders (see Figure 3.8 for an example), the probe consists of 17 words, with new words dictated every 7 seconds for 2 minutes. For example, students receive lined paper that is numbered from 1 to 12 or 1 to 17, depending upon the grade, and told: "We're going to take a 2-minute spelling test. I am going to say some words that I want you to spell on the piece of paper in front of you. Write the first word on the first line, the second word on the second line, and so on. I'll give you 7 [or 10] seconds to spell each word." Students are also instructed to write the new word they hear even if they are not finished with the word they are writing; they are told that they will receive credit for each correct letter written. AIMSweb norms are presented for selected percentiles (e.g., 10th, 50th, 90th). For first, second, and third graders, 50th percentile scores for correct letter sequences at the end of the year are 44, 61, and 100, respectively (Shinn & Shinn, 2002). Student scores at or above the 50th percentile would indicate adequate grade-level development for the given assessment period.

Spelling—CBM Scoring

The examiner scores the number of correct letter sequences in 2 minutes (Shinn & Shinn, 2002). As mentioned earlier, when scoring it is critical to know that there are four possible correct letter sequences in a three-letter word such as *cat* (i.e., ^c^a^t^). For all words, the possible number of correct letter sequences is one more than the total number of letters correctly ordered and spelled.

Written Expression—CBM Administration

The examiner tells the students the following: "You are going to write a story. First, I will read a sentence, and then you will write about what happens next. You will have 1 minute to think about what happens next and 3 minutes to write your story." Students are encouraged to do their best work and prompted halfway through both the thinking and writing times. An example of a story starter for use across grades follows: "I opened the front door very carefully and. . . . " AIMSweb norms are presented for each grade level for both total words written and correct writing sequences. For total words written, end-of-year 50th percentile norms for first, second, and third grades are 19, 27, and 35 words, respectively. For correct word sequences, respective end-of-year norms are 9, 19, and 28 (Powell-Smith & Shinn, 2004).

Written Expression—CBM Scoring

As noted, the examiner has the choice of two scoring options: (1) total words written or (2) correct writing sequences (Powell-Smith & Shinn, 2004).

Math

Teachers have the same options open to them in the area of early math skills development as they do in writing. That is, they can develop and use their own CBM probes, or they can use commercially developed products. Teacher-developed CBM probes generally consist of computation problems (i.e., addition, subtraction, multiplication, division) that are grade appropriate. Grade-level probes can have a singular (e.g., two-digit addition) or multidimensional (e.g., multiplication and division) focus. Probes are developed so that the content of each is proportionally equivalent to the content in each grade's curriculum. That way, grade-level content that is weighted 60% addition and 40% subtraction will have probes that consist of 6 addition and 4 subtraction problems for every 10 problems included. One of the benefits of math instruction is that there is a high level of congruency across basal programs with respect to what should be covered at a given grade (Mercer & Mercer, 2005).

Across computation skills, Smith and Lovitt (1982) suggest that 45–50 correct digits per minute is an indicator of skill mastery. A *correct digit* is a number that matches the right answer for the problem. In problems for which a single digit (e.g., 4 + 4 = 8) is the answer, then there is one potential correct digit (i.e., 8) that a student might write on the probe. The student scores 0 or 1 for that problem. In problems for which the answer has two digits (e.g., 60 + 20 = 80), then a student might score 0, 1, or 2 points, depending on his or her answer to the question. If a student wrote 70 as the answer, then he or she would receive a score of 1 correct digit for correctly writing the 0 where it should go. If a student writes the answer 08, then he or she would receive 0 points for the response because although there is a 0 and an 8 in the answer, the student has written it in the wrong position.

Commercially developed math probes offer ready-made alternative forms at a given grade level along with research-based norms. AIMSweb offers two types of math probes: (1) those that target fluency in computation skill (see Figure 3.9 for an example of a combination addition and subtraction probe); and (2) those that target fluency in the precomputation skills that pave the way for mastering math facts (see Figure 3.10 for an example of a quantity discrimination probe). The following computation probes are available for use across the elementary grades: addition, subtraction, addition and subtraction, multiplication, division, multiplication and division, and a compilation of all four computation skills. The following early numeracy probes are available for kindergartners and first graders: oral counting, number identification, missing number, and quantity discrimination. We highlight administration and scoring procedures for selected AIMSweb system (*www.aimsweb.com*) computation and early numeracy probes here. Administration and scoring manuals, norms, and sample probes are readily available from the website.

Computation—Addition and Subtraction—CBM Administration

For primary-grade students, the examiner places a probe, such as the student copy in Figure 3.9, in front of him or her and says the following: "We're going to take a 2-minute math test. I want you to write your answers to several kinds of math problems. Some are addition and some are subtraction. Look at each problem carefully before you answer it." The examiner continues by telling the student where to start on the page and how to work across and down the page. The examiner also tells the student that if a problem is too difficult, then he or she can place an X through it

AIMSweb® Basic Addition and Subtraction Facts #1—Intermediate Answer Key

4 − 0 **4** (1)	7 + 7 **14** (2)	4 + 7 **11** (2)	4 − 4 **0** (1)	9 + 0 **9** (1)	2 − 0 **2** (1)	5 − 5 **0** (1)	9 (9)
11 − 8 **3** (1)	12 − 6 **6** (1)	7 − 3 **4** (1)	1 + 7 **8** (1)	8 − 6 **2** (1)	9 − 9 **0** (1)	1 + 5 **6** (1)	7 (16)
12 − 8 **4** (1)	10 − 5 **5** (1)	7 − 3 **4** (1)	8 − 6 **2** (1)	12 + 4 **16** (2)	9 + 0 **9** (1)	8 − 1 **7** (1)	8 (24)
3 + 2 **5** (1)	8 + 8 **16** (2)	9 − 7 **2** (1)	12 − 2 **10** (2)	3 + 6 **9** (1)	1 − 1 **0** (1)	10 − 2 **8** (1)	9 (33)
2 + 7 **9** (1)	1 + 8 **9** (1)	9 − 2 **7** (1)	5 − 0 **5** (1)	0 + 3 **3** (1)	9 + 1 **10** (2)	5 + 3 **8** (1)	8 (41)
9 − 9 **0** (1)	8 − 7 **1** (1)	4 + 9 **13** (2)	10 − 6 **4** (1)	3 + 7 **10** (2)	6 + 0 **6** (1)	9 − 5 **4** (1)	9 (50)

FIGURE 3.9. AIMSweb mathematics progress monitoring probe. From AIMSweb. Copyright 2007 by Edformation, Inc. Patent pending. Reprinted by permission. All rights reserved.

and continue to the next problem. During the 2 minutes, the examiner watches to see how the student is working. If the examiner knows the student well, for example, and sees that the student is skipping problems that the examiner believes he or she can do, then the examiner can encourage the student to answer all problems as best as possible. As with the writing probes, norms are presented for selected percentile ranks. For the computation probes, the 50th percentile number of correct digits for the spring across first, second, and third grades is 14, 22, and 29, respectively (Shinn, 2004).

Computation—CBM Scoring

The examiner counts the number of correct digits written during the 2-minute administration (Shinn, 2004). Generally, the examiner underlines each correct digit and then counts the number of underlined numbers. For those who use AIMSweb probes, there are answer sheets that facilitate correct scoring. Figure 3.9 depicts an answer sheet that includes the correct answer, the potential number of digits per problem, the potential total number of digits per line, and the potential cumulative total number of digits per probe. For example, there are 2 potential correct digits for the second problem of the first line; there are 9 possible correct digits for the first line; and there are 50 potentially correct digits on page 1 of the probe. Shinn (2004) notes that it generally takes less than 1 minute to complete the scoring process.

Early Numeracy—Quantity Discrimination Administration

Figure 3.10 reproduces the student probe and examiner recording sheet for a quantity discrimination probe for kindergartners and first graders. The examiner places a model problem in front of them, which consists of a box containing two numbers between 0 and 10 inclusive (e.g., 4 and 7) and says the following: "Look at the piece of paper in front of you. The box in front of you has two numbers in it. I want you to tell me which number is bigger." The examiner waits for a student's response, provides confirmatory or corrective feedback, then tests the student again. Now the examiner gives the student the protocol (see Figure 3.10), tells the student to identify the larger number in each pair, and shows the student how to read across and down the page. The examiner times the student for 1 minute and counts the number of correct responses. Kindergarten and first-grade scores at the 50th percentile in the spring are 27 and 34, respectively (Clarke & Shinn, 2002).

Early Numeracy—Quantity Discrimination Scoring

The examiner counts the number of correct quantity discriminations in 1 minute (Clarke & Shinn, 2002). On the probe in Figure 3.10, a student would provide a cor-

AIMSweb® Quantity Discrimination—Benchmark Assessment #1 (Kindergarten—Fall)

Given To: _____   Given By: _____   Date: _____

| 7 | 1 | 6 | 5 | 10 | 2 | 10 | 0 | / 4 of 4 |

| 1 | 0 | 0 | 5 | 7 | 9 | 9 | 3 | / 4 of 8 |

| 4 | 0 | 3 | 2 | 4 | 5 | 9 | 1 | / 4 of 12 |

| 0 | 7 | 3 | 8 | 7 | 2 | 10 | 1 | / 4 of 16 |

| 2 | 4 | 5 | 9 | 0 | 6 | 2 | 6 | / 4 of 20 |

| 2 | 5 | 10 | 9 | 8 | 9 | 1 | 3 | / 4 of 24 |

| 0 | 3 | 9 | 7 | 10 | 3 | 1 | 5 | / 4 of 28 |

FIGURE 3.10. AIMSweb early numeracy progress monitoring probe. From AIMSweb. Copyright 2007 by Edformation, Inc. Patent pending. Reprinted by permission. All rights reserved.

rect answer if he or she answered 7 for the first box; he or she would receive 1 point for that answer and 4 points if he or she answered all four discriminations correctly on the probe's first line. As the examiner copy indicates, there are 28 discriminations in the probe shown in Figure 3.10.

EXAMPLE OF PROGRESS MONITORING

In this section we provide an example of a special education teacher's use of progress monitoring with students who have BD. Ms. Dierker is a special education teacher who serves K–3 students at City Center Elementary. Currently, she has two students on her caseload who are verified with emotional disturbance. Casey is a first-grade boy with behavioral and academic concerns; the latter are predominantly delays in early reading skills development. Jamie is a third-grade girl with behavioral and math concerns. City Center Elementary conducts benchmark testing three times yearly, in September, January, and May. The school uses the DIBELS system for reading and AIMSweb for math. Students are identified for supplemental (i.e., RTI Tier 2 and/or 3) instruction if they have reading scores in the deficit or at-risk range and/or math scores at or below the 25th percentile. Students who are identified for supplemental instruction as a result of benchmark testing, or through other mechanisms (e.g., assessment for special education), are involved in once-weekly progress monitoring.

Ms. Dierker reviews the September testing results of both Casey and Jamie. Casey demonstrates a deficit in phonological awareness, with an average PSF score of nine phonemes correctly identified in 1 minute. Jamie's math computation scores of 12 correct digits in 2 minutes places her at the 25th percentile. Ms. Dierker then sets middle-of-the-year goals for both students that would place them on track to be considered at low risk by the end of the school year. For Casey, the goal is 22 correct phonemes in a minute by the second benchmark testing. That would place Casey on track to reach the established goal of 35 correct phonemes in a minute by the end of the school year. Once weekly, Ms. Dierker uses a PSF probe to evaluate Casey's phonological awareness development in response to supplemental instruction. Review of Figure 3.11 indicates that the supplemental instruction program is having the desired effect. That is, ongoing progress monitoring data demonstrate that Casey is making sufficient weekly gains to match the goal line set for him.

For Jamie, the goal is 22 correct digits by the second benchmark testing. That would place Jamie between the 25th and 50th percentiles and indicate a reasonable possibility that continued effective intervention would place her at the 50th percentile by the end of the year. Review of Figure 3.12, however, indicates that Jamie is falling short of these goals. The successive progress monitoring data points falling below the goal line suggest that a change in instruction is warranted.

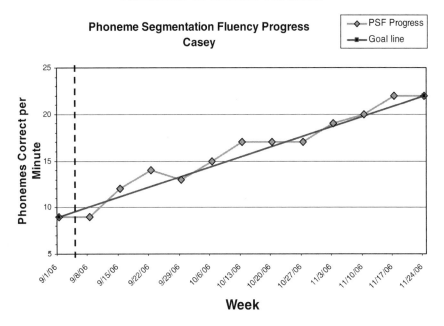

FIGURE 3.11. Casey's responsiveness to intervention in the area of phoneme segmentation fluency.

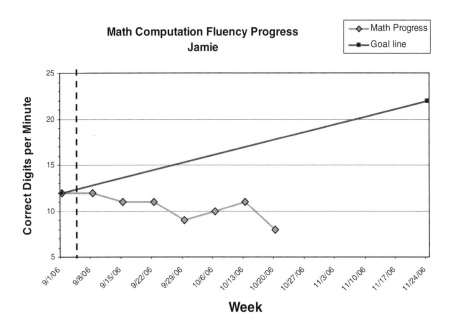

FIGURE 3.12. Jamie's lack of responsiveness to intervention indicating a change in instruction.

OTHER CONSIDERATIONS IN DATA COLLECTION
FOR STUDENTS WITH BD

Given the educational benefit of, and legal and political demands for, in-classroom data collection, it makes sense for all educators to increase its meaningful use. Before concluding the chapter, we address three other issues that might facilitate the increased use of data collection and progress monitoring in classrooms for students with BD: (1) simplifying procedures; (2) establishing educationally meaningful goals; and (3) incorporating self-management of behavior and academics.

Philip Gunter and colleagues (Gunter, Callicott, Denny, & Gerber, 2003) have suggested that one way to increase data collection is to simplify procedures. If recent history is any barometer, then such an assertion has some merit. With the evolution of progress monitoring from teacher-created CBM probes to readily available general outcome measures, the collection of data has skyrocketed in school buildings and districts across the country. For example, school-trained teams in districts across the country gather three times yearly for days or weeks to conduct progress monitoring probes of all their students. Such actions occur, in part, because the progress monitoring procedures of the past (i.e., teacher-constructed CBMs) have been simplified. Gunter et al. provided other examples of ways in which data collection could be meaningfully simplified when working with students who have BD. These include having teachers focus on increasing active student responding via review of 5-minute videotapes of their own instruction and involving students in the data collection process via student collection or data graphing.

Regarding writing IEP goals, Yell and Stecker (2003) have asserted the use of CBM data can facilitate the development of educationally meaningful and legally defensible IEPs for school personnel serving all students with disabilities. Use of such goals ties the IEP to both the comprehensive assessment that was part of the initial—and continuing—eligibility determination and the supplemental intervention activities in which the student, teacher, or parent will engage. For example, in the case of Jamie, the third grader who was described earlier, her comprehensive assessment might have included previous benchmark assessment results. With such results, then, Ms. Dierker could have written the IEP present level of performance in the following manner: "Given grade 3 progress monitoring math computation probes, Jamie currently correctly identifies 12 digits in 2 minutes." Her related end-of-the-year IEP goal, then, could be written as follows: "In 34 weeks, when given a grade 3 computation passage, Jamie will record 30 correct digits in 2 minutes."

Finally, regarding self management, students with BD struggle to meet the behavioral expectations of school and other settings. These struggles are major contributors to their referral for special education services. Self-management interventions have been developed to help students both increase and maintain appropriate behavior (Martella, Nelson, & Marchand-Martella, 2003). That is, teachers can specifically target single behaviors (e.g., verbal outbursts) for reduction or focus on increasing appropriate student responding in the classroom. Research syntheses (e.g., Mooney et al., 2005) have demonstrated that procedures such as self-monitoring and self-instruction can lead to educationally meaningful results for students with BD. Self-management features are discussed in greater detail in Chapter 8.

CONCLUSIONS

We opened this chapter on assessment by defining the term as a process of collecting data to inform decision making. For students with BD, formal decisions begin with eligibility for, and subsequent placement in, special education. The comprehensive assessment that encompasses eligibility determination includes formal and informal assessments, such as standardized achievement tests and classroom observations. Often, a number of school-based assessment professionals team up with teachers, parents, administrators, and others in making these decisions. Once the presence of a disability is verified, the assessment decisions are focused on academic and behavioral concerns.

We devoted most of the chapter to explaining the process of progress monitoring across the basic skill areas of reading, writing, and math. Progress monitoring was defined as a validated repeated process of assessing the academic performance of individuals or groups and evaluating the effectiveness of instruction. Progress monitoring also was placed in the current RTI context. One reason for using progress monitoring with students who have BD is that their combination of academic and behavioral concerns make their deficits hard to remediate and therefore in need of careful attention. Progress monitoring allows teachers to frequently gather data on program effectiveness so as to determine if instructional changes are needed. Teachers can develop their own brief reading, writing, or math probes or use tools readily or commercially available to districts. Regularly applying progress monitoring technologies allows teachers to monitor the skill development of their students by comparing student scores to norms that help discern the existence or nonexistence of risk for failure.

Ongoing data collection and analysis are critical to the effective education of students with and without BD. Ysseldyke and Algozzine (1995) maintain that data collection is "the only way to determine the effectiveness of instruction" (p. 198). For Bushell and Baer (1994), "close, continual contact with relevant outcome data" is a fundamental feature of classroom instruction that results in meaningful student achievement (p. 7). As we now turn our attention to effective supplemental instruction across the areas of reading, writing, language, and math for students with BD, remember that the types of ongoing assessment activities we outlined in this chapter are directly tied to the programs and strategies that we are about to present. In other words, ongoing data collection must be considered part of effective supplemental (i.e., RTI Tier 2 and/or Tier 3) instruction.

CHAPTER 4

Design and Delivery Features
of Commercially Available Early Reading,
Written Language, and Mathematics
Direct Instruction Programs

In the late 1960s and early 1970s, Siegfried E. Engelmann and his colleagues designed and implemented the Direct Instruction model for Project Follow Through (for a complete review of research on Project Follow Through, see Marchand-Martella, Slocum, & Martella, 2004). Involving approximately 100,000 children from 170 communities and costing nearly $1 billion, Project Follow Through was the largest, most expensive study of educational practices ever conducted by the U.S. Department of Education. The overarching goal of the 8-year project (1968–1976) was to compare the relative effectiveness of nine different educational approaches in improving the basic (i.e., language, word recognition, spelling, math computation), cognitive–conceptual (i.e., problem solving, reading comprehension, math concepts), and affective (i.e., self-concept) skills of disadvantaged children.

The models evaluated by Project Follow Through are briefly described in Table 4.1. The Direct Instruction model was the only model to demonstrate educationally significant outcomes on norm-referenced measures of basic, cognitive–conceptual, and affective skills. With the exception of the behavior analysis model, the remaining models produced negative outcomes on these measures. Interestingly, the particular model adopted by a school was not determined by educators. Rather, parents selected the model that would be adopted by their children's school, following a presentation by the sponsor for each model. The Direct Instruction model was the most popular among all of the models, even though it was not the favorite of educators. The prevailing thinking among educators at the time was that children benefit most from more open-ended, child-guided models.

TABLE 4.1. Models Evaluated in Project Follow Through

Model	Description
Direct Instruction	• Curriculum uses carefully sequenced and scripted lessons in reading, mathematics, and language; small-group instructional formats; careful placement of students in similar skill level groups; and frequent monitoring of student learning.
Behavior analysis	• Model uses programmed instructional materials (clearly stated behavioral objectives, self-pacing, active learner response to inserted questions, and immediate feedback regarding the correctness of the response) in reading, writing, spelling, and mathematics and token economy for classroom management, implemented by three to four adults per classroom.
Parent education	• Model trained and encouraged parents to serve as teaching aides in the classroom and involved teacher home visits to teach parents how to enhance the education of their children.
Tucson early education model	• The interests of children guided the specific instructional content, and language was used as the medium with which to develop broad intellectual skills and positive attitudes toward school.
Cognitively oriented curriculum	• Grounded in Piagetian theory, teachers functioned as catalysts rather than providers of information and emphasized reading, mathematics, and science.
Responsive education	• Instruction was self-paced and -determined, emphasizing the development of problem solving, sensory discrimination, and self-confidence.
Bank Street	• Curriculum focused on the development of positive self-image, creativity, coping skills, and formulating and expressing ideas through language.
Open education	• Model focused on providing children with a stimulating environment designed to promote self-respect, imagination, and openness to change.
Language development approach (bilingual)	• Instruction was conducted simultaneously in Spanish and English with an overall positive emphasis on children's primary language and culture.

The Direct Instruction model evaluated in Project Follow Through led to the development of a range of commercially available Direct Instruction programs, which were commonly referred to as "big" Direct Instruction programs and marketed primarily by SRA/McGraw-Hill (*www.sraonline.com*). These programs were referred to as *big* Direct Instruction programs in an effort to distinguish them from the more general use of the term *direct instruction* (summarized by Rosenshine & Stevens, 1986). Generally, *direct instruction* refers to effective teaching functions that teachers apply to any published curriculum, academic skill and application, or content area (see Table 4.2 for brief descriptions of teaching functions). Most of the commercially available early reading, written language, and mathematics Direct Instruction programs from SRA/McGraw-Hill described in this chapter are those derived from the Direct Instruction model developed by Engelmann and

TABLE 4.2. Teacher Functions

Function	Description
Reviews and prerequisite checks	• Teachers initiate a lesson with a series of activities that serve to review the material covered in the previous lesson, check on the prerequisite skills and concepts needed for the new content that will be covered in class, and reteach if a majority of students does not demonstrate mastery of the previous or prerequisite skills and concepts needed to learn the new content.
Presentation of new content	• Teachers present new content by clearly stating the goals of the lesson; focusing on one point or direction at a time; using step-by-step presentation procedures; modeling the skill or concepts; providing concrete and varied examples; and frequently checking for student understanding.
Guided practice	• Teachers provide guided practice activities under their direct supervision to ensure that students master the new skills or concepts.
Independent practice	• Teachers provide independent practice and review activities once students are at least 80% successful under guided practice, to ensure that they consolidate (i.e., 100% successful) the new skills or concepts. Independent practice is designed to facilitate automaticity (i.e., students perform skills successfully, easily, and without much effort) in the case of basic skills.
Weekly and monthly reviews	• Teachers use weekly and monthly reviews to ensure that skills and concepts previously mastered are not forgotten. The weekly and monthly reviews provide an opportunity for students to review the skills and concepts previously taught and give teachers a valid measure of student progress for grading purposes and as feedback on the quality of instruction.

colleagues. The comprehensive and supplementary Direct Instruction programs anchor these effective teaching functions with carefully designed curriculum. Because their effectiveness has been demonstrated directly for students with BD (Marchand-Martella et al., 2002; Nelson, Benner, & Gonzalez, 2005; Nelson, Stage, Epstein, & Pierce, 2005), we describe two additional early literacy and beginning reading supplementary intervention programs available from Sopris West (*www.sopriswest.com*) that include the features of comprehensive and supplementary Direct Instruction programs. Comprehensive Direct Instruction programs address the full range of skills and concepts in an area; supplementary intervention programs address a narrower set of skills and concepts that have been found to be predictive of success in a content area. Additionally, there are other commercially available comprehensive and supplementary early reading and written language programs that include the design and delivery features of the Direct Instruction programs described in this chapter and which could be used successfully for students with BD.

Direct Instruction programs (Barton-Arwood, Wehby, & Falk, 2005; Marchand-Martella et al., 2002; Nelson, Benner, & Gonzalez, 2005; Nelson, Stage, Epstein, & Pierce, 2005; Trout, Epstein, Mickelson, Nelson, & Lewis, 2003; Wehby, Falk, Barton-Arwood, Lane, & Cooley, 2003) have been used effectively with students who have BD. These programs are designed to teach reading, written language, and mathematics skills sequentially and efficiently. Every lesson is planned, prepared, and integrated to ensure that students master a specified set of critical skills and concepts.

The purpose of this chapter is to describe commercially available early reading, written language, and mathematics Direct Instruction programs that have been found to be effective for students whose educational prospects are hindered by BD or other factors (e.g., poverty, race, ethnicity, limited English proficiency, disability). We first provide an overview of the design steps and key features of Direct Instruction programs and then describe key instructional delivery features. Finally, we detail the major commercially available early reading, written language, and mathematics Direct Instruction programs (for a review of all available Direct Instruction programs, see Marchand-Martella et al., 2004).

DESIGN STEPS AND KEY FEATURES
OF DIRECT INSTRUCTION PROGRAMS

Designing instructional lessons is an extremely time-consuming task. Developing a series of daily lessons across time to achieve a specified set of student learning outcomes is a daunting task—even for experienced teachers and expert instructional designers. Consider how difficult it is for teachers who have a relatively small number of hours to plan for and develop instructional lessons across several content areas. Thus, it is not surprising that even experienced teachers struggle in their efforts to improve the academic achievement of students whose education prospects are hindered by BD or other factors. Teaching these students important critical reading, written language, and mathematics skills requires precise instructional design and delivery. Designers of Direct Instruction programs use five steps to ensure that students receive well-designed, well-delivered instruction: (1) thoroughly analyze the curriculum area to identify critical skills and concepts; (2) organize skills and concepts into a scope and sequence; (3) construct instructional formats with which to present skills and concepts; (4) develop in-program progress monitoring procedures; and (5) field-test programs.

First, designers of Direct Instruction programs thoroughly analyze the curriculum area to be taught. The goal of this analysis is to identify critical skills and concepts, including those that would enable students to exhibit generalized performance. The identification of critical skills and concepts ensures that the Direct Instruction program is focused and likely to result in an important outcome (e.g., fluent phonics skills). Many published primary-level curriculum programs used by schools favor broad content coverage over mastery of fewer but critical skills and concepts. For example, we recommend that readers study the scope and sequence of Sopris West's *Stepping Stones to Literacy* (*sopriswest.com*), which is described below and depicted in Figure 4.1. *Stepping Stones to Literacy* is a secondary-level (Tier 2) supplementary prereading intervention program that focuses solely on

Lesson

INSTRUCTIONAL ACTIVITY	1	2	3	4	5	6	7	8	9	10	11	12	13	14	15	16	17	18	19	20	21	22	23	24	25
Identification, Manipulation, and Memory of Environmental Sounds																									
Sounds in Isolation	X	^	^	^	X																				
Sound Relationships	X	^	^	^	X																				
Sounds in Sequence						X	^	^	^	X															
Sound Expectations						X	^	^	V	X															
Omit a Sound											X	^	^	X											
Phonological Awareness																									
Rhyme Identification	X	^	^	^	^	^	X																		
Rhyme Generation								X	^	^	^	^	^	X											
Word Segmentation											X	^	^	X											
Syllable Blending											X	^	^	X											
Onset–Rime Blending															X	^	X								
Phonemic Awareness																									
Phoneme Deletion															X	^	^	X							
Phoneme Identification																		X	^	^	X				
Phoneme Segmentation																									
Initial															X	^	^	X							
Initial and Final																			X	^	^	X			
Initial, Medial, and Final																						X	^	^	X

58

Phoneme Change

Initial															X	>	X					
Final																		X	>	X		
Medial																			X	>	X	

Alphabet Knowledge

Letter Names	X	>	>	>	>	>	>	>	>	>	>	>	>	>	>	>	>	>	>	>	X
Letter Name Distributed Review		X	>	>	>	>	>	>	>	>	>	>	>	>	>	>	>	>	>	>	X
Letter Name Cumulative Review					X					X				X				X		X	X

Serial Rapid Automatic Naming

Serial Rapid Automatic Naming	X	>	>	>	>	>	>	>	>	>	>	>	>	>	>	>	>	>	>	>	X

Print Awareness

Sentence Recognition	X	>	>	>	X																
Sentence Generation				X	>	>	X														

Note. An "X" indicates that a specific instructional activity begins or ends in a particular lesson, whereas a ">" indicates that the activity continues in a given lesson. For example, the instructional activity "Sounds in Isolation" begins (X) in Lesson 1, continues (>) in Lessons 2–4, and ends (X) in Lesson 5.

FIGURE 4.1. Scope and Sequence: High-priority prereading skills (Stepping Stones to Literacy). Reprinted with permission from Sopris West.

early literacy skills predictive of successful reading skill acquisition (i.e., identification, manipulation, and memory of emotional sounds; phonological awareness; phonemic awareness; alphabet knowledge; serial rapid automatic naming; print awareness) (Adams, 1998).

Second, designers of Direct Instruction programs organize the identified skills and concepts into a scope and sequence to ensure that they are taught in an integrated fashion that enables students to master them. For example, teaching letter–sound relationships to students is enhanced when blending, spelling, and reading of decodable storybooks are included. Further, the skills and concepts are ordered within the scope and sequence to enable students to learn in an efficient manner. For example, the scope and sequence of *Stepping Stones to Literacy* are designed to teach young students critical early literacy skills (i.e., identification, manipulation, and memory of emotional sounds; phonological and phonemic awareness; alphabet knowledge; serial rapid automatic naming; print awareness) in twenty-five 20-minute lessons (see Figure 4.1). Prerequisite and easy skills and concepts are taught first. The easier phonological awareness concepts of rhyme identification and generation, word segmentation, syllable blending, and onset–rime blending are taught sequentially before more difficult phonemic awareness concepts (e.g., phoneme deletion, identification, segmentation, change).

Additionally, the scope and sequence allow teachers to systematically fade the amount of scaffolding they give students. *Scaffolding* refers to the support teachers provide to students as they are learning new skills and concepts. Although teachers and peers can provide scaffolding that is independent of the instructional materials and activities, Direct Instruction programs provide scaffolding through an integrated set of instructional activities that gradually and systematically requires students to complete tasks with less prompting or fewer cues. We recommend that readers study examples of the word-blending activity drawn from Sopris West's *Sound Partners*, a secondary (Tier 2) supplementary phonics intervention program. In Figure 4.2 an arrow is used to scaffold students' letter blending in Lesson 5 (top example); this cue is not used in Lesson 18 (lower example). Additionally, Direct Instruction programs provide scaffolding through distributed and cumulative reviews, when necessary, in the design of instruction (see Letter Name Distributed and Cumulative Review activities for *Stepping Stones to Literacy* in Figure 4.1). The distributed review activities provide practice on the immediate skills and concepts being taught; cumulative reviews provide practice on all of the skills and concepts taught to date. These reviews offer further opportunity for students to practice and integrate the skills and concepts they are learning. The reviews also give teachers a chance to check for student mastery of, and fluency with, the skill and concepts taught.

Third, designers of Direct Instruction programs construct the instructional formats for each activity once the critical skills and concepts have been identified and organized into a scope and sequence. The instructional format not only guides the way teachers present the skills and concepts but also provides the necessary instructional stimuli needed to teach the lessons. The instructional formats used in

Direct Instruction programs are consistent; this continuity ensures that the lessons proceed in a very predictable manner for both teachers and students. Consistency in the lesson formats enables teachers to use effective and precise instructional presentation language and to focus on student learning. Consistency in the lesson formats—coupled with instructional scripts—is very helpful to students because it enables them to focus their attention on the skills and concepts they are learning rather than changes in the instructional formats and presentation language that often occur with teacher-designed instructional activities.

Additionally, designers of Direct Instruction programs script each of the activities to facilitate teachers' use of effective and precise instructional presentation language. Direct Instruction programs vary in the degree of scripting used in each lesson. The comprehensive and supplementary Direct Instruction programs available from SRA/McGraw-Hill are hard scripted (i.e., all aspects of teacher–student communication throughout the instructional presentation are scripted). An example of a hard-scripted Direct Instruction lesson, drawn from SRA/McGraw-Hill's *Reading Mastery*, is presented in Figure 4.3. Some programs that include the features of the Direct Instruction programs are soft scripted (i.e., they only provide the major instructional prompts). Soft-scripted Direct Instruction programs rely on teachers to use effective instructional presentation and error-correction practices that are consistent across all instructional activities (i.e., signals and prompts, error-correction procedures). We suggest that readers compare the soft-scripted word-blending activity drawn from *Sound Partners* (Figure 4.2) with the hard-scripted lesson taken from *Corrective Reading: Decoding A* (Figure 4.3).

Fourth, designers of Direct Instruction programs develop in-program progress monitoring procedures to track students' progress toward program learning objectives. The goal of these procedures is to identify early whether students are mastering the skills and concepts being taught. Data from the progress monitoring procedures can be used by teachers to identify students who need additional instruction and practice—and those who are easily mastering the skills and concepts being taught. Teachers can adjust their pacing (i.e., within and across lessons), repeat lessons, or provide students with supplementary instruction when they are having difficulty mastering the skills and concepts being taught. Conversely, teachers may move at a faster pace with those students who are easily mastering the skills and concepts being taught. We suggest that readers study the example of an in-program progress monitoring assessment from SRA/McGraw-Hill's *Reading Mastery Level I*, which is depicted in Figure 4.4. Teachers use this progress monitoring assessment to check whether students have mastered a particular set of letter sounds. Based on the students' responses, teachers directly remediate those letter sounds students have not yet mastered. Teachers also may adjust their pacing within lessons (e.g., provide additional practice for students by repeating instructional activities) and across lessons (e.g., repeat lessons) to ensure that students acquire the critical skills and concepts. Additionally, in-program progress monitoring procedures are often supplemented with the commonly used progress monitoring measures and procedures described in Chapter 3.

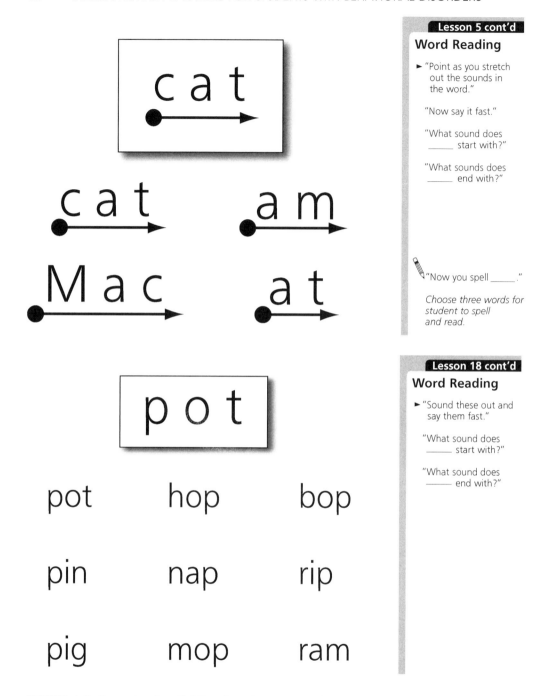

FIGURE 4.2. Example of scaffolding from lessons 5 and 18, provided to students through instructional activities. Reprinted with permission from Sopris West.

EXERCISE 3

• **SAY THE SOUNDS**

Note: Do not write the words on the board. This is an oral exercise.

1. Listen: fffēēē. (Hold up a finger for each sound.)
2. Say the sounds in (pause) fffēēē. Get ready. (Hold up a finger for each sound.) fffēēē. (Repeat until the students say the sounds without stopping.)
3. Say it fast. (Signal.) *Fee.*
4. What word? (Signal.) *Fee.* Yes, **fee.**
5. (Repeat steps 2–4 for **if, fish, sam, at, me, rim, she, we, ship, fat, miff.**)

EXERCISE 4

WORD READING

Task A   Eed

1. You're going to read each word First you sound it out; then you say it fast.
2. (Touch the ball of the arrow for the first word.) Sound it out. Get ready. (Touch under **ee, d.**) *ēēēd.* (Repeat until the students say the sounds without pausing.)

   To correct sound errors:
   a. (Say the correct sound loudly as soon as you hear an error.)
   b. (Point to the sound.) What sound? (Touch.)
   c. (Repeat until firm.)
   d. (Repeat step 2.)
3. Again. Sound it out. Get ready. (Touch under **ee, d.**) *ēēēd.* (Repeat until firm.)

4. (Touch the ball of the arrow.) Say it fast. (Slash right, along the arrow.) *Eed.* Yes, **eed.**
   To correct say-it-fast errors:
   a. (Say the correct word:) **eed.**
   b. (Touch the ball of the arrow.) Say it fast. (Slash right.) *Eed.*
   c. (Return to step 2.)

Task B   Seed

1. (Touch the ball of the arrow for the next word.) Sound it out. Get ready. (Touch under **s, ee, d.**) *sssēēēd.* (Repeat until the students say the sounds without pausing.)
2. Again. Sound it out. Get ready. (Touch under **s, ee, d.**) *sssēēēd.* (Repeat until firm.)
3. (Touch the ball of the arrow.) Say it fast. (Slash right. *Seed.*) Yes, **seed.**
4. (Repeat steps 1–3 for **seem, at, eet, it, if.**)

.eed

.seed

.seem

.at

.eet

.it

.if

FIGURE 4.3. Example of hard-scripted Direct Instruction lesson. From Wright Group/McGroup (1999). Copyright 1999 by The McGraw-Hill Companies. Reprinted by permission.

Finally, designers of Direct Instruction programs conduct field tests to ensure that they achieve the specified program skills and concepts. The field tests typically begin with a series of informal case study outcome and consumer acceptability/satisfaction studies. These studies use a wide array of typical end users who provide the developers with suggestions for improving the curriculum materials and feedback on feasibility of implementation, the amount of time required to teach lessons, difficulties encountered during instruction, and student responsiveness. The case studies are followed with experimental studies to ensure that the Direct Instruction program produces educationally significant student learning outcomes. More than any other commercially available programs, the comprehensive and supplementary Direct Instruction programs detailed in this chapter are supported by research (for a complete research review, see Marchand-Martella et al., 2004).

Mastery Test 13 after lesson 70, before lesson 71

a. When I touch the sound, you say it.
b. (test item) Point to ā. Get ready. Touch ā. *āāā*.
c. (test item) Point to h. Get ready. Touch h. *h*.
d. (test item) Point to u. Get ready. Touch u. *uuu*.
e. (test item) Point to a. Get ready. Touch a. *aaa*.
f. (test item) Point to i. Get ready. Touch i. *iii*.

Total number of test items: 5

A group is weak if more than one-third of the children missed any of the items on the test.

WHAT TO DO

If the group is firm on Mastery Test 13 and was firm on Mastery Test 12:

Present lessons 71 and 72, and then skip lesson 73. If more than one child missed any of the items on the test, present the firming procedures specified below to those children.

If the group is firm on Mastery Test 13 but was weak on Mastery Test 12:

Present lesson 71 to the group during the next reading period. If more than one child missed any of the items on the test, present the firming procedures specified below to those children.

If the group is weak on Mastery Test 13:

A. Present these firming procedures to the group during the next reading period.
  1. Lesson 68, Sounds, page 71, tasks 5, 6.
  2. Lesson 68, Reading Vocabulary, page 73, tasks 12 through 15.
  3. Lesson 69, Reading Vocabulary, page 79, tasks 7 through 11.
  4. Lesson 70, Sounds, page 85, tasks 4, 5.
B. After presenting the above tasks, again give Mastery Test 13 individually to members of the group who failed the test.
C. If the group is firm (less than one-third of the total group missed any items on the retest), present lesson 71 to the group during the next reading period.
D. If the group is still weak (more than one-third of the total group missed any items on the retest), repeat A and B during the next reading period.

FIGURE 4.4. Example of in-program progress monitoring form. From Wright Group/McGraw-Hill (2003). Copyright 2003 by The McGraw-Hill Companies. Reprinted by permission.

DELIVERY FEATURES OF DIRECT INSTRUCTION PROGRAMS

The design features of Direct Instruction programs provide the foundation for student mastery of specified program skills and concepts. However, the effectiveness of Direct Instruction programs is largely dependent upon a number of key delivery features. First, the effective delivery of Direct Instruction programs is enhanced when students are carefully selected and grouped for instruction. Most Direct Instruction programs are designed to be delivered to small groups of students who have similar competence levels. In essence, students benefit most when they receive instruction that is just beyond their current level of competence; this policy ensures that students receive instruction that closely matches their individual needs and allows them to be engaged in tasks they can perform with relatively high levels of success. The grouping of students is especially important in the case of comprehensive Direct Instruction programs designed to address the full range of skills and concepts in a content area. Student selection is critical in the case of Direct Instruction supplementary intervention programs that focus on a narrower set of skills and concepts to achieve a specified set of program learning objectives (e.g., Sopris West's *Stepping Stones to Literacy* and SRA/Mc-Graw-Hill's *Basic Writing Skills*). These programs are designed to address the needs of a specified group of students at the same competence level. Additionally, the effective delivery of Direct Instruction programs is enhanced when the grouping of students is flexible and accommodates individual learning rates. Procedures for selecting and grouping students are specified for each Direct Instruction program.

Second, the effective delivery of Direct Instruction programs is enhanced when teachers allocate sufficient time to complete individual lessons and each lesson has been carefully designed with a set of integrated instructional activities. Direct Instruction lessons are most effective when teachers complete the entire lesson and do not skip days; this outcome requires that adequate time be allocated to complete the lessons on a daily basis. Additionally, teachers must maximize the time allocated to the delivery of Direct Instruction lessons by preparing themselves and actively teaching students the transitions and instructional routines (e.g., "Sit tall," "Look at the lesson book," "Answer on the signal," "Use inside voices"). Brisk pacing of instruction also is important to maximize the time allocated to delivery. A brisk pace improves student engagement by holding attention—which is especially important for students with BD. Further, effective delivery of Direct Instruction programs requires teachers to adjust their instructional pace relative to students' task demands and individual learning rates.

Third, the effective delivery of Direct Instruction programs is enhanced when teachers follow instructional scripts. As mentioned earlier, instructional scripts are designed to facilitate teachers' use of effective and precise instructional presentation language. Teachers, however, must bring the scripts to life by being excited about teaching, building positive and productive relationships with students, and motivating them to reach their full potential. In essence, effective delivery of Direct Instruction programs requires teachers to couple the instructional scripts with the multidimensional art of teaching.

Finally, the effective delivery of Direct Instruction programs is enhanced when teachers ensure that students achieve mastery of the skills and concepts being taught. Direct Instruction includes a number of design features to help students achieve mastery of each lesson, including the thoughtful use of scope and sequence to maximize instruction of critical skills and concepts, selection and grouping procedures, use of consistent and scripted lessons, and in-program progress monitoring procedures. These design features help ensure that students' mastery of a lesson prepares them for the subsequent lesson, and so on. For example, student mastery of lessons 1–10 ensures that students are prepared for lesson 11. Mastery is especially crucial for students who are struggling during the lessons. Thus, it is critical that teachers ensure that *all* students master the skills and concepts in each lesson. Teachers can do this most efficiently by using effective model–lead–test and error correction procedures (see Chapter 2) and by monitoring the mastery level of the lowest-performing students in the group; it is likely that all students are mastering the skills and concepts being taught if low-performing students have. Siegfried E. Engelmann, the original developer of the Direct Instruction model, identified four criteria for assessing student mastery during lessons (cited in Marchand-Martella et al., 2004):

1. Students should be at least 70% correct on skills and concepts being introduced for the first time.
2. Students should be at least 90% correct on skills taught earlier in the Direct Instruction program.
3. At the end of a particular skills and concept instructional sequence, all students should achieve mastery (i.e., virtually 100%).
4. Student error rates should be low enough to ensure that teachers have sufficient time to complete the lesson.

COMMERCIALLY AVAILABLE DIRECT INSTRUCTION PROGRAMS

In this section we discuss commercially available early reading, written language, and mathematics Direct Instruction programs. Two of the supplementary intervention programs—*Stepping Stones to Literacy*, *Sound Partners*—are available from Sopris West (*www.sopriswest.com*); the other comprehensive and supplemental Direct Instruction programs are available from SRA/McGraw-Hill (*www.sraonline.com*). For each program, we provide a general description of the corresponding essential instructional goals, level of intervention (Tier 1, 2, or 3), number of lessons, teacher materials, and student materials. Additionally, we note the primary level of intervention and age level for each program; however, each of the intervention levels can be used at subsequent levels (depending upon the three-tiered model used by the school), and age level depends upon student skill levels. For example, although *Reading Mastery Levels I and II* (described below) are considered Tier 1 beginning reading programs, they can be used as Tier 2 or 3 programs. Furthermore, *Stepping Stones to Literacy*, a Tier 2 early literacy intervention program, could be used at the tertiary level (Tier 3), for example, by increasing opportunities for students to respond though adjustments in grouping (e.g., one-to-one vs. small group) or lesson pacing (e.g., repeating instructional activities and/or lessons).

Early Reading Programs

Stepping Stones to Literacy

Description: *Stepping Stones to Literacy* is a supplementary intervention program designed for pre-K–1 students who have limited prereading or early literacy skills. The six essential instructional goals of the program are to develop identification, manipulation, and memory of emotional sounds; phonological awareness; phonemic awareness; alphabet knowledge; rapid naming (i.e., ability to make quick visual–verbal associations of known sets of colors, digits, and letter names in a left-to-right format); and print awareness. The program can be implemented individually or with small groups (three to five students). The program includes English and Spanish prompts (to accommodate students whose primary language is Spanish) and is intended to be implemented by teachers or paraprofessionals.

Level of intervention: Tier 2

Number of lessons: 25

Teacher materials: An implementation manual and teacher presentation book

Student materials: None

Sound Partners

Description: *Sound Partners* is a supplementary intervention program designed for students in grades 1–3 who have limited phonics skills. The program's three essential instructional goals are to develop decoding, word reading, and fluency skills. The program is administered individually and is intended to be implemented by teachers and paraprofessionals.

Level of intervention: Tier 2

Number of lessons: 100

Teacher materials: An implementation manual, a tutor manual, a teacher presentation book, and sound cards

Student materials: Three sets of decodable books that align with each lesson; the books contain decodable stories that reinforce the decoding and word-reading skills taught in the lessons.

Reading Mastery Plus Levels I, II, and Fast Cycle

Description: *Reading Mastery Plus Levels I* (K–1), *II* (grades 1–2), and *Fast Cycle* (grades 1–2) are part of a comprehensive six-level developmental reading program for K–6 students. Its three essential instructional goals are to develop decoding, word reading, and fluency skills. *Level I* focuses on basic decoding, word reading, and fluency skills; *Level II* expands on these same skills; *Fast Cycle* addresses the same decoding, word reading, and fluency skills taught in *Levels I* and *II* in a shorter period of time. The programs can be administered to the whole class or to small groups (three to eight students) and are intended to be implemented by teachers.

Level of intervention: Tier 1

Number of lessons: Both *Levels I* and *II* contain 160 daily lessons; *Fast Cycle* includes 170 lessons.

Teacher materials: *Level I*—three spiral-bound presentation books, a teacher guide, an annotated edition of the student take-home workbook, three student storybooks, a cassette demonstrating sound pronunciation and sample tasks, a page protector, group progress indicators, a behavioral objectives book, and a skills profile folder. *Level II*—three spiral-bound presentation books, a teacher guide, a spelling book, an annotated edition of the student take-home workbook, two student storybooks, a page protector, group progress indicators, a behavioral objectives book, and a skills profile folder. *Fast Cycle*—four spiral-bound presentation books, a teacher guide, a spelling book, an annotated edition of the student take-home workbook, two student storybooks, a page protector, group progress indicators, a behavioral objectives book, and a skills profile folder.

Student materials: Take-home workbooks and storybooks (*Levels I, II,* and *Fast Cycle*). The take-home workbooks include practice and review activities to reinforce the skills and concepts taught in the lessons. The storybooks contain decodable stories to reinforce the decoding and word-reading skills taught in the lessons.

Corrective Reading

Description: *Corrective Reading* is a supplemental intervention program designed for students in grades 3–12 who are reading 1 or more years below grade level. It includes two major strands: *decoding* and *comprehension*. Both *Corrective Reading Decoding* and *Comprehension* strands have three levels devoted to half-year implementation (*Levels A, B1, B2*) and one level devoted to full-year implementation (*Level C*). The three essential instructional goals of the *decoding* strand are to develop decoding, word reading, and fluency skills and concepts. The two essential instructional goals of the *comprehension* strand are to develop vocabulary and comprehension skills and concepts. The programs can be administered to the whole class or to small groups (three to eight students) and are intended to be implemented by teachers.

Level of intervention: Tier 3

Number of lessons: The *decoding* strand contains 65 lessons each in Levels *A, B1,* and *B2,* and 125 lessons in *Level C;* the *comprehension* strand contains 60 lessons each in *Levels A* and *B1,* 65 lessons in *Level B2,* and 140 lessons in *Level C.*

Teacher materials: For each level of the *decoding* and *comprehension* strands, a spiral-bound presentation book, a series guide, a teacher guide containing reproducible placement tests and sample lessons, blackline masters of additional practice exercises, a Sunshine State standards/benchmarks checklist, standardized test format booklets, and mastery test packages.

Student materials: For each level of the *decoding* and *comprehension* strands, a hardcover student decoding textbook and student comprehension textbook, respectively; workbooks include practice and review activities that reinforce the skills and concepts taught in the lessons.

Early Written Language Programs

Reasoning and Writing: Levels A, B, and C

Description: *Reasoning and Writing Levels A* (K–1), *B* (grades 1–2), and *C* (grades 2–3) are part of a comprehensive six-level developmental combined reasoning and written language program for K–6 students. The essential instructional goals are to develop basic and higher-order reasoning and writing skills. *Level A* focuses on story grammar, temporal sequencing, classification, and higher-order reasoning and writing skills and concepts; *Level B* expands on these same skills; *Level C* focuses on the narrative writing process. *Levels A, B,* and *C* integrate basic writing mechanics throughout the lessons. The programs can be administered to the whole class or to small groups (three to eight students) and are intended to be implemented by teachers.

Level of intervention: Tier 1

Number of lessons: Both *Levels A* and *B* contain 70 daily lessons; *Level C* includes 110 lessons.

Teacher materials: For each level of *Reasoning and Writing*, a spiral-bound presentation book, a series guide, a teacher guide containing reproducible placement tests and sample lessons, blackline masters of additional practice exercises, standardized test and format booklets, and an answer key (*Level C*) for independent student activities.

Student materials: For each of the *Levels A, B,* and *C*, a student workbook. The workbook includes practice and review activities to reinforce the skills and concepts taught in the lessons. *Level C* also includes a hardcover student textbook that contains complete lessons associated with the skills and concepts taught in the program.

Basic Writing Skills Sentence Development and Capitalization and Punctuation

Description: Supplementary intervention programs for writing-deficient students in grades 6–12 who demonstrate third-grade reading and spelling skills. The essential instructional goals are to develop sentence construction, capitalization, and punctuation skills. *Sentence Development* focuses on the construction of a variety of sentences; *Capitalization and Punctuation* teaches basic capitalization and punctuation rules. The programs can be administered to the whole class or to small groups (three to eight students) and are intended to be implemented by teachers.

Level of intervention: Tiers 2 and 3

Number of lessons: *Sentence Development* contains 31 daily lessons; *Capitalization and Punctuation* includes 40 lessons.

Teacher materials: A spiral-bound presentation book and blackline masters of worksheet exercises

Student materials: None

Expressive Writing 1 and 2

Description: *Expressive Writing 1* and *2* are supplementary intervention programs for students in grades 4–8 with written expression difficulties (i.e., who demonstrate third-grade reading and spelling skills). The essential instructional goals are to develop expressive writing skills. *Expressive Writing 1* focuses on the mechanics of sentence and paragraph writing and editing skills; *Expressive Writing 2* expands on these same skills. The programs can be administered to the whole class or to small groups (three to eight students) and are intended to be implemented by teachers.

Level of intervention: Tiers 2 and 3

Number of lessons: *Expressive Writing 1* contains 50 daily lessons; *Expressive Writing 2* includes 10 preprogram lessons and 45 program lessons.

Teacher materials: A spiral-bound presentation book, an answer key to the student workbook, and blackline masters of mastery tests.

Student materials: A student workbook

Early Mathematics Programs

Distar Arithmetic Levels I and II

Description: *Distar Arithmetic Levels I* (K–1) and *II* (grades 2–3) are comprehensive developmental mathematics programs for K–3 students. The four essential instructional goals are to develop skills and concepts in addition, subtraction, multiplication, and fractions. *Level I* focuses on addition, subtraction, and multiplication; *Level II* expands on these skills and concepts to include fractions. The programs can be administered to the whole class or to small groups (three to eight students) and are intended to be implemented by teachers.

Level of intervention: Tier 1

Number of lessons: Both *Levels I* and *II* contain 160 daily lessons.

Teacher materials: *Level I*—three spiral-bound presentation books, a teacher guide, an annotated edition of the student take-home workbooks, four decks of geometric figure cards, 11 form boards, an acetate page protector, and group progress indicators. *Level II*—four spiral-bound presentation books, a teacher guide, an annotated edition of the student take-home workbooks, and group progress indicators.

Student materials: Take-home workbooks that include worksheets for teacher-guided and independent exercises and practice and review activities designed to reinforce the skills and concepts taught in the lessons

Corrective Mathematics

Description: *Corrective Mathematics* is a supplemental intervention program designed for third-grade to postsecondary students who are 1 or more years below grade level. The program includes seven separate modules: *addition, subtraction, multiplication, division, basic fractions, fractions, decimals, percents,* and *ratios and equations.* The nine essential instructional goals are to develop skills and concepts in addition, subtraction, multiplication, division, fractions, decimals, percents, ratios, and equations. The programs can be administered to the whole class or to small groups (three to eight students) and are intended to be implemented by teachers.

Level of intervention: Tier 3

Number of lessons: Each module contains 65 lessons.

Teacher materials: A spiral-bound presentation book, series guide, ExamView software (creates paper- or computer-based tests and worksheets), and answer key booklets

Student materials: Workbooks that include practice and review activities designed to reinforce the skills and concepts taught in the lessons, and summary charts for recording student performance and awarding grades

CONCLUSIONS

The overall purpose of this chapter was to describe commercially available early reading, written language, and mathematics Direct Instruction programs that have been found to be effective for students whose educational prospects are hindered by BD or other factors (e.g., poverty, race, ethnicity, limited English proficiency, disability). We began by distinguishing between big Direct Instruction programs and the general use of the term *direct instruction* to describe effective teaching functions teachers apply to any published curriculum, academic skill and application, or content area (see Table 4.2). The commercially available Direct Instruction programs described in this chapter (as well as others not mentioned here) anchor these effective teaching functions with carefully designed curriculum.

We then described the design steps and key features of Direct Instruction programs. First, these programs focus on critical skills and concepts rather than broad content coverage. This specific focus improves the efficiency and effectiveness of the Direct Instruction program. Second, the programs organize the critical skills and concepts into a scope and sequence, which not only ensures that the skills and concepts are taught in a systematic and integrated manner but also enables teachers to systematically reduce the amount of scaffolding they provide to students. Third, Direct Instruction programs include consistent instructional formats with scripting, which ensure that lessons proceed in a predictable manner. Fourth, in-program progress monitoring procedures are provided to track student mastery of the skills and concepts being taught. Finally, Direct Instruction programs are field-tested to ensure that they produce educationally significant student learning outcomes.

Next, we described the delivery features of Direct Instruction programs, which are most effective when students are carefully selected and grouped for instruction. Most Direct Instruction programs are designed to be delivered to small groups of students with similar competence levels. The effectiveness of Direct Instruction programs is enhanced when teachers allocate sufficient time for instruction, follow the instructional scripts, use brisk pacing during the lessons, and ensure that students achieve mastery of the skills and concepts being taught. Teachers must bring the Direct Instruction lessons to life by being excited about teaching, building positive and productive relationships with students, and motivating them to reach their full potential.

Finally, we described commercially available early reading, written language, and mathematics Direct Instruction programs. For each program we provided a general description of the essential instructional goals, level of intervention (Tier 1, 2, or 3), number of lessons, teacher materials, and student materials. These programs can be used to address the early reading, written language, and mathematics skills of students whose educational prospects are hindered by BD or other factors. Keep in mind that the comprehensive Direct Instruction programs (Tier 1) that were described can be used at subsequent levels (Tier 2 or 3), depending upon the three-tiered model used by the school. The same can be said for the Tier 2 programs. These programs can be used at Tier 3, for example, by supplementing the lessons or giving students more opportunities to respond. In other words, Direct Instruction programs are versatile in that they can be used in a range of school intervention structures.

CHAPTER 5

Early Reading Instruction

We opened this book by describing the characteristics of students with BD and the school and instructional climates in which these students are served. We followed with information on progress monitoring practices that help ensure that instruction is sensitive to the individual needs and performances of students with BD and academic deficits. In the previous chapter, we concentrated on Direct Instruction programs and principles applicable to supplementary instruction for students with BD. The next three chapters focus on empirically validated instructional practices across the basic academic skills. In this chapter, we direct our attention toward developing early reading skills.

We begin with reading skill development for two main reasons. First, current and future teachers understand the importance of learning to read and reading to learn. Students' elementary, high school, and college years are spent reading to learn, be it social studies content, recipes, sports stories, or educational theories and practices. Teachers understand the importance of making sure that students learn to read so they can then read to learn. Anderson, Hiebert, Scott, and Wilkinson (1985) described reading as "a basic life skill . . . a cornerstone for a child's success in school and, indeed, throughout life" (p. 1). Moreover, for the student with BD who is struggling to master the alphabetic system, improvement in reading ability can translate into improvement in communication ability. From that standpoint, improving a student's communication skills can be seen as an effort to develop the student's ability to cooperate and express him- or herself in a way that might otherwise be expressed antisocially (McEvoy & Welker, 2000; O'Shaughnessy, Lane, Gresham, & Beebe-Frankenberger, 2003).

Second, in recent years, significant time, energy, and resources have been invested in improving children's reading outcomes and ensuring that scientifically based reading practices are implemented in U.S. public schools. Unfortunately, teachers of students with BD often do not incorporate scientifically based reading practices into their everyday routines (Vaughn, Levy, Coleman, & Bos, 2002). Guaranteeing that students with BD receive scientifically based instructional practices means that teachers must separate proven practices from unproven practices; this guarantee also requires that evidence-based practices are delivered with integrity in our schools. Implementing scientifically based reading practices is particularly important for students with BD because they are likely to experience reading difficulties. Moreover, students with BD are more likely to be resistant to generally effective reading interventions than other at-risk groups (Al Otaiba & Fuchs, 2002; Nelson, Benner, & Gonzalez, 2003). In this chapter, we describe the evidence base with respect to reading research for students with BD. We follow this description with a theoretical and empirical justification for early and scientifically based intervention, including instructional practices that promote mastery and fluency of critical early reading skills. We conclude with a summary of the chapter's major points.

READING RESEARCH FOR STUDENTS WITH BD

A small body of research documents the effects of reading interventions with students with BD. Three commonalities can be identified in a review of this literature. First, the majority of interventions are peer-mediated ones administered to small groups of students with BD. *Peer-mediated interventions* are those in which student peers are trained to act as direct behavioral change agents (Mooney et al., 2003; Ryan et al., 2004). Peer-mediated interventions include same-age and cross-age peer tutoring and cooperative learning. For example, Barton-Arwood, Wehby, and Falk (2005) included a same-age peer tutoring intervention called *Peer-Assisted Learning Strategies* (PALS; Fuchs et al., 2001) into a multicomponent intervention implemented with 8-year-olds with BD (*n* = 8). Students in this study received instruction in phonological awareness and phonics intervention 3 days a week for 30 minutes each session during the peer-mediated portion of the intervention, which also included a Direct Instruction component (see Chapter 4 for a description of Direct Instruction programs).

Next, the interventions have targeted the major early reading areas of phonological awareness, phonics, and fluency. For example, Dawson, Venn, and Gunter (2000) evaluated text fluency in comparing a teacher-mediated (i.e., teacher-directed) instructional program to computer-directed and no-intervention conditions with four 7- and 8-year-old students with BD. Dawson and colleagues found that fluency and accuracy rates were higher in the teacher-mediated condition than in the other conditions.

Finally, findings across peer- and teacher-mediated interventions have generally been positive, indicating that students with BD do improve their reading skills with systematic intervention (Mooney et al., 2005; Pierce et al., 2004; Ryan et al., 2004). For example, Nelson, Stage, Epstein, & Pierce (2005) studied the effects of a prereading intervention program on the early literacy skills of kindergarten children with concurrent BD and phonological awareness deficits (see Chapter 4 for a description of *Stepping Stones to Literacy*, the program they used). Children who received the prereading intervention program made statistically and educationally significant gains on the standardized measure of phonological awareness and word reading relative to those in the control group.

EARLY READING THEORY AND PRACTICE

We present mastery- and fluency-oriented instructional principles in reading through the prism of Linnea Ehri's four-phase theory of word-reading development. Ehri calls the ability to quickly and correctly read individual words in text or isolation the "hallmark" of skilled reading. The importance of quick and accurate word reading cannot be overstated. As Ehri notes (2005), the automatic reading of words allows readers to spend greater energy on text comprehension.

For teachers of students with BD, the goal should be the development of skilled reading. Skilled readers automatically recognize and understand a seemingly limitless bank of words. Skilled readers also are armed with strategies to recognize unfamiliar words when they come across them in text (Ehri, 2005). For example, skilled readers might be able to sound out individual letter sequences (e.g., /c/ /aaa/ /t/) to make words (i.e., decoding). They also might be able to use words they already know (e.g., *nation*) to read similar-looking words (e.g., *creation*); this skill is known as *analogizing*. They might even use context clues to guess unfamiliar words. The bottom line is that effective readers recognize most pronunciations and meanings instantly and can, therefore, direct their mental energies toward understanding the entirety of the text they are reading. When they come to words they do not immediately recognize, skilled readers decode and flexibly use a range of strategies to understand the meanings. The job of the reading teacher is to develop these skills in students with BD, with the primary emphasis initially on developing word-reading skills.

Ehri's Phases of Reading Development

Ehri (1999) has described four phases involved in reading development: (1) a prealphabetic phase; (2) a partial alphabetic phase; (3) a full alphabetic phase; and (4) a consolidated alphabetic phase. These phases are interconnected, and mastery of one phase is not necessary to initiate movement to the next phase. We describe each of these phases next.

Prealphabetic Phase

Preschoolers and kindergartners are commonly in Ehri's first phase. However, assessment of older students with BD who are experiencing reading difficulties may indicate that their skill level is comparable. Students in the prealphabetic phase lack letter knowledge. With a limited knowledge of letters, children do not understand how letters in written words correspond to sounds in oral language. Children at this phase handle the task of reading words by memorizing their visual features or by guessing words from their context. Ehri and McCormick (1998) believe that mastery-oriented instruction for struggling prealphabetic readers should focus on building letter awareness and phonemic awareness explicitly and incorporate letter and phoneme awareness activities into other classroom literacy tasks. Examples of these instructional activities include studying letters in words in print, counting the number of phonemes in spoken words, blending and segmenting phonemes in spoken words, and saying initial sounds in spoken words. Students who are at this phase of reading development may score poorly on the DIBELS Letter Naming Fluency (LNF) and Initial Sound Fluency (ISF) probes described in Chapter 3 (Good & Kaminski, 2002).

Partial Alphabetic Phase

Ehri's second phase most commonly includes kindergartners and first graders along with older, struggling readers. Students at this level recognize most letters in printed words, sounds in oral language, and connections between letters and sounds, and can read simple decodable text. Essentially, there is an initial working knowledge of the relationship between letters (i.e., graphemes) and sounds (i.e., phonemes) in readers at the partial alphabetic phase. These students, in short, are beginning to crack the code. Ehri and McCormick (1998) indicate that children in this phase know consonant sounds such as *b, d, f, l, m, r, s,* and *t.* Readers at this phase may know the names and sounds of letters and be able, in some instances, to connect sounds to letters in writing, such as writing *JC* for *jake.* The scope of instructional activities necessary for partial alphabetic readers encompasses: (1) mastery of all sounds (phonemes) in words, not just the first and last sounds; (2) mastery of phoneme segmentation and blending; (3) reading of highly controlled text; and (4) writing activities that allow students to create their own stories and teachers to interact afterward with information on correct letter sequences in written text. Students at this phase of early reading development tend to score higher on the DIBELS LNF and ISF probes than the Phoneme Segmentation Fluency (PSF) and Nonsense Word Fluency (NWF) probes.

Full Alphabetic Phase

Readers at this phase—typically, first graders—possess extensive working knowledge of the graphophonemic (i.e., letter–sound) system and can use this knowledge to fully analyze the connections between graphemes and phonemes in words (Ehri, 1999). This understanding enables readers to decode unfamiliar words and store fully analyzed sight words in memory. Moreover, these readers now have the beginnings of a reservoir of sight words that can be pulled from memory nearly instantly when encountered. The scope of instructional activities in this phase encompasses much controlled practice reading decodable text; learning and practicing word families; and dividing words into syllables, including onsets (i.e., the part of a syllable that comes before the vowel; e.g., the *r* in *read*) and rimes (i.e., the rest of the letters in the syllable; e.g., *ead* in *read*). Students at this phase of early reading development tend to score high on the DIBELS PSF and NWF probes and may meet grade-level benchmarks on the Oral Reading Fluency (ORF) probe.

Consolidated Alphabetic Phase

Second-grade and older readers typically advance to this phase, which is characterized by the strengthening of the known grapheme–phoneme blends and the identification of word patterns in more complex words (Ehri, 2005). The important alphabetic acquisition at this phase consists of a working knowledge of letter sequences that recur in different words and how they are pronounced as blended units. These consolidated units might include affixes, root words, onsets, rimes, and syllables. The value of consolidated units is that they facilitate word decoding accuracy and speed and sight-word learning. Whereas full alphabetic readers operate primarily with grapheme–phoneme relations, consolidated alphabetic readers operate primarily with larger units; the total number of units to be processed in words is therefore reduced. For example, the word *interesting* contains 10 graphophonemic units (NG is one phoneme) but only four graphosyllabic units (IN-TER-EST-ING). The focus of instruction at this phase is building mastery of syllable recognition and manipulation in complex words (i.e., those with three or more syllables). It is critical that teachers of students with BD continue to offer explicit instruction in, and ample practice opportunities working with, complex words. Ehri and McCormick (1998) note that without continued instruction, the likelihood that struggling readers will become fluent in recognizing patterns in complex words is reduced. Students at this phase of reading development may meet grade-level benchmark standards on the ORF probe.

MASTERY INSTRUCTION

In Chapter 2 we introduced the two major components used to guide the process of developing students' skill mastery. First, a well-defined scope and sequence of skills needs to be developed. Second, an instructional design that applies a model–lead–test presentation and includes systematic error-correction procedures for use in group or one-on-one settings is necessary. It is important to note that the skills described in this chapter center on those critical to word-reading development. As such, the skills and associated instructional practices fit in approaches used at Tiers 2 and 3 of RTI models. The National Reading Panel (2000) articulated core beginning reading skills from kindergarten through grade 3. Vaughn and Linan-Thompson (2004) provide a detailed scope and sequence to the full range of literacy skills, based directly on the core skills identified by the National Reading Panel, included in core Tier 1 reading programs (see Table 5.2. on p. 98). As discussed in Chapter 2, comprehensive instructional approaches address the full range of skills in early reading development, whereas supplementary (Tiers 2 and 3) intervention approaches address a narrower set of skills critical to successful reading in the primary grades.

According to Ehri's phase-theory model, skilled reading evolves as readers develop knowledge of letter names, phonemes, letter sounds, spelling patterns, and whole words and then apply that knowledge with increasing efficiency in text that initially is highly predictable and controlled and eventually involves real-world reading of expository and narrative texts. We noted earlier that research in effective reading instruction for students with BD has indicated that both teacher- and peer-mediated formats have proven beneficial for supplemental instruction. In presenting scientifically based reading practices across the prealphabetic, partial alphabetic, and full alphabetic phases of Ehri's model, we incorporate teacher- or peer-mediated formats to highlight the respective instructional practices.

Letter Naming: Prealphabetic Phase—Teacher-Mediated

Scope and Sequence

The scope of instruction depends on the needs of the individual learner. For one student, the focus might be on mastery of all 26 letters in both lowercase and uppercase formats. For another student or for a group of students, instruction might focus on a small subset of upper and lowercase letters not readily identified during screening. Figure 5.1 provides a screening instrument that includes all 52 letter formats. The DIBELS LNF probe also can be used to screen for mastery of letter names. Teachers can place a copy of the sheet in front of the student and keep their own copy in order to record correct and incorrect responses. Teachers can point to the first letter and ask the child to name it, along with the others on the line, moving from left to right. Teachers can place a line through those letters incorrectly named and use that list to inform the scope of instructional activities.

Figure 5.2 includes a potential introduction sequence for all 52 lowercase and uppercase letters, as suggested by Carnine, Silbert, Kame'enui, and Tarver (2004). The order is guided by the following three principles. First, introduce lowercase letters first; most words in text are composed of lowercase letters. Second, introduce letters that are most useful first; letters that are most often seen in text give students a chance to decode more words. For example, the letters *a*, *m*, and *d* are used much more frequently in general text than the letters *q*, *x*, and *z*. Third, separate letters that look or sound similar. Examples of letters that look similar to each

j	e	H	m	P	u	r
X	c	G	I	Q	v	Z
g	K	r	U	y	E	i
O	s	W	f	L	p	Y
j	R	a	D	n	B	k
V	z	J	t	F	x	I
w	M	d	T	o	A	h
c	q	C	S	b	N	L

FIGURE 5.1. Probe of lower and uppercase letter names to direct mastery instruction.

From J. Ron Nelson, Gregory J. Benner, and Paul Mooney. Copyright 2008 by The Guilford Press. Permission to photocopy this figure is granted to purchasers of this book for personal use only (see copyright page for details).

other include *b* and *d*, and letters that sound similar include *f* and *v*. Figure 5.3 illustrates a sequence of four explicit lessons that incorporate these principles and can be used to introduce letter names and their symbols.

Grouping

In teacher-mediated instruction, students with BD are provided individualized instruction or are grouped with other students whose screening results are similar. For example, if four kindergarten students struggling to meet classwide benchmarks in the regular curriculum are screened midway through the year for letter-naming mastery, and three of the four correctly identify fewer than 15 letters and the fourth identifies 26, then it may be possible to group all four students together and prepare for additional supplemental instruction. However, if there are wide

a m t s i f d r o g l h u c b n k v e w j p y T L M F D I N A R E H G B x q z J Q

FIGURE 5.2. An acceptable sequence for introducing letters. From Carnine, Silbert, Kame'enui, and Tarver (2004, p. 61). Copyright 2004 by Pearson Education, Inc. Reprinted by permission.

Lesson 1

	a, m		
a	a	m	m
m	a	a	m
m	a	m	a
a	m	m	a

Lesson 2

	t		
a	t	t	s
a	t	a	s
t	a	t	m
t	m	a	t

Lesson 3

	s		
s	m	s	a
s	a	m	s
s	s	a	m
m	s	s	a

Lesson 4

	l		
i	i	a	s
t	i	a	i
i	t	s	i
a	i	m	i

FIGURE 5.3. Sequential set of four mastery instructional lessons for the letters.

disparities in the number of letter names correctly identified, then there may be a need for more individualized instruction.

Presentation

Teachers should use a model–lead–test format for introducing letter names. Discrimination training involves the use of model–lead–test instructional presentation procedures for the sequential and systematic movement from acquisition to mastery of letter naming. The teacher begins each instructional activity by modeling the naming of the letter and then immediately asking students to do the same (lead). Students then practice the new letter independently with practice examples (test). We detail the model–lead–test format to build mastery with the lowercase letters *a* and *m* in Figure 5.3, Lesson 1.

We begin with the steps involved with modeling the letter names to students. The teacher prepares a visual representation of the letter being introduced while saying the letter name at the same time—this is considered the model. The teacher may display Lesson 1 in Figure 5.3 using an Elmo, overhead transparency, white/blackboard, PowerPoint, or easel. Two letter names are introduced in the first lesson to allow students to discriminate the names. Subsequent lessons typically introduce one new letter name in the context of two to five known letter names to allow students to discriminate the new letter name and practice discriminating previously learned letter names. The teacher introduces the lesson by saying, "We are going to learn the letter names for *a* and *m* today. First it is my turn. This is the letter *a*." The teacher uses a verbal (e.g., "Ready") and physical prompt (e.g., pointing under the lowercase letter *a*) to engage students. Pointing under the lowercase letter *a*, the teacher says, "What letter?" In unison, the students say "*a*." This process is then repeated with the letter *m*. Finally, the students practice discriminating the letter names for *a* and *m* independently with practice examples. The teacher points beneath another letter found in the 20 practice examples beneath the model prompt in Figure 5.3. Pointing under the letter *a* in the first row and column of the practice examples, the teacher asks, "What letter name?" The teacher repeats this process until students are able to correctly discriminate the letter names for *a* and *m* every time. In implementing the model–lead–test sequence, the teacher moves to the next letter (i.e., the lowercase *m*) if the student successfully meets all tests; that is, if the student (or group of students) discriminates correctly all instructional requests.

The pace of new letter introduction is adjusted to meet the needs of the individual student or group being taught. Pacing and testing mastery of the letter names can increase as children are able to identify the letter names more quickly. Vaughn and Linan-Thompson (2004) suggest that teachers incorporate games, songs, and writing activities into letter-name instruction. It is also important to monitor individual responses and correct errors (described below). Mastery is reached when those letters that are taught (e.g., the *a* and *m* in Lesson 1 of Figure 5.3) are correctly discriminated at least 90% of the time during instruction and any periodic progress monitoring that takes place.

Error Correction

As we mentioned in Chapter 2, it is important to be systematic about error correction to reduce the number of incorrect statements uttered by students. Error detection and subsequent reteaching of targeted skills are critical if students are to attain mastery of any given letter name or instructional task. Error-correction procedures also follow a model–lead–test format (see Chapter 2 for a more detailed discussion). For example, if the student does not correctly identify the letter name for *a* during instructional activities, the teacher should point under the letter *a* and say "This is the letter *a*" (model). The teacher immediately redelivers the verbal prompt (lead), "What letter?" The student should respond with "*a*." The teacher then points under the letter *a* again and says, "Your turn, what letter?" The teacher returns to testing mastery of the letter name for *a* within several instructional trials (test). Stated differently, if the teacher is testing for mastery of letter names for *a* and *m*, then the student is tested on mastery of the letter *a* shortly after following the model–lead–test error-correction procedure above.

Letter–Sound Knowledge: Partial Alphabetic Phase—Peer-Mediated

Scope and Sequence

Teachers should build on the guiding principles of sequencing alphabetic knowledge instruction in designing a sequence of mastery-oriented activities related to letter–sound knowledge. That is, teachers should still introduce more useful and lowercase letters before less useful and uppercase letters; they also should separate letters that look or sound similar to each other. However, teachers also should remember a fourth principle: Focus initial instruction on the most common sounds for each letter, not *all* sounds (Carnine et al., 2004). For example, the most common sound for /a/ is the short-vowel pronunciation as read in *fat*. For /y/ and /j/, the most common sounds are spoken in the words *yes* and *jet*, respectively. A sequence identical to that for letter names is appropriate (Carnine et al., 2004). Teachers also can use the same assessment tool (see Figure 5.1).

For peer-mediated instruction, the scope of letter sounds should include all those common sounds a student has or group of students have yet to master. No matter how the groupings are organized, it is imperative that the teacher remove those letters that have been correctly identified from the instructional sequence and gear instruction toward those letter sounds that were incorrectly identified. As can be seen in Figure 5.3, however, students will continue to encounter previously taught letters during instructional practice opportunities. We use the first grade PALS (Mathes, Torgesen, Allen, & Allor, 2001) program, which includes a well-designed instructional sequence of mastery-oriented activities related to letter–sound knowledge, to highlight peer-mediated instruction. Each letter sound activity in PALS offers practice on previously presented letter sounds while introducing a new sound. In the letter–sounds activity, a series of letters is listed that not only includes the new sound but also previously presented sounds.

Teaching letter sounds in PALS involves three phases. The first phase is student training. Teachers introduce students to the general PALS procedures and materials during this phase. Comprised of Lessons 1 and 2, most teachers complete this phase in 1 week. The second phase consists of 12 teacher-directed sounds and words preparation exercises. An example of the visual presentation sheet used to provide teacher-directed instruction during presentation exercises is found in Figure 5.4. Each sounds and words preparation exercise takes 10–15 minutes. The goal of the preparation exercises is to reach mastery of 12 letter sounds, starting with the sounds /a/ and /m/ in the first exercise. The final phase involves peer-mediated

Sounds and Words Preparation Exercise 1—Visual Presentation Sheet

Activity 1

Activity 5

FIGURE 5.4. PALS visual presentation sheet for sounds and words preparation exercise 1. Reprinted by permission of Sopris West.

practice of the letter sounds mastered during the preparation exercises and teacher-directed instruction on new sounds. This phase begins during week 5 and continues through week 16. The sounds and words practice takes 15 minutes during this phase.

Grouping

During PALS, higher-performing students with or without BD are paired with lower-performing students with or without BD and take turns serving as coach and reader. The more skilled student is always the coach first and the less skilled, the reader. This method permits the stronger reader to take on the role of teacher and the weaker student to benefit from a model of good reading. The coach is essentially the tutor and presents the tasks and tallies points when motivational systems are incorporated. The reader serves in the role of tutee and responds to all coach requests. Again, during an instructional session, each student serves as both coach and reader. Placement into groups occurs by rank ordering of all targeted students from highest to lowest performing on the screening instrument (see Figure 5.1), and then matching the highest performer with the lowest performer, the second highest performer with the second lowest performer, and so on. Adjustments in pairings occur when a given pair does not work well together. Pair assignments continue for at least 4 weeks.

Presentation

As mentioned previously, peers are the primary teachers in PALS, and teachers serve three roles. First, teacher-directed discrimination training procedures are used to introduce and build mastery of new letter sounds. For example, the teacher builds mastery of the letter sounds /a/ and /m/ corresponding to the letters *a* and *m* that were mastered in Figure 5.3. As was the case with introducing letter names, above, discrimination training using model–lead–test instructional presentation procedures are used to facilitate the sequential and systematic movement from acquisition to mastery of letter sounds. The visual presentation sheet in Figure 5.4 provides an example of a tool used to introduce and build mastery of two new letter sounds (/aaa/ and /mmm/). Second, once students are able to correctly identify the letter sounds every time in the group instructional format, peer-mediated instruction is used for practicing the new letter sounds. The role of the teacher during peer-mediated instruction is to monitor the pairs. Finally, the teacher shows students how to carry out their respective roles and use the PALS materials. The child serves two roles in each session: one time as a coach, and the other time as a reader. Then, the teacher models appropriate procedures for carrying out each role and observes students to ensure that they can complete both sets of responsibilities. Once each student is proficient in both roles, then peer-mediated instruction begins in dyads and teachers serve the role as monitor. PALS instruction begins with the teacher distributing the PALS folders, which contain the Scorecard (see Figure 5.5) in one pocket and the Game Sheet (see Figure 5.6) in the other pocket. The teacher begins by saying, "It's time for Peer-Assisted Literacy Strategies. Let's get ready for sounds and words. Today the new sound is /aaa/. Say it with me, /aaa/. By yourselves, /aaa/. Readers, get out your Game Sheets. Find where you left off. Coaches, remember to fill in the happy face and, Readers, mark 5 points when you complete a row without making a mistake. If the reader finishes the Game Sheet before I say to stop, you should switch jobs, and the first coach should take a turn reading the Game Sheet." It is important to note that the letter in the box in Figure 5.6 is the new sound /aaa/. The teacher then sets the timer for 15 minutes and says "Begin."

Using the PALS Game Sheet in Figure 5.6, for example, the coach should point under the letter *a* in the first row and column of the practice examples in Figure 5.6 and say, "Say the sound." The coach should then continue from left to right in the first row of the practice examples in Lesson 1, then with the letter sounds in row 2, and so on. The teacher can suggest changes in the pace of delivery depending on the success of the pairs in mastering knowledge of letter sounds. The teacher monitors pairs and provides feedback during the 15-minute session. Pairs earn points for successfully completing each PALS activity during each session. If readers say all of the sounds correctly, the pair earns 5 points and coaches fill in a happy face on the lower right corner of each session activity in the Game Sheet. After 15 minutes the teacher says, "Stop. Put your Game Sheets in your folder." As seen in Figure 5.5, the goal is to fill up the entire 150-point scorecard.

SCORECARD

Coach _____   Reader _____

Starting Date _____

1	2	3	4	5	6	7	8	9	10
11	12	13	14	15	16	17	18	19	20
21	22	23	24	25	26	27	28	29	30
31	32	33	34	35	36	37	38	39	40
41	42	43	44	45	46	47	48	49	50
51	52	53	54	55	56	57	58	59	60
61	62	63	64	65	66	67	68	69	70
71	72	73	74	75	76	77	78	79	80
81	82	83	84	85	86	87	88	89	90
91	92	93	94	95	96	97	98	99	100
101	102	103	104	105	106	107	108	109	110
111	112	113	114	115	116	117	118	119	120
121	122	123	124	125	126	127	128	129	130
131	132	133	134	135	136	137	138	139	140
141	142	143	144	145	146	147	148	149	150

FIGURE 5.5. PALS Scorecard. Reprinted by permission of Sopris West.

Game Sheet 1

						Coach says:
a	m	a	m	a	m	"Say the sound."
m	t	a	m	t	m	
a	t	m	a	t	m ☺ 5 points	

FIGURE 5.6. PALS Game Sheet for sounds in lesson 1. Reprinted by permission of Sopris West.

Error Correction

With one important exception, error-correction procedures used by coaches are identical to those practiced in teacher-mediated instruction as students learn how to fill the roles of coach and reader. The exception for coaches is that after an error is corrected, the coach should return to the beginning of the row in which the error was made. In the PALS program, the error-correction strategy is to *tell*, *ask*, and *start again*. For example, if the reader makes an error on the final (last column) letter sound of the second row (/mmm/) of Game Sheet 1 in Figure 5.6, the coach should say, "That sound is /mmm/" (tell). The next part of the strategy is to ask, "What sound?" The reader says the correct sound, */mmm/*. The coach then directs the reader to start again at the first letter sound of the second row, and to continue with each letter sound in that row, and so on. As teachers monitor instruction following student role training, they will observe how error-correction procedures are being implemented by their students and provide praise for correct implementation or corrective feedback for incorrect usage.

Word Family Instruction: Full Alphabetic Phase— Teacher-Mediated

Scope and Sequence

Gaskins, Ehri, Cress, O'Hara, and Donnelly (1996–1997) provide a 28-week scope and sequence of activities that teach 93 key words with varying word patterns. Figure 5.7 displays the 93 key words across each of the 28 weeks of word family instruction. The purpose of the program is to provide students with "key word" models they can use to decode and analyze unknown words they encounter. Essentially, when students encounter unknown words, they search their minds for analogous word patterns. The word patterns introduced become increasingly more complex over time. For example, Week 1 words include *in*, *and*, and *up*. In Week 4, students encounter letter combinations that make one sound, such as the ck in *truck* and *black*. By Week 10, students are becoming aware of hard to decode but consistent letter patterns such as /igh/ in *right*. Over the course of 28 weeks, students see a consistent visual map that connects the spelling of the given word to its pronunciation (see Figure 5.8).

Grouping

As mentioned previously, teacher-mediated instruction allows for the choice of individualized or small-group instruction.

Presentation

"Word detective" students are guided by the teacher through an activity based on the specific word pattern introduced. For example, in Week 10, the /igh/ pat-

Week	Key words			
1	IN	AND	UP	
2	KING	LONG	JUMP	
3	LET	PIG	DAY	
4	TRUCK	BLACK	NOT	
5	CAT	IT	GO	LOOK
6	RED	FUN	HE	
7	NAME	SWIM	MY	MAP
8	CAR	VINE	SEE	CAN
9	TENT	ROUND	SKATE	TEN
10	OLD	FROG	RIGHT	
11	SLIDE	STOP	TELL	HER
12	AN	SMASH	BRAVE	
13	COW	SLEEP	SCOUT	
14	FOR	ALL	SAW	
15	HAD	KICK	SNAIL	GLOW
16	BOAT	THINK	NEST	
17	TREAT	MAKE	THANK	
18	MICE	LITTLE	MORE	
19	SHIP	CLOCK	WASH	STATION
20	SKUNK	WHALE	BOY	BABY
21	SQUIRT	SCHOOL	COULD	
22	CAUGHT	COIN	TALK	
23	PAGE	FLEW	FLU	
24	USE	BUG	RAIN	
25	PAL	FUR	PLACE	
26	PHONE	QUEEN	WRITE	
27	KNIFE	PLANE	GUESS	
28	BABIES	TAX	DELICIOUS	

FIGURE 5.7. Word family instruction of 93 key words across 28 weeks. From Gaskins, Ehri, Cress, O'Hara, and Donnelly (1996–1997). Reprinted with permission from the authors and the International Reading Association.

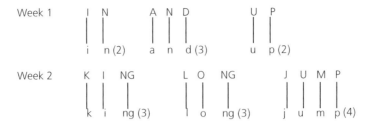

FIGURE 5.8. Example of visual map connecting spelling words to pronunciation over 2 weeks. Numbers in parentheses are the number of individual sounds in the word. Adapted from Gaskins, Ehri, Cress, O'Hara, and Donnelly (1996–1997). Reprinted with permission from the authors and the International Reading Association.

tern is introduced using the key word *right* (Gaskins, 2004). The teacher begins the lesson by saying, "Today we are going to learn the word *right*. Stretch the word." The teacher leads the students through an activity in which they collectively sound out the word while holding up a finger each time they hear a sound. Once the group has determined the correct number of sounds, the teacher draws that number of boxes on an overhead or chalkboard and places the chosen word (e.g., *right*) so it can be seen as well. Students are asked to indicate which letter goes in which box. Once the first and last boxes have been filled, the teacher asks the student detectives to solve the "problem" of having one box left and three letters. Ultimately, the group has to come to understand that the /igh/ represents one sound and fits in the remaining middle box. This process is practiced several times and reviewed periodically. Students are exposed to numerous words that follow the key word pattern. Teachers can place key words and matches on classroom walls so that they are readily available to students during reading and writing activities.

Error Correction

As previously mentioned, error-correction procedures occur immediately after an incorrect student response and follow a model–lead–test format. Mastery is reached with correct response rates above 90%. Error detection and subsequent reteaching of targeted skills are critical to students' reaching that level across instructional tasks.

FLUENCY INSTRUCTION

In Chapter 2 we introduced the six steps used to guide the process for developing students' skill fluency. In this section, we describe the six steps more fully using early reading examples to highlight how to design and deliver fluency instruction to students. The six steps are:

1. Select observable pivotal skills directly related to the content being taught.
2. Select the range of skill practice items the student has mastered.
3. Develop fluency instructional sheets.
4. Establish daily performance standards.
5. Conduct a series of short, timed instructional trials.
6. Have students chart the number of correct responses.

Select Observable Pivotal Skills

Two considerations should be made when selecting observable pivotal skills for fluency instruction. First, the observable skills must be directly related to the content being taught. For example, if students were at the prealphabetic phase and are being taught initial letter–sound correspondence through a variety of instructional activities (e.g., blending decodable words, reading controlled passages), teachers would not target letter names for fluency instruction. Rather, teachers might target letter sounds, one-syllable decodable words, or highly controlled text for fluency instruction. Second, the skills selected for fluency instruction also must involve observable behavior that can be counted and recorded. We recommend that readers review the potential observable key pivotal skills that could be targeted for fluency instruction across Ehri's (2005) four phases of reading development (see Table 5.1).

Select the Range of Skill Practice Items

Teachers should consider the range of skill practice items that will be used for fluency instruction. Review of Table 5.1 reveals that the observable pivotal skills that can be targeted for fluency building involve either text or discrete items (e.g., letter sounds). In the case of text, the selection of the skill practice items is based on the students' reading level. Independent-level text, which is used for fluency instruction, is relatively easy text for the reader, with no more than approximately one in 20 difficult words. Thus, text selected for fluency instruction will range from highly controlled (all decodable words) to uncontrolled grade-level text. For example, a teacher who is working with students at the partial alphabetic phase of reading

TABLE 5.1. Potential Observable Pivotal Skills That Can Be Targeted for Fluency Building across the Phases of Reading

Prealphabetic	Partial alphabetic	Full alphabetic	Consolidated alphabetic
Letter names	Letter sounds	Simple sight words	Multisyllabic sight words
Initial phoneme identification	One-syllable decodable words	Word families	
Phoneme segmentation	Highly controlled text	Controlled text	Uncontrolled text

would select text comprised of highly decodable text that students can read independently with little difficulty. Additionally, the text used for fluency instruction can be drawn directly from passages used during mastery instruction or from those students have not yet encountered. The key is to use text that matches students' independent reading levels.

The selection of discrete skill practice items is based on what is being taught and what students have mastered. Suppose a teacher is working with students at the prealphabetic phase of reading. The teacher is using a variety of instructional activities to teach children letter names (among other important prereading skills), but does not have to wait until students have mastered all 26 letter names to initiate fluency instruction. The teacher can construct a fluency instructional sheet that has a limited set of the letter names students have mastered. For example, the teacher has taught, and students have mastered, the following letter names in order: *a*, *m*, *s*, *t*, *i*, and *d*. The teacher would then construct a fluency instructional sheet using these six letter names and initiate fluency instruction. After the students achieve a high degree of fluency, the teacher can construct another fluency sheet that contains the next six letter names that were being taught during the time the teacher was doing fluency instruction on the previous six letter names. The teacher also may elect to systematically introduce one new mastered letter name for fluency instruction on a regular basis. In this case, the teacher would remove one letter name in conjunction with the introduction of the new letter. Additionally, the teacher should construct cumulative fluency instructional sheets. For example, the teacher has taught and students have mastered 15 letter names. The teacher could construct fluency instructional sheets that include a random selection of 6–8 of the 15 mastered letter names.

Develop Fluency Instructional Sheets

The development of fluency instructional sheets is straightforward. The first point that teachers should consider when developing fluency instructional sheets is the optimal counting time for this instruction. *Counting time* refers to the amount of time the students will practice the observable pivotal skill. Typically, fluency instruction has 1-minute counting times. Of course, the counting time may be longer in the case of text (e.g., 2–3 minutes) and the independent reading level of the student. Teachers also may use a shorter counting time as an intervention for facilitating fluency. Teachers should use the same counting time each day. This consistency aids student learning and allow teachers to monitor changes in students' fluency rates from day to day.

Next, teachers develop the actual fluency instructional sheets. In the case of text, the passages should be long enough that the student will not finish them within the identified counting time. Teachers can run a photocopy of the text and indicate the number of words in each line in the right-hand margin to facilitate counting of correct words read during the established time period. Many teachers retype passages using a computer and include the number of words in each line in the right-hand margin. The electronic version can then be adjusted to meet the learning needs of students. For example, teachers can use larger type sizes and increase the spacing between lines of text for students, if necessary. Additionally, electronic versions are also easier to store as well as share among colleagues. An example of a text fluency instructional sheet focusing on long vowel sounds, created from *Bob Books Steps to Reading* (Maslen & Maslen, 2006), is provided in Figure 5.9.

In the case of discrete stimuli, teachers should select a set of items students have mastered (95–100% accurate). The total number of items used to develop the fluency instructional sheet should range from five to eight. These items should be distributed randomly in a serial format (i.e., either left to right or top to bottom). The density of the items (i.e., space between items and lines) can be adjusted to meet the individual learning needs of the student. The number of items in a line should be indicated in the right-hand margin. Teachers can use the "table" function in their computer programs to create the fluency instructional sheets; they also can use a free downloadable file to create fluency instructional sheets for discrete stimuli (available at *www.johnandgwyn.co.uk/probe.html*). This file enables teachers to create discrete item fluency instructional sheets by simply typing in each item just once. The file randomly fills in the sheet. The file gives teachers the option of creating fluency instructional sheets ranging from 4 to 20 discrete items. An example of a fluency instructional sheet for five discrete letter sounds (i.e., /a/, /m/, /s/, /c/, and /t/) is presented in Figure 5.10.

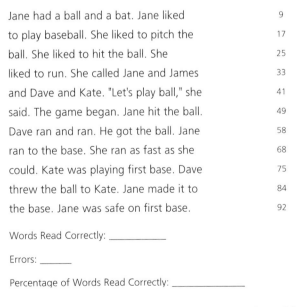

Jane had a ball and a bat. Jane liked	9
to play baseball. She liked to pitch the	17
ball. She liked to hit the ball. She	25
liked to run. She called Jane and James	33
and Dave and Kate. "Let's play ball," she	41
said. The game began. Jane hit the ball.	49
Dave ran and ran. He got the ball. Jane	58
ran to the base. She ran as fast as she	68
could. Kate was playing first base. Dave	75
threw the ball to Kate. Jane made it to	84
the base. Jane was safe on first base.	92

Words Read Correctly: _____

Errors: _____

Percentage of Words Read Correctly: _____

FIGURE 5.9. Text fluency instructional sheet. Used with permission from Scholastic—Bob Books Set 5, book 1—long vowels.

M	C	t	c	a	5
a	m	T	a	S	10
A	c	s	T	S	15
T	m	M	C	A	20
a	S	t	s	a	25
m	C	s	M	T	30
c	A	C	t	m	35
M	T	S	c	a	40
t	a	m	M	A	45
C	s	T	t	c	50

FIGURE 5.10. Example of discrete-item fluency instructional sheet.

From J. Ron Nelson, Gregory J. Benner, and Paul Mooney. Copyright 2008 by The Guilford Press. Permission to photocopy this figure is granted to purchasers of this book for personal use only (see copyright page for details).

Establish Daily Performance Standards

Establishing a student's baseline score is the first step in creating daily performance standards. A student's baseline score provides the teacher's best estimate of the student's level of performance prior to fluency instruction. Typically, this estimate is obtained by determining the median number of words read correctly on the first three fluency instructional trials conducted on the first day of fluency instruction. Although fluency instruction can be conducted individually or in small groups of students who have similar competence levels, establishing a student's baseline score is done individually. Students with higher scores may need no or few fluency instructional trials; those with lower scores may need a high number of instructional trials each day.

    The teacher uses the initial baseline performance of students to establish the first daily performance goal and subsequent goals are based on students' daily performance. A key component of fluency instruction involves establishing reasonable daily performance goals that can be attained by students. Meeting the daily performance goal is very motivating for students. However, it is also important for the teacher to encourage students to set ambitious daily performance goals. Each day's performance goal is established through an interactive process with students. An example of dialogue between a teacher and students setting a daily performance goal for letter sounds follows:

TEACHER: Yesterday you identified 22 letter sounds correctly. How many do you think you can learn today?

JORGE (student): I don't know—24?

TEACHER: I think you can do more than that. You are getting faster every day. I think you can do 26. What do you think?

SEVERAL STUDENTS: OK! We can get 26 at least one time today.

TEACHER: Excellent!

It is important for teachers to have in mind a fluency goal and to communicate it to students. A *fluency goal* refers to a performance level that indicates that the student is fluent. The easiest way is to use the scores obtained by fluent peers. This will occur naturally in those cases in which the general education teacher establishes the baseline performance of an entire class. Those students in the upper 25th percentile will provide a reasonable estimate of the fluency goal for a particular fluency instructional sheet. Special education and other specialists working with students who have reading problems can sample from fluent peers in the general education classroom. The process of establishing fluency goals for each fluency instructional sheet only needs to occur once. Thus, it is important for teachers to keep records of their fluency goals.

Conduct Short, Timed Instructional Trials

After setting the daily performance standard, the teacher conducts several (i.e., three to five) instructional trials each day, depending upon the learning needs of students. The teacher also may be working on more than one skill at a time. For example, a teacher working with students at the prealphabetic phase might conduct a number of instructional trials for a group of letter sounds, one-syllable decodable words, and a passage (highly controlled text). The entire instructional session should range from 15 to 20 minutes in length. Instructional sessions should be conducted on a regular basis and be integrated into students' literacy instruction block. Another instructional session can be conducted at another point in the day for those students who need additional fluency scaffolding.

Teachers initiate each instructional trial with consistent beginning (e.g., "Begin") and ending (e.g., "Time") prompts. The examples in the figure apply to both individual and small-group instructional formats. Teachers should not correct student errors during the instructional trial. However, teachers may elect to review incorrect responses with students following each trial. Student errors should be due to carelessness, given that they have achieved mastery of the skill prior to fluency instruction. Teachers should reteach students if the errors are numerous and not of a careless nature. After the instructional trial, teachers should provide immediate feedback to students. The feedback should include praise for engaging in the instructional trial and recognition of beating or getting close to the daily performance standard (e.g., "You got it!" or "You were so close!").

As previously noted, fluency instruction can be delivered individually or with small groups of students who have similar competence levels. Teachers, peer partners, paraprofessionals, classroom volunteers, and cross-age tutors can be used to provide fluency instruction to individual students. Some tips for organizing small groups of students for fluency instruction include the following:

1. Students sit on chairs in a curved row in front of the teacher, so that they are able to see the fluency instruction form without much effort. This seating arrangement also ensures that the teacher is able to observe students easily.
2. Students who need the highest degree of instructional scaffolding should sit directly in front of the teacher. This will help them pay attention and reduce management issues.
3. Teachers assign seats to ensure that students are seated where they will benefit from instruction. Assigning seats also decreases the amount of time needed to transition from the previous instructional activity.
4. Teachers start the first instructional trial quickly and present each trial in a consistent and predictable manner, using a brisk pace in and across lessons.

A small-group instructional format requires teachers to use a combination of group and individual student responses. A group signal should be used to cue students to respond in unison (choral response). Teachers can then call on individual students (individual turns) to respond during the instructional session. Although teachers should engage all students individually at some point during the instructional session, they should focus on those students who need additional fluency instruction. Teachers should not move to individual turns until the group has had two or three instructional trials and members are fluent in their responses. This process will increase the success rate of instructionally needy students. We recommend that readers review the beginning prompts for small-group instruction detailed in Figure 5.11.

Have Students Chart Correct Responses

The task of students charting their performance actively engages them in the fluency building process. Indeed, simply focusing students' attention on their own performance should, in itself, have a positive effect on performance. The positive

Text	**Discrete stimuli**
Individual	*Individual*
Please read this out loud. I will tell you the word if you get stuck so you can keep reading until I say "time." Remember to do your best reading. Put your finger on the first word. Ready, begin.	Please say the . . . [e.g., letter sounds] out loud as fast as you can. I will tell you the . . . if you get stuck so you can keep going until I say "time." Remember to do your best. Put your finger on the first. . . . Ready, begin.
Small group	*Small group*
Please read this passage out loud with me. Remember to follow along with me until I say "time." Eyes up here (*point to passage*). Ready (*finger pointing at the first letter of the initial word*), begin (*slide your finger* [the rate should meet the daily performance standard] *under the word in the passage to prompt students to read the passage in unison*).	Please say the . . . out loud with me. Remember to follow along with me until I say "time." Eyes up here (*point to fluency sheet*). Ready (*finger pointing at the first . . .*) begin (*slide your finger* [the rate should meet the daily performance standard] *under the . . . to prompt students to say the . . . in unison*).
Use the "individual" prompt above for individual turns. Peers can follow along with their fingers as the individual student reads the passage.	Use the "individual" prompt above for individual turns. Peers can follow along with their fingers as the individual student reads the passage.

FIGURE 5.11. Sample beginning prompts for instructional fluency trials of text and discrete stimuli.

effects of self-observing and self-recording performance can be further enhanced with overt reinforcers for meeting the established performance goal. The procedure for student charting is straightforward and, in general, simply requires the student to self-observe and self-record the total number of correct responses he or she achieves for the specified count period.

The first step in the process of student charting of correct responses involves teachers setting up and labeling a graph for students (see Figure 5.12). Individual graphs are used even in the case of small-group instruction in which the rate is, in part, a function of the performance rate of the group. That is, the rate of performance is guided by the teacher and students. The bottom, or horizontal, axis of the graph is labeled *school days*. The graph is divided into 5-day school weeks. There should be space provided at the bottom of the graph to record the date that corresponds with each Monday. The vertical axis of the graph should include a label for the pivotal skill (e.g., correct letter names, correct letter sounds, correct sight words) being targeted. The left side of the graph should also include the unit of measurement. Additional information should include space for the name(s) of students, the subject area, and the pivotal skills. Teachers can use standard graph paper, Excel, or word-processing software to create graphs. Further, teachers need a relatively small number of graphs to cover the potential range of student performance across skill areas.

Student Name(s): _____

Skill(s): Letter Names _____

	50	M	T	W	Th	F	M	T	W	Th	F	M	T	W	Th	F	M	T	W	Th	F
	48																				
	46																				
	44																				
	42																				
	40																				
	38																				
	36																				
	34																				
	32																				
Number of Correct Letter Names	30																				
	28																				
	26																				
	24																				
	22																				
	20																				
	18																				
	16																				
	14																				
	12																				
	10																				
	8																				
	6																				
	4																				
	2																				
		M	T	W	Th	F	M	T	W	Th	F	M	T	W	Th	F	M	T	W	Th	F

School Days

Week of _____ Week of _____ Week of _____ Week of _____

FIGURE 5.12. Example of Student Charting Graph

Students then chart their performance on a daily basis, recording their highest rate of performance across the instructional trials. They begin by placing a dot in the square on the graph that represents their baseline performance, then they place a dot in the square next to the number that marks their rate of performance for the day. For example, a group of students' highest performance scores on a 1-minute letter-naming fluency instructional activity for the letters *a, m, s, t,* and *c*, across 5 consecutive days in 1 week, were 25, 30, 35, and 38. The students placed dots in the squares for 25, 30, 35, and 38 on each of their individual graphs and then connected the data points with a line. Days are skipped when there is no count for the day (e.g., student is absent). Students should connect the data points in those cases in which there is only one missing data point, but not when there are two or more missing data points. The last step in student charting involves indicating changes in fluency instruction (i.e., new text or set of discrete items). Whenever a new fluency instructional sheet is introduced, a vertical line should be drawn from the top to the bottom and a short note explaining the change included on the top.

OTHER CONSIDERATIONS IN PLANNING AND DELIVERING READING INSTRUCTION FOR STUDENTS WITH BD

Before concluding our discussion of scientifically based skills instruction in reading, we want to make two additional points. One, our presentation of mastery- and fluency-oriented supplemental instruction highlighted both teacher- and peer-mediated delivery systems. Research has demonstrated that both instructional formats can produce educationally significant and meaningful effects on the learning of students with BD (i.e., Pierce et al., 2004; Ryan et al., 2004). In offering model interventions across the phases, we chose either teacher- or peer-mediated formats to introduce interventions in the areas of letter, letter sounds, and word family awareness. However, teachers should understand that they are free to include both teacher- and peer-mediated instructional formats in the reading programs. For example, teachers of students with BD could incorporate reciprocal peer tutoring into their mastery- and fluency-oriented instructional programming in the area of letter naming. Teachers could use the model–lead–test format in a large group setting to show students how to be teachers. Once the teacher is comfortable that students can effectively deliver lessons, reinforce correct responses, and correct errors, then the teacher could pair more knowledgeable students with less knowledgeable students to provide additional presentation and practice opportunities on letters that are not mastered in small-group or whole-class instructional formats. In this manner, students with BD receive more minutes of instruction targeted at a skill deficit and an opportunity to practice and present relevant course material (i.e., the names of letters yet to be mastered). In the area of fluency, reciprocal peer tutoring pairs also could be useful during discrete and extended practice opportunities.

Two, although we have focused on targeted skills such as letter naming and letter–sound recognition in developing our mastery and fluency sections, it is imperative to understand that this targeted instruction for students with BD is but one piece of a larger literacy and language program that includes reading, writing, speaking, and listening instruction. Multitiered models, such as those discussed in Chapter 2, often devote at least 30–60 minutes of supplemental instruction in each tier, in addition to the 90–120 minutes of core instruction offered to all students in a classroom. Moreover, the National Reading Panel (2000) suggested that comprehensive beginning reading instruction focus on the essential areas of phonemic awareness, phonics, fluency, vocabulary, and comprehension. Table 5.2 provides a potential reading scope and sequence across the primary grades, suggested by Vaughn and Linan-Thompson (2004). Teachers need to know that *all* areas must be addressed as they design and deliver instruction. For students with BD, there is a greater likelihood that explicit instruction in one or more of these areas will be necessary.

TABLE 5.2. Timeline for Teaching Literacy

	Kindergarten	First grade	Second grade	Third grade
Phonological awareness	Syllables Onset–rime Phoneme level	Phonemic awareness		
Phonics and word study	Print awareness Alphabetic knowledge Alphabetic principle Decoding Irregular word reading	Alphabetic principle Decoding Irregular word reading Decodable text reading		
Fluency		Connected text (second semester)	Connected text	Connected text
Vocabulary	Oral vocabulary	Oral and reading vocabulary	Reading vocabulary	Reading vocabulary
Comprehension	Listening comprehension Sense of story	Listening comprehension Reading comprehension	Reading comprehension in narrative and expository texts	Reading comprehension in narrative and expository texts

Note. From Vaughn and Linan-Thompson (2004). Reprinted with permission from the Association for Supervision and Curriculum Development.

CONCLUSIONS

In this chapter we focused on basic reading skill improvement for students with BD. The importance of early and effective reading instruction in the primary grades cannot be overstated. A small body of reading research with students who have BD informs practice. This literature base indicates that peer- and teacher-mediated supplemental reading interventions can be successful in developing beginning reading skills. Ehri's phase theory of reading development provides a context for the design of supplemental intervention for students with BD. The chapter discussed mastery- and fluency-oriented instruction across selected phases and targeting specific essential skills. The two key elements of mastery instruction are a well-defined scope and sequence and an instructional design that includes a model–lead–test format and systematic error-correction procedures. We then provided examples of applying these elements in teacher- and peer-mediated formats to build mastery of letter names, letter–sound correspondence, and word family knowledge.

The observable pivotal skills that can be targeted for fluency building involve independent reading level text (less than one error in 20 difficult words for the student) or discrete items that the student has mastered. The remaining steps to guide the process for developing students' reading skill fluency include developing fluency instructional sheets, establishing performance standards, conducting short, timed instructional trials, and having students chart their beginning reading skill progress. We concluded our discussion of reading instruction by recommending the inclusion of both teacher- and peer-mediated instructional formats in supplemental reading intervention to ensure a comprehensive program for students with BD.

CHAPTER 6

Early Math Instruction

Mathematics, like reading and writing, is an important gateway skill to economic access and improved quality of life. Success in any academic area (e.g., business or science), job (e.g., construction), or day-to-day activity (e.g., paying bills, using a vending machine) depends on at least basic mathematic skill (Choate, 1987; National Research Council, 2005). Moreover, scholars have argued that mathematical fluency is the most urgent social issue affecting disadvantaged populations in the United States (Moses & Cobb, 2001); it is very difficult to achieve economic access and full citizenship in the 21st century without this area of fluency. Thus, because only 30% of U.S. eighth graders were "proficient" in mathematics, based on the 2005 National Assessment of Educational Progress (NAEP), improving mathematics achievement is a national priority, as articulated in the reauthorization legislation of NCLB (U.S. Department of Education, Office of the Under Secretary, 2002).

As with reading and writing, students with BD are likely to evidence math deficits. Reviewing the academic status research conducted during a 40-year period, Epstein, Nelson, Trout, and Mooney (2005) reported that prevalence of math deficits for students receiving special education services for BD ranged from 42 to 93%. The magnitude of math deficits ranged from 1 to 2 years below expected grade level (Epstein et al., 2005). Further, the math deficits evidenced by students receiving special education services for BD appear to be stable across the school years (Greenbaum et al., 1996; Mattison et al., 2002; Nelson et al., 2004). In this chapter we describe the evidence base with respect to math research for students with BD. We follow this description with a theoretical and empirical justification for early and scientifically based intervention, including instructional practices that promote mastery and fluency of critical early mathematics skills. We conclude with a summary of the chapter's major points.

MATH RESEARCH FOR STUDENTS WITH BD

A small body of research documents the effects of math interventions for students with BD (Mooney et al., 2003). Three conclusions can be drawn from a review of this literature. First, the majority of the interventions are self-regulation interventions (e.g., Carr & Punzo, 1993; Levendoski & Cartledge, 2000; Skinner, Bamberg, Smith, & Powell, 1993; Skinner, Ford, & Yunker, 1991; Skinner, Turco, Beatty, & Rasavage, 1989). These types of interventions include self-evaluation, self-monitoring, strategy instruction techniques, self-instruction techniques, and multiple-component strategies (i.e., involving elements of more than one self-regulation intervention). For example, Skinner et al. (1991) compared the effects of written and verbal cover, copy, and compare (CCC) responses on two students (ages 9 and 11) in a residential school for students with BD. The CCC strategy involves four steps: (1) the student silently reads the first problem on a worksheet and the corresponding answer on the left side of the paper; (2) the student covers the problem and the answer with an index card; (3) the student writes or verbalizes the problem and the answer; and (4) the student uncovers the problem and the answer on the left side to check the written response. The four-step procedure is repeated before proceeding to the next item if the problem or answer is written or verbalized incorrectly. CBMs of multiplication facts are frequently used to compare the effects of written and verbal CCC formats. Skinner and colleagues (1991) found that verbal CCC resulted in double the opportunities to respond and greater improvements on CBMs of basic multiplication facts.

Next, the interventions have targeted basic mathematical facts, operations, and problem solving (e.g., Franca, Kerr, Reitz, & Lambert, 1990; Scruggs, Mastropieri, & Tolfa-Veit, 1986). Fluency with basic math facts involves the automatic recall of addition, subtraction, multiplication, and division answers. Fluent operations involve the accurate and efficient use of procedures or algorithms for math computations (i.e., procedural fluency). Problem-solving fluency consists of the ability to formulate, represent, solve, and explain mathematical problems (i.e., strategic competence and reasoning). For example, Franca and colleagues (1990) investigated the effects of a same-age tutoring procedure on the math facts and operations of eight middle school students with BD, ages 13–16, delivered in a self-contained classroom in a private school. Tutors and tutees were given nine 20″ × 12″ index cards arranged in an easel-like format. The side of the index card facing the tutee showed the math problem and the steps required to solve it, and the side facing the tutor included written instructions about the steps necessary to solve the problem. Problems included addition and subtraction facts and operations and multiplication and division of fractions. Tutor presentation consisted of four steps: (1) the students were given the problem on an index card; (2) the tutor read the instructions to the students; (3) the tutor corrected student errors; and (4) the students received reinforcement for effort and problem completion. Results indicated that the tutoring procedure was effective in building mastery of addition and subtraction facts and operations and multiplication and division of fraction operations (Franca et al., 1990).

Finally, findings across teacher-directed, peer-mediated, and self-regulation interventions have generally been positive, indicating that students with BD do improve their math skills when provided with systematic intervention (Franca et al., 1990; Lee, Sugai, & Horner, 1999; Penno, Frank, & Wacker, 2000). For example, Lee and colleagues (1999) reported that explicit teacher-directed instruction of difficult tasks was effective in improving the math performance of two 9-year-olds with BD. Each student's basic math facts and operations were assessed using the Math Skills Assessment (MSA), which was developed as a modified version of the Instructional Sequence and Assessment Chart in Direct Instruction Mathematics (Silbert, Carnine, & Stein, 1981). Two sets of difficult tasks were selected from tasks for which the participant had scored lower than 33% on the MSA. Teachers used error analysis to identify component skills that students lacked. Students then received individualized mastery instruction on the component skills in need of improvement. Students' performance on measures of basic math facts and operations increased after receiving teacher-directed instruction on the difficult tasks (Lee et al., 1999).

EARLY MATH THEORY AND PRACTICE

We present mastery- and fluency-oriented instruction principles in early math through a four-phase developmental skill framework articulated by a number of researchers (Gersten & Chard, 1999; National Research Council, 2001, 2004, 2005; National Council of Teachers of Mathematics, 2006). You may note similarities between this four-phase math framework and Linnea Ehri's four-phase theory of word reading development (see Chapter 5). Indeed, there are direct parallels between mastery- and fluency-oriented instruction in early math skills and word reading. Students must achieve mastery of basic math facts to solve complex math problems.

The four phases involved in early math development are: (1) early number sense; (2) partial number sense; (3) full number sense; and (4) a consolidated number sense. These four phases are interconnected; however, mastery of skills at one phase is not necessary to initiate movement to the next phase. The goal of the first phase is to develop the central conceptual understanding of number sense necessary for mastery of addition and subtraction facts. Such mastery begins during the partial number sense phase and extends through the full number sense phase. The two overarching goals of the consolidated number sense phase are: (1) fluency with addition and subtraction operations and problem solving; and (2) mastery of multiplication and division facts, operations, and problem solving. A scope and

MORE COMPLEX

Skill	Tasks	Scope and sequence
Problem solving	Analyze and solve practical problems. Explain math concepts and vocabulary. Analyze numerical relationships.	• Write story problems. • Solve problems using an organized list. • Identify the missing number in a sequence. • Act out, draw pictures, and write number sentences to solve story problems.
Operations	Perform simple to complex computations.	• Multiply multidigit numbers. • Divide by 2. • Multiply by 2. • Add three or more multidigit numbers. • Subtract multidigit numbers with and without regrouping. • Add two multidigit numbers with regrouping. • Add three or more single-digit numbers. • Add two multidigit numbers without regrouping. • Subtract 10 from a two-digit number. • Add 10 to a two-digit number.
Math facts	Achieve math fact fluency. Calculate single-digit math facts.	• Division fact fluency • Multiplication fact fluency • Subtraction fact fluency • Addition fact fluency • Division facts • Multiplication facts 6 through 9 (up to $9 \times 9 = 81$) • Multiplication facts through 5 (up to $9 \times 5 = 45$) • Addition and subtraction facts

LESS COMPLEX

FIGURE 6.1. Scope and sequence for K–3 math facts, operations, and problem-solving tasks.

sequence for math facts, operations, and problem solving from kindergarten through third grade is presented in Figure 6.1. The scope and sequence advances from the least complex task of calculating single-digit math facts to the most complex task of analyzing and solving practical problems. The scope and sequence aligns well with the four phases of early math development. Next, we describe each of the phases.

Early Number Sense

Preschoolers and kindergarteners commonly experience early number sense (the first phase of early math skill development). However, older students with BD who experience math difficulties may lack fluency of the skills associated with the early number sense phase. There are two learning targets for mathematical understanding at the early number sense phase. First, students develop oral counting skills. The ability to count orally demonstrates an understanding of the one-to-one correspondence rule: that is, a particular number is matched to each counted object. Further, students begin to demonstrate the rule of cardinality (i.e., the last word they state in counting tells "how many"). Second, students develop the ability to recognize quantity as the total number within a set or group of objects. For example, students understand that "3" refers to a set with three members. Students also can compare the size of two sets of objects that differ in size and tell which is larger. The scope of instructional activities in this phase encompasses the one-to-one correspondence rule, the rule of cardinality, counting objects to 10, isolating sets of objects, and quantity and size discrimination of objects. Students at this phase of number sense development should score well on CBMs of oral counting, but they may have difficulty with number identification (see Chapter 3).

Partial Number Sense

Kindergarteners, first graders, and some older students with BD tend to experience the second phase of early math skill development: partial number sense. There are three learning targets for mathematical understanding at the partial number sense phase. First, students begin to solve problems involving single-digit numbers and quantities independent of real objects. The emerging ability to solve problems is a major change from the early number sense phase in which students count objects orally. The least advanced students at this phase will use the "count on from 1" strategy by starting their count at 1 and counting to 3 using their fingers on one hand. They will then count to 2 in the same manner with the fingers on their other hand and count the total raised fingers. When asked how many cats they would have if they had 3 and someone gave them 2 more, the most advanced students at this phase will know this basic addition fact and say 5 because 3 plus 2 equals 5.

Second, students acquire the ability to identify the missing number in a sequence. They use the same range of strategies as applied when counting without objects orally (e.g., "count on from 1" strategy) to determine the missing number in a sequence. Finally, students at this phase can discriminate the quantity between two single-digit numbers. Students with the ability to discriminate quantity understand that numbers indicate amount, that numbers occupy fixed positions in the counting sequence, and that numbers that come later in the sequence indicate larger quantities. The scope of instructional activities in the partial number sense phase includes counting without using objects, identifying the missing number in a sequence, comparing and ordering whole numbers, joining and separating sets, and quantity discrimination using numbers. Students at this phase of development of number sense should perform well on CBMs of number identification, quantity discrimination, and missing number, but they may have difficulty with math facts in subtraction and addition (see Chapter 3).

Full Number Sense

First and second graders and many older students with BD tend to exhibit math performance that is characteristic of full number sense (the third phase of early math development). There are two learning targets for students at the full number sense phase. First, students need to understand the central conceptual structure of number sense: written numerals are symbols for number words that represent distinct quantities and positions on the number line. This understanding of the conceptual structure of number sense includes the symbols for addition, subtraction, and equality. Second, students master addition and subtraction facts (see Figure 6.1: Math Facts). This is a foundational learning target because students who do not memorize the basic math facts will flounder as operations that are more complex and involve additional problem solving are required, and the students' progress will likely slowly stop by the end of elementary school (Klein et al., 2005).

The scope of instructional activities in the full number sense phase includes understanding number names and symbols, adding or subtracting quantities smaller than four, using the commutative principle (i.e., the order in which two or more numbers are added does not affect the answer) for single-digit addition, and mastering addition and subtraction facts. Mastery of addition facts, for example, begins with adding 0 to single-digit numbers and progresses to adding 1, 2, 3 and doubles through 6 plus 6. When these addition facts are firm, the student then progresses to adding 10, 9, 6, 4, 5, 7, and 8, respectively, to single-digit numbers. Addition and subtraction facts are presented in Figures 6.2 and 6.3. Students at this phase of development of number sense should perform well on CBMs of missing number and math facts in addition and subtraction, but they may not score well on multiplication and division facts and math computation (as described in Chapter 3).

Consolidated Number Sense

Second- and third-grade students tend to perform at the final phase of early math development: the consolidated number sense phase. The focus of the consolidated phase shifts from the mastery of math facts at the full number phase to the use of operations and problem solving (i.e., addition, subtraction, multiplication, division, fractions). There are four learning targets for students at the consolidated number sense phase.

First, students master addition and subtraction operations (see Figure 6.1: Operations). Mastery of addition operations begins with adding 10 to a two-digit number and progresses to determining the sum of up to four one-, two-, three-, or four-digit numbers and solving word problems associated with them. Mastery of subtraction operations begins with subtracting 10 from a two-digit number and advances to determining the difference of two numbers that require regrouping and associated word problem solving.

ZERO				
0 + 0 = 0	0 + 1 = 1	0 + 2 = 2	0 + 3 = 3	0 + 4 = 4
0 + 5 = 5	0 + 6 = 6	0 + 7 = 7	0 + 8 = 8	0 + 9 = 9
ONE				
1 + 0 = 1	1 + 1 = 2	1 + 2 = 3	1 + 3 = 4	1 + 4 = 5
1 + 5 = 6	1 + 6 = 7	1 + 7 = 8	1 + 8 = 9	1 + 9 = 10
TWO				
2 + 0 = 2	2 + 1 = 3	2 + 2 = 4	2 + 3 = 5	2 + 4 = 6
2 + 5 = 7	2 + 6 = 8	2 + 7 = 9	2 + 8 = 10	2 + 9 = 11
THREE				
3 + 0 = 3	3 + 1 = 4	3 + 2 = 5	3 + 3 = 6	3 + 4 = 7
3 + 5 = 8	3 + 6 = 9	3 + 7 = 10	3 + 8 = 11	3 + 9 = 12
FOUR				
4 + 0 = 4	4 + 1 = 5	4 + 2 = 6	4 + 3 = 7	4 + 4 = 8
4 + 5 = 9	4 + 6 = 10	4 + 7 = 11	4 + 8 = 12	4 + 9 = 13
FIVE				
5 + 0 = 5	5 + 1 = 6	5 + 2 = 7	5 + 3 = 8	5 + 4 = 9
5 + 5 = 10	5 + 6 = 11	5 + 7 = 12	5 + 8 = 13	5 + 9 = 14
SIX				
6 + 0 = 6	6 + 1 = 7	6 + 2 = 8	6 + 3 = 9	6 + 4 = 10
6 + 5 = 11	6 + 6 = 12	6 + 7 = 13	6 + 8 = 14	6 + 9 = 15
SEVEN				
7 + 0 = 7	7 + 1 = 8	7 + 2 = 9	7 + 3 = 10	7 + 4 = 11
7 + 5 = 12	7 + 6 = 13	7 + 7 = 14	7 + 8 = 15	7 + 9 = 16
EIGHT				
8 + 0 = 8	8 + 1 = 9	8 + 2 = 10	8 + 3 = 11	8 + 4 = 12
8 + 5 = 13	8 + 6 = 14	8 + 7 = 15	8 + 8 = 16	8 + 9 = 17
NINE				
9 + 0 = 9	9 + 1 = 10	9 + 2 = 11	9 + 3 = 12	9 + 4 = 13
9 + 5 = 14	9 + 6 = 15	9 + 7 = 16	9 + 8 = 17	9 + 9 = 18
TEN				
10 + 0 = 10	10 + 1 = 11	10 + 2 = 12	10 + 3 = 13	10 + 4 = 14
10 + 5 = 15	10 + 6 = 16	10 + 7 = 17	10 + 8 = 18	10 + 9 = 19
10 + 10 = 20				

FIGURE 6.2. Addition facts.

ZERO				
0 – 0 = 0				
ONE				
1 – 0 = 1	1 – 1 = 0			
TWO				
2 – 0 = 2	2 – 1 = 1	2 – 2 = 0		
THREE				
3 – 0 = 3	3 – 1 = 2	3 – 2 = 1	3 – 3 = 0	
FOUR				
4 – 0 = 4	4 – 1 = 3	4 – 2 = 2	4 – 3 = 1	4 – 4 = 0
FIVE				
5 – 0 = 5	5 – 1 = 4	5 – 2 = 3	5 – 3 = 2	5 – 4 = 1
5 – 5 = 0				
SIX				
6 – 0 = 6	6 – 1 = 5	6 – 2 = 4	6 – 3 = 3	6 – 4 = 2
6 – 5 = 1	6 – 6 = 0			
SEVEN				
7 – 0 = 7	7 – 1 = 6	7 – 2 = 5	7 – 3 = 4	7 – 4 = 3
7 – 5 = 2	7 – 6 = 1	7 – 7 = 0		
EIGHT				
8 – 0 = 8	8 – 1 = 7	8 – 2 = 6	8 – 3 = 5	8 – 4 = 4
8 – 5 = 3	8 – 6 = 2	8 – 7 = 1	8 – 8 = 0	
NINE				
9 – 0 = 9	9 – 1 = 8	9 – 2 = 7	9 – 3 = 6	9 – 4 = 5
9 – 5 = 4	9 – 6 = 3	9 – 7 = 2	9 – 8 = 1	9 – 9 = 0
TEN				
10 – 0 = 10	10 – 1 = 9	10 – 2 = 8	10 – 3 = 7	10 – 4 = 6
10 – 5 = 5	10 – 6 = 4	10 – 7 = 3	10 – 8 = 2	10 – 9 = 1
10 – 10 = 0				
ELEVEN				
11 – 1 = 10	11 – 2 = 9	11 – 3 = 8	11 – 4 = 7	11 – 5 = 6
11 – 6 = 5	11 – 7 = 4	11 – 8 = 3	11 – 9 = 2	11 – 10 = 1

(continued)

FIGURE 6.3. Subtraction facts.

TWELVE				
12 – 2 = 10	12 – 3 = 9	12 – 4 = 8	12 – 5 = 7	12 – 6 = 6
12 – 7 = 5	12 – 8 = 4	12 – 9 = 3	12 – 10 = 2	
THIRTEEN				
13 – 3 = 10	13 – 4 = 9	13 – 5 = 8	13 – 6 = 7	13 – 7 = 6
13 – 8 = 5	13 – 9 = 4	13 – 10 = 3		
FOURTEEN				
14 – 4 = 10	14 – 5 = 9	14 – 6 = 8	14 – 7 = 7	14 – 8 = 6
14 – 9 = 5	14 – 10 = 4			
FIFTEEN				
15 – 5 = 10	15 – 6 = 9	15 – 7 = 8	15 – 8 = 7	15 – 9 = 6
15 – 10 = 5				
SIXTEEN				
16 – 6 = 10	16 – 7 = 9	16 – 8 = 8	16 – 9 = 7	16 – 10 = 6
SEVENTEEN				
17 – 7 = 10	17 – 8 = 9	17 – 9 = 8	17 – 10 = 7	
EIGHTEEN				
18 – 8 = 10	18 – 9 = 9	18 – 10 = 8		
NINETEEN				
19 – 9 = 10	19 – 10 = 9			
TWENTY				
20 – 10 = 10				

FIGURE 6.3. *(continued)*

Second, students begin to understand place value. For example, students recognize that the number in the 10's place of each problem has a much bigger value than the number in the 1's place.

Third, students master multiplication and division facts and operations and solve problems. Students are able to solve problems involving multiplication facts, operations (i.e., product of one-, two-, or three-digit numbers), and word problem-solving tasks that include the product, sum, or difference. Mastery of multiplication operations is first demonstrated by determining the product of a two-digit and a one-digit number, followed by the product of one-, two-, or three-digit numbers. Mastery of division operations involves dividing four-digit by two-digit numbers, and problem solving involves determining the quotient, product, sum, or difference in word problems. Multiplication and division facts are presented in Figures 6.4 and 6.5, respectively.

Fourth, students develop an understanding of fractions and fraction equivalence by the end of third grade; this understanding is the capstone target of stu-

| ZERO | | | | |
(Any number multiplied by 0 equals 0)				
0 × 0 = 0	1 × 0 = 0	2 × 0 = 0	3 × 0 = 0	4 × 0 = 0
5 × 0 = 0	6 × 0 = 0	7 × 0 = 0	8 × 0 = 0	9 × 0 = 0

| ONE | | | | |
(Any number multiplied by 1 equals that number)				
0 × 1 = 0	1 × 1 = 1	2 × 1 = 2	3 × 1 = 3	4 × 1 = 4
5 × 1 = 5	6 × 1 = 6	7 × 1 = 7	8 × 1 = 8	9 × 1 = 9

TWO				
0 × 2 = 0	1 × 2 = 2	2 × 2 = 4	3 × 2 = 6	4 × 2 = 8
5 × 2 = 10	6 × 2 = 12	7 × 2 = 14	8 × 2 = 16	9 × 2 = 18

THREE				
0 × 3 = 0	1 × 3 = 3	2 × 3 = 6	3 × 3 = 9	4 × 3 = 12
5 × 3 = 15	6 × 3 = 18	7 × 3 = 21	8 × 3 = 24	9 × 3 = 27

FOUR				
0 × 4 = 0	1 × 4 = 4	2 × 4 = 8	3 × 4 = 12	4 × 4 = 16
5 × 4 = 20	6 × 4 = 24	7 × 4 = 28	8 × 4 = 32	9 × 4 = 36

FIVE				
0 × 5 = 0	1 × 5 = 5	2 × 5 = 10	3 × 5 = 15	4 × 5 = 20
5 × 5 = 25	6 × 5 = 30	7 × 5 = 35	8 × 5 = 40	9 × 5 = 45

SIX				
0 × 6 = 0	1 × 6 = 6	2 × 6 = 12	3 × 6 = 18	4 × 6 = 24
5 × 6 = 30	6 × 6 = 36	7 × 6 = 42	8 × 6 = 48	9 × 6 = 54

SEVEN				
0 × 7 = 0	1 × 7 = 7	2 × 7 = 14	3 × 7 = 21	4 × 7 = 28
5 × 7 = 35	6 × 7 = 42	7 × 7 = 49	8 × 7 = 56	9 × 7 = 63

EIGHT				
0 × 8 = 0	1 × 8 = 8	2 × 8 = 16	3 × 8 = 24	4 × 8 = 32
5 × 8 = 40	6 × 8 = 48	7 × 8 = 56	8 × 8 = 64	9 × 8 = 72

NINE				
0 × 9 = 0	1 × 9 = 9	2 × 9 = 18	3 × 9 = 27	4 × 9 = 36
5 × 9 = 45	6 × 9 = 54	7 × 9 = 63	8 × 9 = 72	9 × 9 = 81

(continued)

FIGURE 6.4. Multiplication facts.

TEN				
0 × 10 = 0	1 × 10 = 10	2 × 10 = 20	3 × 10 = 30	4 × 10 = 40
5 × 10 = 50	6 × 10 = 60	7 × 10 = 70	8 × 10 = 80	9 × 10 = 90
10 × 10 = 100	11 × 10 = 110	12 × 10 = 120		

ELEVEN				
0 × 11 = 0	1 × 11 = 11	2 × 11 = 22	3 × 11 = 33	4 × 11 = 44
5 × 11 = 55	6 × 11 = 66	7 × 11 = 77	8 × 11 = 88	9 × 11 = 99
10 × 11 = 110	11 × 11 = 121	12 × 11 = 132		

TWELVE				
0 × 12 = 0	1 × 12 = 12	2 × 12 = 24	3 × 12 = 36	4 × 12 = 48
5 × 12 = 60	6 × 12 = 72	7 × 12 = 84	8 × 12 = 96	9 × 12 = 108
10 × 12 = 120	11 × 12 = 132	12 × 12 = 144		

FIGURE 6.4. *(continued)*

dents at the consolidated number sense phase. Students at this phase develop an understanding of the meanings and uses of fractions to represent parts of a whole, parts of a set, or points or distances on a number line. The scope of instructional activities in the consolidated number sense phase includes double-digit addition and subtraction operations, equality problems, multiplication and division facts, multiplication and division operations, and fractions. Students at this phase of development of number sense should score well on mixed and single-skill CBMs of math facts in addition, subtraction, division, and multiplication, but they may struggle with mixed-skill computation (described in detail in Chapter 3).

MASTERY INSTRUCTION

We center our discussion of mastery instruction procedures on math facts (partial and full number sense), operations (consolidated number sense), and problem-solving (consolidated number sense) concepts and skills. It is important to note that the concepts and skills described in this chapter are limited to those found to be critical to the development of mathematics applications and reasoning. As such, the math facts, operations, and problem-solving skills and concepts fit into approaches used at Tiers 2 and 3 of RTI models. See the National Council of Teachers of Mathematics (2006) list of benchmark math skills, or curriculum focal points included in comprehensive Tier 1 math programs, from preschool through grade 8 (*www.nctm.org/*). As discussed in Chapter 2, comprehensive instructional approaches address the full range of skills and operations needed in early math development, whereas supplementary (Tiers 2 and 3) intervention approaches address a narrower set of skills and operations that are critical to early math success.

ZERO				
(Numbers cannot be divided by zero because it is impossible to make zero groups of a number.)				

ONE				
(Any number divided by one equals that number. If you divide by one you have one group and so everything is in that group)				
0 ÷ 1 = 0	1 ÷ 1 = 1	2 ÷ 1 = 2	3 ÷ 1 = 3	4 ÷ 1 = 4
5 ÷ 1 = 5	6 ÷ 1 = 6	7 ÷ 1 = 7	8 ÷ 1 = 8	9 ÷ 1 = 9

TWO				
0 ÷ 2 = 0	2 ÷ 2 = 1	4 ÷ 2 = 2	6 ÷ 2 = 3	8 ÷ 2 = 4
10 ÷ 2 = 5	12 ÷ 2 = 6	14 ÷ 2 = 7	16 ÷ 2 = 8	18 ÷ 2 = 9

THREE				
0 ÷ 3 = 0	3 ÷ 3 = 1	6 ÷ 3 = 2	9 ÷ 3 = 3	12 ÷ 3 = 4
15 ÷ 3 = 5	18 ÷ 3 = 6	21 ÷ 3 = 7	24 ÷ 3 = 8	27 ÷ 3 = 9

FOUR				
0 ÷ 4 = 0	4 ÷ 4 = 1	8 ÷ 4 = 2	12 ÷ 4 = 3	16 ÷ 4 = 4
20 ÷ 4 = 5	24 ÷ 4 = 6	28 ÷ 4 = 7	32 ÷ 4 = 8	36 ÷ 4 = 9

FIVE				
0 ÷ 5 = 0	5 ÷ 5 = 1	10 ÷ 5 = 2	15 ÷ 5 = 3	20 ÷ 5 = 4
25 ÷ 5 = 5	30 ÷ 5 = 6	35 ÷ 5 = 7	40 ÷ 5 = 8	45 ÷ 5 = 9

SIX				
0 ÷ 6 = 0	6 ÷ 6 = 1	12 ÷ 6 = 2	18 ÷ 6 = 3	24 ÷ 6 = 4
30 ÷ 6 = 5	36 ÷ 6 = 6	42 ÷ 6 = 7	48 ÷ 6 = 8	54 ÷ 6 = 9

SEVEN				
0 ÷ 7 = 0	7 ÷ 7 = 1	14 ÷ 7 = 2	21 ÷ 7 = 3	28 ÷ 7 = 4
35 ÷ 7 = 5	42 ÷ 7 = 6	49 ÷ 7 = 7	56 ÷ 7 = 8	63 ÷ 7 = 9

EIGHT				
0 ÷ 8 = 0	8 ÷ 8 = 1	16 ÷ 8 = 2	24 ÷ 8 = 3	32 ÷ 8 = 4
40 ÷ 8 = 5	48 ÷ 8 = 6	56 ÷ 8 = 7	64 ÷ 8 = 8	72 ÷ 8 = 9

NINE				
0 ÷ 9 = 0	9 ÷ 9 = 1	18 ÷ 9 = 2	27 ÷ 9 = 3	36 ÷ 9 = 4
45 ÷ 9 = 5	54 ÷ 9 = 6	63 ÷ 9 = 7	72 ÷ 9 = 8	81 ÷ 9 = 9

(continued)

FIGURE 6.5. Division facts.

TEN					
0 ÷ 10 = 0	10 ÷ 10 = 1	20 ÷ 10 = 2	30 ÷ 10 = 3	40 ÷ 10 = 4	50 ÷ 10 = 5
60 ÷ 10 = 6	70 ÷ 10 = 7	80 ÷ 10 = 8	90 ÷ 10 = 9	100 ÷ 10 = 10	

ELEVEN					
0 ÷ 11 = 0	11 ÷ 11 = 1	22 ÷ 11 = 2	33 ÷ 11 = 3	44 ÷ 11 = 4	55 ÷ 11 = 5
66 ÷ 11 = 6	77 ÷ 11 = 7	88 ÷ 11 = 8	99 ÷ 11 = 9	110 ÷ 11 = 10	121 ÷ 11 = 11

TWELVE					
0 ÷ 12 = 0	12 ÷ 12 = 1	24 ÷ 12 = 2	36 ÷ 12 = 3	48 ÷ 12 = 4	60 ÷ 12 = 5
72 ÷ 12 = 6	84 ÷ 12 = 7	96 ÷ 12 = 8	108 ÷ 12 = 9	120 ÷ 12 = 10	132 ÷ 12 = 11
144 ÷ 12 = 12					

FIGURE 6.5. *(continued)*

As noted earlier, there are direct parallels between reading and math instruction. Thus, we focus on cognitive strategy procedures for teaching operations and problem solving in this chapter, because teaching math facts directly parallels teaching students beginning reading skills (e.g., letter–sound correspondence, sight words). Briefly, the first key element of mastery instruction in math facts is a well-defined scope and sequence. The introduction of addition, subtraction, multiplication, and division facts occurs at the full and consolidated number sense phases of early math development. As indicated in Figure 6.1, mastery of math facts begins with addition (Figure 6.2), followed by subtraction (Figure 6.3), multiplication (Figure 6.4), and division (Figure 6.5).

Instructional procedures for discrimination training are used to build mastery of math facts (see Chapter 2 for a complete description). Further, the use of these kinds of procedures to teach math facts mirrors those articulated to teach letter names to mastery in Chapter 5. The teacher then moves to fluency instruction of math facts—the repeated presentation of known math facts designed to produce fluent performance (i.e., performance at or near 100% accurate). Given that discrimination instructional procedures were detailed in prior chapters, here we focus our discussion of mastery-oriented instruction on cognitive strategy instruction for math operations and problem solving.

Mastery instruction, in relation to math operations and problem solving, involves a controlled presentation of cognitive strategies (low to moderate levels of accuracy) that are designed to help students master and accurately apply the steps in operations and problem solving. Thus, instruction centers on knowing what problems require use of the strategy and mastering the necessary components in the strategy, or algorithm, to solve a given problem. The scope and sequence for math operations and problem solving is provided in Figure 6.1. We begin a teacher-directed example of cognitive strategy instruction using the self-regulated strategy development (SRSD) implementation model for column addition requiring regrouping. Mastering the regrouping rule for double-digit addition problems is an important skill at the consolidated number sense phase. We continue with an application of the SRSD implementation model on a word problem-solving strategy. We conclude with correction procedures for fact, component, and strategy errors. These same procedures can then be applied across the full range of operations and problem solving detailed in Figure 6.1.

Full Number Sense: Using the SRSD Regrouping Strategy for Column Addition

Scope and Sequence

There are two important reasons for the use of the SRSD as a model for building mastery of early mathematical operations and problem solving. First, the SRSD is an instructional model designed to make the multiple steps involved in mathematical operations and problem solving habitual, flexible, and automatic. Mastery of the steps involved in mathematical operations and problem solving can take a lot of time, practice, and effort. Fortunately, the SRSD model gives teachers an instructional template to follow to teach the needed steps in a simple and systematic fashion. Second, SRSD is an implementation model for cognitive strategy instruction, which has more than 20 years of empirical support (Brophy & Good, 1986; Pressley et al., 1995; Reid & Lienemann, 2006).

There are six stages in the SRSD instructional sequence: (1) develop and activate background knowledge, (2) discuss the strategy, (3) model it, (4) memorize it, (5) support it, and (6) provide independent performance. The SRSD model includes mnemonics to facilitate recall of a strategy for column addition requiring regrouping. Frank and Brown (1992) developed a self-regulation strategy, based on the SRSD model, for remembering the steps for column addition problems involving regrouping (the consolidated number sense phase), using the acronym SASH as a mnemonic strategy: (1) Start in the 1's column; (2) Add together the numerals in each column; (3) Should I carry a numeral?; and (4) Have I carried the correct numeral? Now we describe the procedures for teaching the SASH mnemonic strategy at each stage of the SRSD model.

Stage 1: Develop and Activate Background Knowledge

Stage 1 of the SRSD implementation model is to develop and activate the background knowledge necessary to learn the SASH strategy. This stage begins with a task analysis of the key prerequisite math facts and operations necessary to apply the SASH strategy: These include mastery of place value up to three-digit numbers and addition facts adding 1, 2, 3, 10, and 9 to single-digit numbers. The teacher can use CBM or AIMSweb Addition Math Facts probes to ascertain whether the student has sufficiently mastered these addition facts (see Chapter 3).

Mastery of two prerequisite math operations is necessary to apply the SASH strategy. First, students need to demonstrate mastery of adding two two-digit numbers involving no regrouping (e.g., 21 + 32 = 53), starting with the 1's column, or right to left, as opposed to working such problems from left to right. Second, students must learn to keep a running total (e.g., cross out values that have already been added) for column addition of three single-digit numbers (e.g., 1 + 4 + 7 = 12). This type of problem is critical to regrouping problems, which often involve adding three values in a column, and often the first value is 1. Mastering these important math facts and operations sets the stage for learning the SASH regrouping strategy. Students with mastery of these prerequisite skills should be taught in a small-group arrangement, whereas those students who have not yet mastered these skills might be taught individually.

Stage 2: Discuss the Strategy

Discussion of the SASH strategy (Stage 2 of the SRSD implementation model) begins with demonstrating its importance. The teacher begins by writing a single-digit addition problem on the board:

$$\begin{array}{r} 9 \\ + \ 6 \\ \hline \end{array}$$

The teacher reads the problem: "9 (*pointing to 9*) plus (*pointing to the plus sign*) 6 (*pointing to 6*) is (*pointing to the line*) 15 (*pointing under the line*)." The teacher then says, "Your turn to read the problem [test]." The teacher points to each number and addition symbol as students read the problem and answer.

Next, the teacher asks, "What is the first digit of 15?" The students respond with "1." The teacher states, "I need to write *1* in the 10's column and *5* in the 1's column." The teacher writes *15* as follows:

$$\begin{array}{r} 9 \\ + \ 6 \\ \hline 15 \end{array}$$

Finally, the teacher explains: "This works when you don't have to add other numbers in the 10's column. But watch this." The teacher changes the problem as follows:

$$\begin{array}{r} 29 \\ + \ 16 \\ \hline 15 \end{array}$$

The teacher explains that the answer in the 1's column is still 15, but writing both digits in the answer will give us the wrong answer. The teacher asks the students if they have ever encountered a problem like this one and explains that a strategy is important to solving such problems.

Stage 3: Model the Strategy

During Stage 3 of the SRSD implementation model, the teacher models the strategy, beginning with writing each step of the strategy on the board and underlining each letter of the SASH mnemonic. Next, the teacher models the first step in the regrouping strategy, "Start in the 1's column." The teacher states, "The first step of the SASH strategy is to *Start (pointing to the S in the word Start on the board)* in the 1's column." The teacher points to the 1's column and states, "This is the 1's column." Next, the teacher asks the students, "What column is this?" The students should respond, "1's." The teacher points to the column and states, "This is the 10's column." Next, the teacher asks the students, "What column is this?" The students should respond, "10's." The teacher restates that the first step in the SASH strategy is to *start* in the 1's column. The teacher asks, "What is the first step in the SASH regrouping strategy?"

Next the teacher explains: "The next step is to *Add (pointing to the A in the word Add on the board)* the numbers in the 1's column." The teacher asks, "Students, what is 9 plus 6?" The students should respond with 15. The teacher explains, "Yes, 9 plus 6 is 15. So, the answer is *15.*"

The teacher asks, "What is the second step in the SASH regrouping strategy?" and answers, "The next step is *Should (pointing to the S in Should).* Should I carry a numeral?" The teacher explains, "We can't write both digits of our answer. We have to write the digit for the 10's somewhere else. So, we write it at the top of the 10's column *(pointing to the top of the 10's column)*, not at the bottom. Watch me."

$$
\begin{array}{r}
1 \\
29 \\
+\ 16 \\
\hline
15
\end{array}
$$

The teacher says, "Get ready to answer yes or no. Should *(pointing to the S in Should)* I carry a numeral after adding 9 plus 6 *(pointing to ones column)*?" Students respond, "Yes." The teacher asks, "Students, what is the third step in the SASH regrouping strategy?"

Stating the last step in the strategy, "The last step is to ask: *Have* I carried the correct numeral?", the teacher explains, "We have the one 10 we carried in the column with the other 10's." Finally, the teacher asks, "Yes or no? Have *(pointing to the H in Have)* we carried the correct numeral?" Then the teacher explains that the one 10 in 15 has been carried above the column with the other 10's.

Stage 4: Memorize the Strategy

It is critical that students commit the SASH strategy steps to memory in order to focus on the task rather than remembering the steps of the strategy. Memorization means more than just reciting the steps in the strategy; it includes knowing and understanding what is involved with each step in the process (Reid & Lienemann, 2006). Thus, memorization of the SASH strategy will likely not occur with one or two practice opportunities, but through consistent repetition and varied practice.

To review student understanding of each step in the SASH strategy, the teacher says, "Let's review. What is the first step in the SASH regrouping strategy?" The students respond, "Start with the 1's column." The teacher says, "Yes. The first step of the SASH strategy is to *Start* (*pointing to the S in the word* Start *on the board*) in the 1's column." The teacher repeats this presentation format for the remaining steps in the strategy. After the last step, the teacher should say, "Let's review the steps in the SASH strategy quickly. The steps are?"

Stage 5: Support the Strategy

The teacher provides support for the SASH strategy. An example of guided support for the SASH strategy is providing a worksheet containing the following problems:

$$
\begin{array}{llll}
\text{a.} \quad 29 & \text{b.} \quad 39 & \text{c.} \quad 19 & \text{d.} \quad 49 \\
\quad\ +16 & \quad\ + 18 & \quad\ + 76 & \quad\ + 29
\end{array}
$$

The teacher says, "Use the SASH strategy to solve these problems. When we add the numbers in the 1's column for each of these problems, we get two-digit answers. Therefore, you will need to carry the first digit to the top of the 10's column. You will write the digit you carry at the top of the 10's column. Let's do the first problem together. Put your finger on the 1's column in problem 'a'; 9 plus 6 is 15 (*pointing to each number in the 1's column*). The answer is 15. What is the first digit of 15?" The students respond, "1." The teacher says, "This digit goes to the top of the 10's column (*writes 1 at the top of the 10's column*). What is the second digit of 15?" The students respond, "5." Finally, the teacher should say, "Let's write 5 at the bottom of the 1's column. Do it just like I did on the board." Then the teacher checks individual student responses to the first problem.

Step 6: Independent Performance

After students accurately complete the first part of problem "a," they should be asked to continue with the other problems. The teacher should carefully monitor student responses and provide error correction.

Consolidated Number Sense: Using the SRSD for Word Problem Solving

Amanda VanDerHeyden at the University of California, Santa Barbara, has outlined a good example of cognitive strategy instruction for solving word problems. Details about VanDerHeyden's math word problem-solving strategy are available on the "Scientifically Based Research" webpage (*www.gosbr.net/*). The following steps are used to solve word problems:

1. Underline what is known.
2. Circle what is unknown.
3. Write the operation(s) next to the problem.
4. Write the problem and the answer, and then label the answer.

This strategy for teaching word problem solving parallels the first four of the six stages of the SRSD implementation model detailed in the previous example; however, it does not include steps for supporting the strategy (Stage 5) or independent performance (Stage 6). As such, we turn the focus of our discussion of mastery instruction toward the word problem-solving strategy of Stages 5 and 6 of the SRSD implementation model.

Stage 5: Support the Strategy

Peer tutoring is used to support the word problem-solving strategy at Stage 5 of the SRSD implementation model. Two tasks are necessary to implement peer-tutoring. The first task is to create a worksheet with as many as six word problems for students (several online sources can be used to create such worksheets, including Math Playground (*www.mathplayground.com*) and edHelper.com (*www.edhelper. com/math.htm*). For example, to create word problems for addition of two-digit numbers that require regrouping, select the word problems tab on the Math Playground webpage. A worksheet with five two-digit addition word problems that require regrouping will open. An example of such problem is: "Kayla ran in 15 races last year. Paula ran in 17 races. How many races did they run altogether?" The worksheets can be printed and distributed to students (and students should write their names near the top of the worksheet).

The second task to support the word problem-solving strategy is arranging for the peer tutoring. Students should be directed to assemble in working pairs and to complete as many worksheet problems as possible in 5 minutes with the help of a peer buddy. Each of the four stages involved in solving word problems should be completed, and the student writing the answers should explain, out loud, how he or she got the information for each stage. After each problem, the peer buddy should ask, "How did you solve the problem?" and the student should explain the answer (e.g., "We started with 14 apples and bought 17 more, so 14 plus 17 equals 31; 31 apples is the answer"). The peer buddy should complete a checklist of the four stages of the word problem strategy as the partner explains the answer. A check is made on the checklist for each stage correctly explained. After 5 minutes, the students should switch roles. The other student should complete as many problems as possible in 5 minutes with help from his or her peer buddy. The teacher should monitor each pair carefully to make sure that partners are going through the stages correctly.

Stage 6: Independent Performance

After 10 minutes of peer tutoring on the word problem strategy, the teacher should distribute another copy of five two-digit addition problems that require regrouping. Students should be timed for 2 minutes. After the probe is completed, students should trade papers and score each other's work. As the teacher gives the correct answer, students should chorally respond with each of the four word problem-solving strategy stages. The teacher should review a missing stage if many students missed it, and students should record the correct answer for each of the problems they missed.

Error Correction

There are three primary types of mathematical errors (Snider & Crawford, 2004). The first type, *fact errors*, stems from lack of proficiency with basic math facts. If fact errors are frequent or repeated, teachers should first give students the answer to a problem (e.g., "2 plus 1 is 3") and immediately redeliver the verbal prompt (e.g., "What is 2 plus 1?"). The teacher should then instruct the student to state the whole problem ("Say the whole problem"). The student should respond, "2 plus 1 is 3." The teacher should return to the math fact that was incorrect after several instructional trials.

The second type of error, *strategy errors*, involves omitting one or more steps in an operation. For example, a student may forget one of the steps of the SASH mnemonic strategy for column addition that requires regrouping. Strategy error correction involves reminding students of the steps in a procedure and allowing sufficient practice until students are able to conduct all the steps independently. A precorrective statement, used prior to students' completing the problem independently, may be beneficial (e.g., "Be careful. What do you do first to solve this problem?").

The final type of error, *component errors*, indicates deficits in the prerequisite skills required to complete an operation or solve a math problem (Stage 1 of the SRSD model). An example of a component skill error would be not keeping a running total (e.g., crossing out values that have already been added) for column addition of three single-digit numbers (e.g., 1 plus 4 plus 7 equals 12). If students lack this component skill, adding three one-digit numbers in the 10's place on column addition problems that require regrouping will be very difficult. This type of error should be corrected immediately by first repeating the task that was missed and then reteaching the entire part of the lesson in which the mistake was made.

FLUENCY INSTRUCTION

In this section we discuss how to design and deliver fluency instruction of math facts, operations, and problem solving, using the six steps for fluency instruction discussed in Chapter 2. We highlight a number of online technologies available for developing fluency instruction in this chapter. These online technologies can be used across reading, math, and writing. Remember, the six steps of fluency instruction include:

1. Select observable pivotal skills that are directly related to the content being taught.
2. Select the range of skill practice items the student has mastered.
3. Develop fluency instructional sheets.
4. Establish daily performance standards.
5. Conduct a series of short, timed instructional trials.
6. Have students chart correct responses.

Select Observable Pivotal Skills

There are pivotal skills for fluency instruction of math facts, operations, and problem solving. The pivotal skill areas for math fact fluency are addition, subtraction, multiplication, and division facts (see Figure 6.1). The pivotal skill area for math operations is computation (e.g., multiply multidigit numbers, add and subtract two multidigit numbers with regrouping). Pivotal skill areas for problem solving include analyzing and solving practical problems, explaining math concepts and vocabulary, and analyzing numerical relationships. Fluent problem solving and operations center on high levels of accuracy with the application of cognitive strategies.

Select the Range of Skill Practice Items

The observable pivotal skills that can be targeted for math facts, operations, and problem-solving fluency involve applied problems or discrete items. There are two types of applied math fluency skills: cumulative skills and applied word problem skills. Cumulative skill fluency focuses on building fluent application of math facts and operations (National Research Council, 2001, 2004). If students have recently mastered all of the addition and subtraction facts, an example of practice in cumulative skill fluency would be instruction that includes these facts. A teacher might generate a probe with these facts randomly distributed and time student fluency performance for 2 minutes. The purpose of applied word problem fluency is to build automatic application of cognitive strategies for problem solving (National Research Council, 2001, 2004). Using the same content (addition and subtraction facts), a teacher might generate a probe of two to six word problems and time student fluency performance for 5 minutes. An example might be: "Amanda told on her brother because he put four bugs on her arms and one bug on her leg. How many bugs did her brother put on her in all?"

In the case of discrete items, the selection of skill practice items is based on what is being taught and what students have mastered. For example, a teacher has taught, and students have mastered, addition facts for adding 1 to single-digit whole numbers up through five (i.e., 0 + 1, 1 + 1, 2 + 1, 3 + 1, 4 + 1, 5 + 1). The teacher would then construct a fluency instruction sheet that has these six addition facts and initiate fluency instruction. After the students achieve a high degree of fluency, the teacher could construct another fluency sheet that contains the next four addition facts (i.e., 6 + 1, 7 + 1, 8 + 1, 9 + 1) being taught during the time the teacher is doing fluency instruction on the previous six addition facts. Furthermore, teachers should construct fluency instructional sheets that are cumulative in nature. For example, a teacher has taught, and students have mastered, 20 addition facts (e.g., all the + 0 and + 1 single-digit addition facts). The teacher could then construct fluency instructional sheets that include a random selection of 6–8 of the 20 mastered addition facts.

Develop Fluency Instructional Sheets

The first point teachers should consider when developing fluency instructional sheets is the optimal counting time for this instruction. Typically, math fluency instruction has 2-minute counting times. There are two primary considerations for raising the counting time to 4–5 minutes. The first consideration is whether the fluency instructional sheet involves more than one skill, such as addition and subtraction or word problems. The second consideration involves students' proficiency in independent math skills. For students above the third grade, a general guideline is 4-minute timings for cumulative skill fluency and 5-minute timings for applied problem fluency. Teachers should use the same counting time each day. We now describe the specific steps involved in creating applied problem and discrete-item fluency sheets.

Creating Applied Problem Fluency Sheets

There are several online resources designed to aid teachers in the development of applied problem fluency sheets (cumulative and word problem). Sources for cumulative skill fluency probes include SuperKids® Educational Software Review (*www.superkids.com/aweb/tools/math*), edHelper.com (*www.edhelper.com/math.htm*), Free Math Worksheets (*www.math-drills.com*), and the worksheet generator at Intervention Central (*www.interventioncentral.org/tools.php*). Sources for generating word problem fluency probes include Math Playground (*www.mathplayground.com*) and edHelper.com. With the exception of edHelper.com, teachers are able to generate math probes and worksheets using these sites at no charge.

To create a cumulative skill fluency math worksheet using the math worksheet generator found at Intervention Central, first open the following webpage: *www.interventioncentral.org/tools.php*. Next, scroll down the page to the math worksheet generator and left-click on "Select a probe generator." The math probe types menu appears: single-skill addition, single-skill subtraction, single-skill multiplication, single-skill division, and mixed skill—all problem types. The teacher should highlight or select the "mixed skill—all problem types" menu option. A new webpage should open with the following title: Curriculum-Based Assessment Math Computation Probe Generator: Multiple-Skill Worksheets in Mixed Skills (*www. interventioncentral.org/htmdocs/tools/mathprobe/allmult.php*). The options on the top of the webpage allow a teacher to choose the number of rows, columns, font size (small, medium, large, X-large, and XX-Large), and item of the cumulative skill fluency sheet. If the teacher would like to create a probe with 40 items, for example, he or she could select 4 rows and 10 columns. To choose the number of rows, the teacher should left-click the columns menu under the Advanced Settings section at the top of the page. Four column options (1–4 columns) are listed. The teacher selects *4* to create a worksheet with four columns. The same procedures used to select the number of columns are used for rows and font size. The menu options for number of rows range from 1 to 10. The teacher should select *10* for a worksheet with 10 rows. The two choices for item order are "present items in order selected" or "present items in randomized order." To select "present items in randomized order," the teacher should left-click on the radio button to the left of the order option. Presenting items in a randomized order means that the math facts will be randomly distributed as opposed to problems of one item type being grouped together.

The next step is to select item types within each of the four pivotal skills for whole-number proficiency: addition, subtraction, multiplication, and division. Drawing upon the example used previously, consider the teacher who wants to create an applied problems fluency probe of single-digit addition and subtraction facts. The teacher would left-click in the box to the left of two addition problem types: "two 1-digit numbers: sums to 10" and "two 1-digit numbers: sums to 18." The box to the left of one subtraction item type is checked "—two 1-digit numbers: 0 to 9." The final step is to click on the bar reading "Multiple Skill Computation Probe." The student copy of the probe, with four columns and ten rows of randomly distributed single-digit addition and subtraction problems, will open. The title of the student copy will be: "Curriculum-Based Assessment Mathematics Multiple-Skills Computation Probe: Student Copy." A space for student names is found on the left side of the page beneath the title. A line for the date is found below the title. The teacher (or examiner) copy of the probe, with an answer key, is provided on a separate webpage. The title of the teacher copy is: "Curriculum-Based Assessment Mathematics Multiple-Skills Computation Probe: Examiner Copy." The teacher answer key includes the correct digits possible and a cumulative count of the total correct digits possible above each item. The items and structure (number of rows, columns) will parallel the student copy. The teacher and student copies of the cumulative applied problems fluency probe can be printed for easy distribution.

Creating Discrete-Item Fluency Sheets

In the case of discrete stimuli, teachers should select a set of items that their students have mastered with 95–100% accuracy. The total number of items used to develop a fluency instructional sheet should range from five to eight and be distributed randomly in a serial format. There are two primary options for the creation of discrete fluency instructional sheets. The first option allows teachers to use the "table" function of their word-processing software to create the discrete-item fluency instructional sheets. The second option is for teachers to use an information technology product such as SuperKids Educational Software Review (*www.superkids.com*). To create a fluency instructional sheet using SuperKids, a teacher should open the SuperKids Math Worksheet Creator by clicking on the math worksheets link found on the left side of the SuperKids homepage. A new page will open (*www.superkids.com/aweb/tools/math*) with the following menu options: Addition, Subtraction, Mixed Addition and Subtraction, Multiplication, Division, Order of Operations, Fractions, Percentages, Greater than/Less than, Odd or Even, Rounding, Averages, Exponents, Factorials, Is It Prime?, and Telling Time. Using the previous example, consider a teacher interested in creating a discrete-item fluency instructional sheet for adding 1 to single-digit numbers up through 5. The teacher should click on the Addition menu option. Another webpage with five addition options (basic addition, advanced addition, horizontal addition, addition with more than 2 addends, and addition tables) will appear. The teacher should select *basic addition*, and the following webpage will open: *www.superkids. com/aweb/tools/math/add/plus1.shtml*.

At this point, creating discrete-item fluency instructional sheets is a five-step process. First, the teacher should select the maximum value of numbers used. The maximum value of any digit should be 5 because this is the highest single-digit whole number to which 1 will be added. Next, the teacher should left-click on the menu options to the right of "Select maximum value of numbers used." Nineteen maximum value choices will appear, ranging from 1 to 1,000. The teacher should move the mouse over the number *5* and left-click on it. The second step is to choose the minimum value of numbers used. This value should be 0 because it is the lowest single-digit number to which 1 will be added. The teacher should left-click on the menu options to the right of "Select minimum value of numbers used." Except for the addition of 0, the menu options are identical to those for maximum value. Thus, there are 20 number menu options. The teacher selects *0* by left-clicking on it (the menu option at the top of the list).

The third step is to choose one number in all problems. The teacher should left-click on the menu options to the right of "Optional: Use one number in all problems." With the exception of the no number (or blank space) option, the 21 options parallel those for selecting the minimum value of numbers used. Selecting one from the menu will create problems that add 1 to single-digit numbers from 0 to 5. The teacher then chooses the number of problems by left-clicking the menu options to the right of "Number of problems on page." The teacher can choose 5, 10, 15, 20, 25, 30, or 50 items, applying the same procedure used to select values. It is important that the sheet include enough items to occupy students throughout the fluency period (e.g., 2 minutes).

The final step is to left-click on the "Make My Worksheet" bar, directly below the "Number of problems on page" selection option. A worksheet will open with the following title: "SuperKids Math Worksheet: Addition using 1 and values between 0 and 5." The student's name goes in the upper left corner and the date in the upper right. The number of columns will always be five. However, the number of rows will depend upon the teacher's selection for the "Number of problems on page" option. If 30 problems were selected, for example, there will be six rows. All of the problems have 1 added to 0–5, if 1 was selected at the "Optional: Use one number in all problems" option. If 0 and 5 were selected as minimum and maximum values, respectively, all of the problems will include 1 being added to randomly chosen numbers from 0 to 5. At this point, the teacher can print and distribute the student copy of the discrete-item fluency probe.

To create an answer sheet, the teacher should first scroll to the bottom of the worksheet using the scroll bar on the right of the page. Next, the teacher should left-click on the "Create Answer Sheet" bar. An answer sheet with a key number (e.g., Key #79145) in the upper-left corner and date in the upper-right will emerge. The answer key number will match that found on the "Create Answer Sheet" bar at the bottom of the student discrete-item fluency worksheet.

Establish Daily Performance Standards

Establishing a student's baseline score is the first step in determining daily performance standards. A student's baseline score is the teacher's best estimate of the student's level of performance prior to fluency instruction. Teachers use a student's initial baseline performance to establish the first daily performance goal. Subsequent performance goals are established based on the student's daily performance. It is important for teachers to have in mind a fluency goal and to communicate it clearly to students. The process of establishing a fluency goal is discussed in Chapters 3 and 5.

Conduct Short, Timed Instructional Trials

After setting the daily performance standard, teachers conduct several (i.e., three to five) instructional trials each day, depending upon student learning needs. Teachers also may be working on more than one mathematics skill at a time. For example, a teacher may conduct separate fluency timings on addition facts and subtraction facts. The entire instructional session should range from 15 to 20 minutes in length. Another instructional session can be conducted at another point in the day for those students who need additional math instruction.

Teachers should initiate each instructional trial with a consistent beginning (e.g., "Begin") and ending (e.g., "Time") prompt. Sample beginning prompts for instructional fluency trials for applied problems and discrete items are presented in Table 6.1. Whether in small groups or working with individual students, the same

TABLE 6.1. Sample Beginning Prompts for Applied Problems and Discrete Stimuli

Applied problems	Discrete stimuli
Individual Please write your answers to different kinds of math problems. Look at each problem carefully before you answer it. I will tell you the answer if you get stuck, so you can keep going until I say "time." Remember to do your best. Get ready to do the first problem (*pause*). Begin. At the end of 2–5 minutes say, "Stop. Put your pencils down."	*Individual* Please write your answers to these . . . (e.g., addition facts). Look at each one carefully before you answer it. I will tell you the answer if you get stuck, so you can keep going until I say "time." Remember to do your best. Get ready to do the first problem (*pause*). Begin. At the end of 2–5 minutes say, "Stop. Put your pencils down."
Small group Please say these different math facts with me. Remember to follow along with me until I say "time." Eyes up here (*point to problems*). Ready (*finger pointing at the first item*), begin (*slide your finger under each part of the fact* [the rate should meet the daily performance standard] *to prompt students to say the fact in unison*). Use the "individual" prompt above to track fluency for individual students. The individual prompt can be delivered to more than one student at a time.	*Small group* Please say the . . . out loud with me. Remember to follow along with me until I say "time." Eyes up here (*point to problems*). Ready (*finger pointing at the first item*), begin (*slide your finger under each part of the fact* [the rate should meet the daily performance standard] *to prompt students to say the fact in unison*). Use the "individual" prompt above to track fluency for individual students. The individual prompt can be delivered to more than one student at a time.

beginning prompt should be used for math instructional fluency trials. Teachers should not correct student errors during these trials. After an instructional trial, a teacher should provide students with immediate feedback that focuses on praise for engaging in the instructional trial and for correct performance or for beating or getting close to the daily performance standard (e.g., "You got it!" or "You were so close!").

Have Students Chart Correct Responses

The primary purpose of evaluating and modifying instructional support is to determine whether the intervention is effective at improving early mathematics skills. Evaluating and modifying instructional support requires that math fluency data inform instruction. Data-based decision-making procedures are used for evaluating current performance in relation to the fluency goal and to past performance. The procedures for determining if the intervention is working well enough to achieve the fluency goal are described in Chapter 3.

OTHER CONSIDERATIONS IN PLANNING AND DELIVERING MATHEMATICS INSTRUCTION FOR STUDENTS WITH BD

Before concluding our discussion of mastery and fluency instructional procedures in mathematics, we want to underscore the importance of developing strong early and partial number sense (phases 1 and 2) for the prevention of math difficulties. Students who demonstrate later difficulties with mathematics lack strong early and partial number sense when compared to their typically developing peers (Geary, Bow-Thomas, & Yao, 1992). Remediating math difficulties in the elementary grades and beyond is very challenging if students lack the building blocks for number sense. Teachers should screen students to determine whether these skills are intact prior to focusing instruction on math facts, operations, and problem solving. The resource with the most extensive and inexpensive collection of early numeracy measures is CBM warehouse at Intervention Central (*www.interventioncentral.org*).

CONCLUSIONS

In this chapter we focused on building and enhancing the early mathematics skills of students with BD. Improving mathematics achievement is a national priority, given that less than one-third of eighth graders in the United States were "proficient" in mathematics, based on the 2005 National Assessment of Educational Progress (NAEP; Perie, Grigg, & Dion, 2005). Students with BD tend to experience math fact, operations, and problem-solving deficits that persist throughout their academic careers (Greenbaum et al., 1996; Mattison et al., 2002; Nelson et al., 2004). The research on math interventions with students who have BD indicates that teacher-directed, peer-mediated, and self-regulation interventions have generally improved fluency in math facts, operations, and problem solving. The majority of researchers have examined the effects of self-regulation interventions on this population.

We presented mastery- and fluency-oriented instructional principles in early math through a four-phase developmental skill framework: (1) early number sense phase; (2) partial number sense phase; (3) full number sense phase; and (4) a consolidated number sense phase. The goal of the early number sense phase is to develop the central conceptual understanding of number sense necessary for mastery of addition and subtraction facts. Mastery of addition and subtraction facts begins during the partial number sense phase and extends through the full number sense phase. The two overarching goals of the consolidated number sense phase are fluency with addition and subtraction operations and problem solving and mastery of multiplication and division facts, operations, and problem solving.

We centered our discussion of mastery instruction procedures on math facts (partial and full number sense), operations (consolidated number sense), and problem solving (consolidated number sense). We focused on cognitive strategy procedures for teaching operations and problem solving in this chapter because teaching math facts directly parallels teaching students beginning reading skills. Instructional procedures for discrimination training are used to build mastery of math facts. In the case of math operations and problem solving, mastery instruction centers on mastering the necessary steps in the strategy, or algorithm, to solve the problem. We discussed a teacher-directed example of cognitive strategy instruction using the SRSD implementation model for column addition requiring regrouping. We also provided a peer-mediated example of the SRSD implementation model to teach a word problem-solving strategy. Math fact, strategy, and component error-correction procedures were detailed.

Finally, we discussed the two types of applied math fluency problems: cumulative skill and applied word problems. We described the development of fluency instructional sheets and the specific steps involved in creating two types of applied problem fluency sheets: cumulative skill and word problem fluency. We detailed each step in the creation of a cumulative skill fluency using the math worksheet generator found at Intervention Central. We also detailed the creation of discrete fluency instructional sheets using SuperKids Educational Software Review. We concluded the chapter by highlighting the importance of early and partial number sense to the prevention of math difficulties.

CHAPTER 7

Early Writing Instruction

In the last two chapters the instructional processes that enable students to become proficient primary school readers and mathematicians were presented as cornerstones of successful schooling. We think the same is true of the methods educators use to help students become skilled writers. Indeed, writing "is an indispensable tool for learning" (Graham, 2006, p. 457). So much can be accomplished by proficient writers, from investing a great deal of time and energy in composing a holiday letter to send to friends and family across the country, to responding quickly and almost effortlessly to an e-mail from a coworker or friend. Students who are adept at written communication can impress instructors through their biology lab reports, history term papers, or preservice teaching reflections. These students also are more likely to earn better grades because a great deal of what is expected of them as they advance through elementary, middle, and high school—and through postsecondary programs of study—involves the effective written communication of ideas or content. Additionally, we believe a focus on the development of writing skills in primary grades students with BD is important for two other reasons. One, much as is the case with reading, students with BD have a difficult time communicating through the written word. Two, writing instruction is a complex, multifaceted process that promotes academic development in all areas.

Students with BD often struggle to manage the parts of school that involve writing. Reviewing status research conducted across a 40-year period, Epstein et al. (2005) reported that almost half of students verified with emotional disturbance and included in research studies evidenced written expression deficits. The magnitude of writing delays in students with emotional disturbance ranged from 0.48 to 2.4 years below expected grade level (Epstein et al., 2005). Nelson, Benner, Lane, and Smith (2004) advanced the status literature by incorporating more technically adequate (i.e., norm-referenced) measurement procedures than had been included in previous studies. Testing a random sample of 155 K–12 students with emotional disturbance, Nelson and colleagues found the average writing delay to be about two-thirds of a standard deviation on a standardized test of writing achievement. Further analyses of student scores indicated equivalence across both grade level (i.e., elementary vs. secondary) and gender (i.e., male vs. female), meaning that the delays were widespread. Research on the writing status of students with BD has contributed to the view of this population as among the toughest to teach (Dixon, Isaacson, & Stein, 2007).

The difficulties faced when intervening academically with students who have BD are only exacerbated by the complexities of teaching writing skills in public school settings. Writing instruction can be impacted by myriad factors. We highlight two of those factors here. One, consider the many skills involved in writing. Students must learn to spell words correctly if they are to produce works judged acceptable by instructors. Students also must employ appropriate conventions of grammar and mechanics when they compose stories or reports. Additionally, given assignments such as writing fictional stories or fact-based reports, students often must simultaneously plan, compose, and revise their thoughts or material and regulate their own thinking in order to generate meaningful products.

Two, consider the many components of writing that exist "outside" the student—components that must be addressed in order for the student to be able to produce a meaningful text. These components include a written text's form, purpose, and audience. For instance, the current collection of words you are reading is organized as a book chapter. As such, this chapter's contents have been planned and written by its authors to relate to the accompanying chapters. This chapter's purpose (i.e., to inform) is similar to the book's other chapters; its audience is likely identical to the audience of the book's other chapters. Although the chapter's structure is similar to some chapters (e.g., early reading and math skills development), it is different from others (e.g., instructional management). Overall, both individual factors and writing components may comprise the early writing instruction provided to primary grade students with BD. It is critical that such instruction be effective. Graham and Harris (2002) have noted that quality of instruction is a major determinant in the success of struggling writers. Graham and Harris's assertion also is a bit unnerving when one considers that researchers (e.g., Dixon et al., 2007) report that writing instruction is often absent from general classroom settings.

We begin this chapter on early writing instruction with a discussion of research targeted at improving the writing skills of students with BD; models on which to base writing instruction; mastery- and fluency-based instructional activities designed to improve the spelling, handwriting, and written expression of struggling writers; and other considerations in the planning and delivery of writing instruction. We conclude the chapter with a summary of its major points.

WRITING RESEARCH FOR STUDENTS WITH BD

As was the case with reading and math (see Chapters 5 and 6, respectively), there is a small body of intervention studies targeting writing improvement for students with BD. Two related conclusions can be drawn from a review of the empirical findings. The overwhelming majority of writing studies: (1) target spelling improvement; and (2) are teacher directed (i.e., mediated) and aimed at individuals or small groups of students with BD. In teacher-mediated studies, teachers either maintain control throughout the intervention process or strategically allow students to exert greater control by having them self-manage their own academic performance (Mooney et al., 2003, 2005; Pierce et al., 2004). Teachers were the primary managers of writing interventions for students with BD. For example, McDougall and Brady (1995) implemented a spelling intervention with three boys ranging in age from 5 years, 11 months to 8 years, 7 months. A self-monitoring intervention was targeted at new word acquisition for the three boys. During baseline, the boys were expected to carry out the following procedure—known as the "hand method"—for each word during the 8 minutes preceding their spelling lesson: (1) look at the word; (2) say the word while looking at it; (3) spell the word while looking at it; (4) cover the word; (5) say the still covered word; (6) spell the still covered word; and (7) uncover the word to check for accuracy (Graham, 1983). During intervention, students incorporated into the 8-minute study period a self-monitoring procedure involving a cassette recorder, a prerecorded tape, a set of headphones, and a paper taped to the desk. When cued by the tape, each student was expected to look at the piece of paper and silently answer the question written on it: "Am I using the hand method to study?" After answering the question, the student was expected to record his answer on the piece of paper and return to his studies. Results of the study indicated immediate increases in oral words spelled correctly for two of the three boys and eventual increases for all three students following individual adjustments in the intervention for the third boy. More importantly, all three boys showed score improvement on written probes administered the day after instruction, indicating response generalization.

EFFECTIVE WRITING MODELS AND PRACTICE

We frequently refer to Chapter 5 (which was focused on early reading instruction), and we do so again here for the following reasons. One, early reading and writing instruction both fall under the literacy umbrella. Two, because of that relationship, comparisons and contrasts can be made in terms of the theoretical and empirical advancements in the two literacy practices. In Chapters 5 and 6, we presented developmental models of early reading and math achievement that clearly connected theory to practice across the primary grades. However, in terms of early writing skills, such a comprehensive model has yet to be articulated (Graham, 2006). Therefore, we highlight two theoretical perspectives. The first perspective addresses spelling development and, because of its obvious focus on the alphabetic principle, has parallels to Ehri's (1999) model of sight-word reading discussed in Chapter 5. The second perspective draws on the work of Graham (2006) by highlighting components of two writing models that impact composition instruction.

In the area of spelling, Mercer and Mercer (2005) describe five stages of development. The first stage, precommunicative spelling, encompasses children's scribbles and efforts to form letters. In this stage, which is typical of preschoolers, there is no understanding of phoneme–grapheme correspondence or print conventions. The precommunicative stage can be compared to Ehri's prealphabetic phase in early reading. In the second stage, semiphonetic spelling, children ages 5 and 6 demonstrate some knowledge of the connection between phonemes and graphemes and an initial awareness of a left-to-right progression in terms of writing. Ehri's parallel period is the partial alphabetic phase. In the third stage, phonetic spelling, typical 6-year-olds demonstrate alphabetic principle by representing all phonetic features when spelling words. These children are advanced to the point where they choose letters on the basis of sounds. In Ehri's model, these children have reached the full alphabetic phase of development. In the fourth stage, transitional spelling, children ages 7 and 8 evidence recognition and application of letter patterns in words. Transitional spelling leads into the final stage, correct spelling, in which 8- and 9-year-olds spell most words correctly and are skilled enough to identify incorrect letter sequences when they see them.

In terms of composition (writing) processes, there are no theoretical models that highlight development in the primary grades. However, models do exist that have influenced intervention research in improving composition skills and strategies. The two models we highlight were proposed by Bereiter and Scardamalia (1987) and Zimmerman and Risemberg (1997). The first model addresses the composing process; the second model describes motivational and related factors involved in the composing process.

Simplifying the influential model of skilled writing developed by Hayes and Flower (1980), Bereiter and Scardamalia (1987) focused on the composing process for novice—as opposed to skilled—writers. Whereas the Hayes and Flower model emphasizes planning, writing, and revising, the Bereiter and Scardamalia model focuses on writing. Essentially, theirs is the "here's what I know about the subject matter all at once" approach to writing (Graham, 2006). According to Graham and Harris (2003), the scaled-down version accurately reflects the writing of many students with disabilities. The second model focuses on the personal skills necessary to carry out the composition described in Bereiter and Scardamalia (1987). Zimmerman and Risemberg (1997) describe a given writer's self-control, motivation, and beliefs about competence as a writer. These personal skills and beliefs work together to facilitate or hinder the writer's composition. For example, a student's negative feelings about him- or herself as a writer may contribute to a situation wherein he or she does not listen well to instructions given by teachers. The student's failure to understand the writing assignment may then lead him or her to direct less effort toward the task that night at home. Believing that there is a lack of effort on the part of the student, teachers may not offer as much help as they might if they thought the student was giving maximal effort. In this example, personal efficacy, skills, and motivation interact with external variables (i.e., teacher assistance) to contribute to a less than adequate writing process and written product. Zimmerman and Risemberg's model taps into the individual motivation that contributes to the composition's end product. The combination of models, then, allows us to focus on both the process of composition and individual motivation when addressing instructional issues related to students with BD.

MASTERY INSTRUCTION

As we have noted throughout this book, it is critical that primary-grade students with BD, who are at high risk of early and continued school failure, receive instruction that teaches mastery of the early academic skills of reading, writing, and math prior to developing skill fluency. Remember from Chapter 2 that mastery instruction is aimed at skill acquisition. In this type of instruction teachers focus on developing student accuracy by applying a well-defined scope and sequence that incorporates a model–lead–test presentation format and systematic error-correction procedures (see Chapter 2 for a more detailed description).

Mastery instruction in writing is multifaceted. A comprehensive writing scope and sequence in the primary grades includes instruction in spelling, handwriting, and composing. Because students with BD are considered among the toughest to teach, it is essential that all three areas receive attention. In describing scientifically based and mastery-oriented writing instruction, we begin with spelling.

Spelling: Center on Accelerating Student Learning Program

Scope and Sequence

The Center on Accelerating Student Learning (CASL) spelling program (Graham, Harris, & Fink-Chorzempa, 2002) consists of eight units (see Table 7.1 for a description) collectively designed to teach children basic sound–letter combinations and short- and long-vowel spelling patterns (Graham, Harris, & Fink-Chorzempa, 2003). Each unit focuses on two or more spelling patterns and consists of six lessons. The unit lessons are similarly sequenced and target both skill mastery and fluency. In the area of mastery, students are directed through the following six activities over the course of a unit:

1. Teacher-directed word sorting, designed to teach the unit's featured spelling rule
2. Peer-mediated word sorting
3. Individual study of eight spelling words commonly misspelled in student writing

TABLE 7.1. Spelling Patterns Taught in Each Unit of the Spelling CASL Program

Unit	Spelling patterns
1.	Short-vowel sound for /a/, /e/, and /i/ in CVC-type words
2.	Short-vowel sound for /o/ and /u/ in CVC-type words
3.	Short-vowel sound for /a/ in CVC-type words; long-vowel sound for /a/ in CVCe-type words
4.	Short-vowel sound for /o/ in CVC-type words; long-vowel sound for /o/ in CVCe-type words
5.	Short-vowel sound for /i/ in CVC-type words; long-vowel sound for /i/ in CVCe-type words
6.	Short-vowel sound and /ck/ at the end of monosyllabic words; long-vowel sound and /ke/ at the end of monosyllabic words
7.	Adding the suffix -ed to monosyllabic words with a short- or long-vowel sound
8.	Adding the suffix -ing to monosyllabic words with a short- or long-vowel sound

Note. CVC, consonant–vowel–consonant; CVCe, consonant–vowel–consonant–e. Adapted from Graham, Harris, and Fink-Chorzempa (2003). Copyright 2003 by the Council for Exceptional Children. Adapted by permission.

4. Teacher-directed targeted sound–letter combination identification
5. Peer-mediated word development incorporating the unit's spelling pattern
6. Testing on eight spelling words identified earlier

Grouping

For teacher-mediated supplemental instruction, students with BD are matched on the results of an initial screening. For example, those students with similar AIMSweb spelling probe scores (see Chapter 3 for more information about standardized skill-based probes) might be taught in a small-group arrangement, whereas those whose scores differ significantly from peers might be taught individually.

Presentation

Each of the eight CASL spelling program units consists of the six mastery-oriented activities, noted above, incorporated into six lessons. As described by Graham et al. (2003), in Lesson 1 the teacher presents students with one or two "master word cards" depending upon how many spelling patterns are featured in the unit. For example, master word cards in Unit 3 (see Figure 7.1) include *mad* (i.e., short-vowel /a/ sound) and *made* (i.e., long-vowel /a/ sound). During the activity, the teacher (1) pronounces each word twice, regularly the first time and with an emphasis on the targeted sound (e.g., m/aaaaa/d) the second time; (2) points out the pattern's critical features (e.g., the different sounds of /a/ due to the presence or absence of the ending *e*); (3) uses 12 other word cards, with equal numbers of short- and long-vowel words, to direct a think-aloud as to where each word goes; (4) leads students

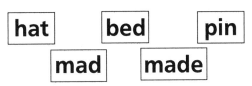

FIGURE 7.1. Master word card examples for CASL spelling program Units 1 (top) and 3 (bottom).

through their own think-aloud sorting; (5) leads students through a process in which the group collectively states the rule; (6) assists students in developing and sorting their own words cards, including exception words (e.g., *may*), which are placed into a third pile; and (7) encourages students to search for words that fit the pattern while engaging in other classwork (e.g., reading social studies materials). If time warrants, teachers may direct peer groups to redo the word sorting activity for practice.

In Lessons 2–5 the teacher directs students to learn the previously unknown spelling words, practice sound–letter combinations, and identify words that contain the unit's spelling pattern. For each word, students can be taught to: (1) say the word with eyes open and study the letters; (2) say the letters with eyes closed; (3) study the letters again with eyes open; (4) write the word three times without looking at it; and (5) check the spelling of each written word and correcting any misspellings. When practicing sound–letter combinations, the teacher spends 2 minutes completing such tasks as holding up a card with a picture of a dog on it and asking students to identify letters associated with the beginning, middle, or ending sounds in the picture word. During the peer-mediated word development activity, the teacher gives students a card that contains a rime (i.e., all the letters in a given word following the initial vowel, such as *-ate*) and shows them how to create real words using the rime and various consonants (e.g., *f*), blends (e.g., *pl*), or digraphs (e.g., *ai* or *ay* for the long /a/ song). Students are instructed to create as many real words as they can. The teacher remains involved by letting students know if they have created nonsense words. During Lesson 6, the teacher directs students to take a spelling test on the eight identified words, grade the test, correct misspellings, graph their score, and set a goal for the number of words spelled correctly in the next unit. With the goal known, the teacher can reward students for meeting their goal.

Error Correction

We cannot emphasize enough how systematic error correction must be. Because an orientation toward mastery denotes correct responses at least 90% of the time before moving forward, keeping errors to a minimum is included among a teacher's critical roles. While mediating the CASL spelling program, there are a number of situations in which errors are likely to take place, including during the initial word-sorting activity, sound–letter practice, word development activity using rimes, and the spelling test. When errors are made, a model–lead–test format is followed. For example, if a student misses two out of eight spelling words on a test, the teacher might spell one of the misspelled words correctly verbally *to* the student (i.e., model), spell the word verbally *with* the student (i.e., lead), and *ask the student* to spell the word (i.e., test). The teacher also might follow by writing the word, writing the word with the student, and then having the student write the word. In this particular situation, the teacher also might want to make sure that the student repeats the word-learning process highlighted earlier in this section, when discussing Lessons 2–5. The model–lead–test sequence should be repeated for all misspelled words.

Handwriting: CASL Program

Scope and Sequence

The scope of the CASL handwriting program (Graham, Harris, & Fink, 2000) involves accurate and fluent writing of all 26 letters in lower-case form. The program consists of nine units, each of which comprise three lessons. Each 15-minute lesson includes the following four activities: (1) Alphabet Warm-Up (2 minutes); (2) Alphabet Practice (6 minutes); (3) Alphabet Rockets (5 minutes); and (4) Alphabet Fun (2 minutes). Table 7.2 illustrates the program's sequence. As shown in Table 7.2, the first eight units comprise three letters that are introduced and practiced, with the ninth unit including two letters. Letters were placed in each group based on the following criteria: (1) letters formed in similar ways were grouped together; (2) letters occurring more frequently in children's writing were introduced before those occurring less frequently; (3) letters that are easier for children to produce are introduced before the more difficult ones; and (4) letters that are easy to confuse are placed in different units.

TABLE 7.2. Letters Introduced in Each Unit of the CASL Handwriting Program

Unit	Letters
1.	l, i, t
2.	o, e, a
3.	n, s, r
4.	p, h, f
5.	c, d, g
6.	b, u, m
7.	v, w, y
8.	x, k, z
9.	j, q

Note. Adapted from Graham, Harris, and Fink (2000). Copyright 2000 by the Council for Exceptional Children. Adapted by permission.

Grouping

Teacher-mediated instruction serves as the starting point for the CASL handwriting program. Teachers group students in small groups or individually, based upon the results of an initial screening. Teachers might consider using the letter probe in Chapter 5 as a guide and having students write down each letter as it is said to them. There are instructional options from which teachers can choose. Teachers can either make a determination as to the legibility of a letter and whether or not it needs to be included in a student's program, or they can choose to introduce the entire program as it is described here.

Presentation

As we noted previously, the CASL handwriting program consists of four activities implemented across each of 27 lessons. With our emphasis in this section on mastery instruction, we focus on the first two activities. We address the other two activities in the section on fluency instruction. Teachers begin with Alphabet Warm-Up. During this activity, which evolves as the lessons unfold, the teacher initially has students sing the alphabet song while pointing to the corresponding letters on a chart. Once students have mastered the simultaneous singing and pointing, that task is replaced by an activity in which the teacher says the name of a letter and a student points to the corresponding letter on the alphabet chart. When students can accurately and fluently point to and name all the letters on the chart, the teacher modifies the task expectation by pointing to a letter and asking the student to name it. Ultimately, Alphabet Warm-Up evolves to an activity in which the teacher points to a letter and the student names that letter and the letters before and after it. Such a focus on letter identification is designed to build students' fluency in letter naming and access, because it is believed that the name of a letter serves as a cue for the letter writing (i.e., motor retrieval) process (Graham et al., 2000).

Alphabet Practice is the instructional activity in which the student is explicitly taught how to form lower-case manuscript letters and given opportunities to practice writing letters in isolation and in words. Alphabet Practice includes the following sequence of activities for Lesson 1 of each unit:

1. The teacher models, in words and actions, how to form each letter in the unit by using cards that show the order and direction of strokes for each letter.
2. The teacher has the child trace each letter while describing the motor actions that are taking place.
3. The teacher and student discuss how their versions of the traced letters are similar and different.
4. The student traces a copy of the letter that contains the numbered arrows while saying the name of the letter.

5. The student traces three copies of the letter without the numbered arrows, each time saying the name of the letter.
6. The student writes the letter three times, each time saying the name of the letter.
7. The student writes the letter three times on regular-lined paper, each time saying the name of the letter.
8. The student circles the best formed letter for each letter practiced.

In Lessons 2 and 3 of each unit, the discussion of similarities and differences is omitted. Also, the writing activities all take place on regular-lined paper and incorporate the writing of letters within words.

Error Correction

As with spelling instruction, handwriting instruction affords the teacher multiple opportunities to use the model–lead–test sequence for correcting errors. For example, during Alphabet Warm-Up, the teacher listens and looks closely to ensure that the correct letter is being spoken by the student. During Alphabet Practice, the teacher makes sure that the student is following the order and sequence of the arrows from the beginning of the unit to the end. (Procedures related to Alphabet Rockets and Alphabet Fun are addressed in the "Fluency Instruction" section.)

Written Expression: SRSD

Scope and Sequence

As it relates to writing, SRSD (Harris & Graham, 1996) is an instructional model designed to enhance students' strategic behaviors, self-regulation skills, knowledge, and motivation (Graham & Harris, 2003). SRSD's scope, then, is the creative writing process, which includes planning, composing, revising, and publishing. Its sequence incorporates the following six instructional stages: (1) develop and activate background knowledge; (2) discuss the process; (3) model it; (4) memorize it; (5) support it; and (6) perform it independently (see Table 7.3). However, the preceding order is described as only "a general guideline for instruction" (Graham & Harris, 2003, p. 330). Instructors are encouraged to reorder, combine, or modify the stages to meet students' collective or individual needs. Researchers have successfully incorporated modifications for students with BD, such as providing increased opportunities to develop background knowledge and discuss SRSD and moving the self-evaluation and graphing tasks back in the instructional sequence (Lane, Graham, Harris, & Weisenbach, 2006). A more complete description of the SRSD instructional stages is provided in Chapter 6.

The SRSD model includes mnemonics (i.e., a system to improve memory) to facilitate recall of a general writing strategy (i.e., POW) and a planning procedure (i.e., WWW; What = 2, How = 2; see Figure 7.2). *POW* stands for "Pick my idea,"

TABLE 7.3. Stages of Instruction in the Self-Regulated Strategy Development Model

Stage	Description
1. Develop background knowledge.	Students are taught any background knowledge or skills needed to use the strategy successfully.
2. Discuss it.	Students examine their current writing performance and discuss the purpose and benefits of the new strategy.
3. Model it.	The teacher models how to use the strategy and self-regulation techniques.
4. Memorize it.	Students memorize the steps of the strategy.
5. Support it.	Students practice using the strategy with decreasing levels of teacher support and scaffolding.
6. Perform it independently.	Students use the strategy with little or no support.

Note. These stages are designed to be flexible and should be combined, repeated, or reordered, as needed. From Santangelo, Harris, and Graham (2007). Reprinted with permission from the coeditors of *Learning Disabilities: A Contemporary Journal*, published by Learning Disabilities Worldwide Inc. (LDW).

"Organize my notes," and "Write and say more," and is a three-step strategy that can be applied to all types of story writing. WWW, *What = 2, How = 2*, is taught to help cue memory of seven questions students can ask themselves as they plan a story:

1. Who is the main character?
2. When does the story take place?
3. Where does the story take place?
4. What does the main character do or want to do? What do other characters do?
5. What happens when the main character tries to do it? What happens with other characters?
6. How does the story end?
7. How does the main character feel? How do other characters feel?

Grouping

Because the tasks associated with written expression are so complex, teachers are likely best served by teaching all targeted students with BD in small-group settings.

Presentation

In order to evaluate instructional effectiveness, teachers ask students to write a story for them. Teachers begin SRSD by developing background knowledge in the components of a comprehensive story (Lane et al., 2006). The goal of this stage is to

POW

Pick my Idea

Organize my Notes

Write and Say More

W-W-W What = 2 How = 2

Who is the main character?

When does the story take place?

Where does the story take place?

What does the main character do or want to do? What do other characters do?

What happens then? What happens with other characters?

How does the story end?

How does the main character feel? How do other characters feel?

FIGURE 7.2. Wall chart for POW and W-W-W, What = 2, How = 2 mnemonics. Courtesy of Karen R. Harris and Steve Graham.

ensure that students are familiar with the seven components represented by the preceding questions. Time is spent writing and recalling the mnemonics. Flash cards can be developed for use throughout the early stages of instruction. At the next stage, teachers continue "teaching" the mnemonics, but direct considerable energy in discussing how: (1) POW and WWW, What = 2, How = 2 are useful tools for developing comprehensive stories; and (2) those tools can be utilized in other writing assignments that students are given. In the modeling stage, teachers incorporate verbal and motor models in demonstrating how to use the POW and WWW, What = 2, How = 2 strategies. Specifically, teachers talk out loud while planning, writing, and revising a story. During their verbal models, teachers comment not only on the writing process but also on individual goal setting (e.g., "I want to include all seven components this time, not just five like I did last time") and self-reinforcement (e.g., "I did a great job of describing the main character"). In the memorizing stage, teachers ensure that students are familiar with the two mnemonics and their meanings.

In the supporting stage, teachers work with each student to apply all the strategies and write a story. The teacher's role during this stage is to provide as much support as is necessary in order to develop a comprehensive story (Lane et al., 2006). Once the story has been written, then the teacher and student evaluate it by

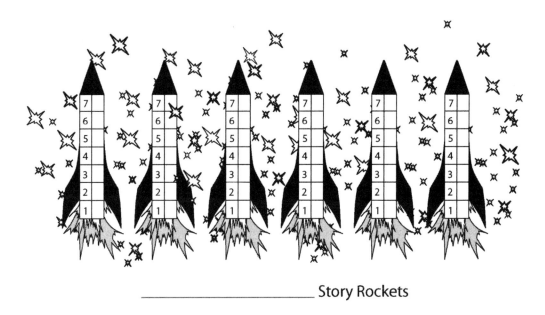

Story Rockets

FIGURE 7.3. Motivational chart for use in recording the number (out of seven) of story grammar components included in student writing. Story components are summarized in the WWW, What = 2, How = 2 mnemonic.

determining the number of story components (out of seven) that were included. Students then graph the number of elements incorporated into the story using the rockets shown in Figure 7.3. Each rocket can be divided into seven pieces and students can color in the number of elements included. Teachers conclude the process for a given story by comparing the number of elements in the newest rocket with the number of elements in the original rocket. As time progresses, teachers gradually decrease their support of students until they are directing the process. In the independent performance stage, students apply the learned strategies themselves.

Error Correction

The traditional model–lead–test procedure we have described can easily be applied to the initial SRSD stages, given that content information (e.g., the mnemonics) is being learned. During the latter stages of SRSD, the "support" role delineated in this stage is likely to be the best approach to "error" correction. That is, teachers can provide the assistance necessary in order to ensure that all necessary components are included in students' story-writing actions.

FLUENCY INSTRUCTION

The instructional goal of fluency instruction is to firm up student accuracy and speed. Fluency instruction involves selecting observable pivotal skills and a range of student-mastered skill practice items, developing fluency instructional sheets, establishing daily performance standards, conducting short, timed instructional trials, and charting student performance. In fluency-oriented instruction, rate-based measures are appropriate measurement tools.

An attractive instructional feature of the spelling, handwriting, and written expression programs we have highlighted is that fluency activities are explicitly incorporated. That is, they are built into the scope and sequence of the three writing programs. Specifically, the spelling program includes activities involving student review of previously learned spelling words and patterns. In Units 2–8 of the CASL spelling program, for example, Lesson 6 concludes with students' review of material previously taught. Review materials include the spelling rules that students discovered collectively and the words developed using rimes that mirrored a particular spelling pattern.

In handwriting, two of the four activities of the CASL handwriting program (i.e., Alphabet Rockets and Alphabet Fun) are geared toward fluency. Alphabet Rockets is aimed at increasing students' speed in copying text and incorporates reinforcement procedures. Students copy, for 3 minutes, unit-specific sentences that contain multiple instances of the target letters and then graph the number of letters they copied on a rocket chart. Over three lessons, students are encouraged to beat their previous score by three letters. If that feat is accomplished during Lessons 2 and 3, then the teacher draws a star above the rocket for that lesson. A gradual increase in the number of letters copied is desired so legibility does not suffer (Graham et al., 2000). Alphabet Fun, designed to allow students to end handwriting instruction with an enjoyable task, completes each lesson (Graham et al., 2000). Students are asked to pick a letter from the unit and write it in an unusual way or as part of a picture.

In written expression the SRSD program incorporates multiple forms of fluency instruction flexible enough to meet an individual student's learning needs. First, as part of its six instructional stages, SRSD includes an independent performance stage. Once student writing process skills have been developed, students are expected to apply the learning strategies themselves. Second, teachers are expected to spend much time as is needed in any one of the six stages. Students with BD, for example, may need to spend considerable time learning the appropriate mnemonics, particularly if their learning histories have not included extensive formal writing instruction. Third, as noted earlier, the SRSD model can be modified to meet individual or group learning needs. Research by Lane and colleagues (2006) indicated that additional opportunities to develop background knowledge and delays in introducing self-evaluation and graphing activities were beneficial for second-grade students with BD.

OTHER CONSIDERATIONS IN PLANNING AND DELIVERING WRITING INSTRUCTION FOR STUDENTS WITH BD

As with early reading instruction, teachers should take into account a number of additional considerations when planning and delivering supplemental writing lessons. We open this section by focusing on two components that directly impact students with BD, and we close it by highlighting three writing instructional principles Graham (2006) suggests are informed by research and should be incorporated into classroom writing instruction.

It is important that the writing program of students with BD be comprehensive and integrated within a broader effective school program (see our discussion of Response to Intervention on pp. 13–21). Supplemental early writing instruction is bolstered when it is one piece of a strong core curriculum. Such a core curriculum must focus on scientifically based literacy instruction that not only includes comprehensive writing instruction (i.e., spelling, handwriting, composition) but also effective reading instruction across the areas of phonemic awareness, phonics, fluency, vocabulary, and comprehension. Given that Dixon et al. (2007) noted that effective writing instruction is often absent in classrooms, it may be necessary for teachers of students with BD to make school administrators aware of situations in which "supplemental" instruction is the only instruction in a student's educational program. It is also important that teachers realize that supplemental instruction in areas such as spelling and handwriting can be integrated. For example, Graham and Harris (2006) discussed a program for at-risk first graders that provided additional handwriting and spelling instruction, incorporating their CASL programs with positive effects in the targeted areas but also in sentence construction skills and vocabulary diversity as well. Moreover, Table 7.4 offers some examples of

TABLE 7.4. Examples of Instructional Adaptations Made by Primary-Grade Teachers for Teaching Writing

	Type of adaptations
Basic writing skills	Extra handwriting instruction
	Extra spelling instruction
	Extra grammar instruction
	Extra punctuation and capitalization instruction
	Extra instruction for writing sentences
	Permit students to dictate compositions
	Permit students to compose on a keyboard
	Extra time to practice writing skills
Writing processes	Extra revising instruction
	Teach specific strategies for planning
	Extra time to practice using planning and revising skills
Instructional modifications that support learning to write	Extra conferencing with students
	Extra mini-lessons
	Additional reteaching of skills and strategies
Other adaptations	Writing or tutoring assistance from a peer
	Encourage the use of invented spelling
	Alternate writing assignments
	Extra encouragement

Note. From Fink-Chorzempa, Graham, and Harris (2005). Copyright 2005 by the Council for Exceptional Children. Reprinted by permission.

adaptations targeted at specific student needs that teachers can incorporate into supplemental writing instruction.

In addition, supplemental early writing instruction should be considered within the broader context of a positive behavioral support (PBS) model. PBS models are designed to provide multiple, increasingly intense levels of behavioral, social, and academic support to all students in a school system, depending on each student's demonstrated need. For students with BD, multitiered programs provide an existing framework designed to deliver intensive and long-term academic and behavioral support to the small percentage of students with the greatest need. Furthermore, the comprehensive and ongoing screening component that is part of multitiered systems provides students at risk for BD with a means of receiving preventive academic and behavioral supports in the hopes of "catching them up" before they fall too far behind. Lane and colleagues (2006) implemented SRSD as a preventive intervention.

It also is important that we meld goal setting and attainment and data-based decision making into all of our instructional programming for students with BD. Goal setting and ongoing progress monitoring should be integrated into the regular teaching routine, because students with BD are likely to evidence negative attitudes toward writing. For example, a third-grade boy with BD, served in a primary school with which one of us (P.M.) is familiar, has described his hatred of writing to teachers on numerous occasions. The student's primary teacher also observed that when the student was required to compose a response for the yearly standardized assessment, he counted the numbers of words he was expected to write in the response and discontinued his writing when he had reached the required minimum number of words. The teacher was able to observe the behavior because the student provided prior indication of his plans for completing the assessment response.

Although such feelings and responses to writing requests are likely not isolated to students with BD, they are noteworthy in the sense that supplemental writing instruction must not only improve writing skill but also students' opinions of themselves as writers. During the primary grades, students need to learn to write words that are legible and spelled correctly; they also must begin the process of composing comprehensive stories. Intervention, then, must include goal setting and monitoring of progress to determine if goals are being attained. The CASL spelling and handwriting programs and SRSD have built into their everyday programming a focus on goal setting, evaluation, and reinforcement for goal attainment.

In terms of overall instructional principles guided by theory and research, we close this section by describing three suggestions recently offered by noted writing researcher Steve Graham (2006). First, Graham calls for explicit instruction in writing strategies, skills, and knowledge for struggling writers. His suggestion can be applied appropriately to the writing instruction of students with BD. That is, primary-grade students with BD, for example, have benefited from explicit instruction in spelling (McDougall & Brady, 1995) and composition planning strategies (Lane et al., 2006). Second, Graham believes that teachers must structure the writing environment in ways that maximize students' success and learning. Effective structures provide students with necessary supports across the skills being taught; such structures also foster meaningfulness in the writing and encourage students' enjoyment of the process. (We have reinforced this point on several occasions, both in this chapter and throughout the book.) Finally, Graham contends that peer interaction that promotes effective writing experiences should be encouraged. For example, teachers can teach students to assist each other in the composition processes of planning, drafting, and revising. Peers, then, can serve as both tutors and tutees in developing written compositions. The suggestion has particular merit for intervention efforts designed for students with BD, given that peer-mediated instruction in reading and math has evidenced positive findings (Ryan et al., 2004) and peer-mediated intervention research across spelling, handwriting, and composition has been underutilized.

CONCLUSIONS

This chapter focused on early writing instruction for students with BD. We concur with Graham (2006) that good writing skills are essential for success in school. In particular, writing development affords students with BD the chance for a socially accepted means of self-expression across all aspects of life. In the school setting, writing improvement gives these students a chance to earn good grades and teacher recognition. However, research on the writing status of students with BD indicates delays of up to two grade levels—two-thirds of a standard deviation—when compared to normally achieving populations. Intervention research in writing for students with BD has focused on spelling improvement and has yielded positive findings in supplemental interventions directed by teachers.

A broad body of writing intervention literature across the domains of spelling, handwriting, and composition exists, however, and has the potential to improve the academic performance of students with BD. This chapter described teacher-mediated spelling and handwriting programs and a comprehensive intervention for writing composition strategy development (i.e., SRSD). The CASL spelling program targets development of short- and long-vowel patterns in words. The CASL handwriting program teaches manuscript writing across all letters. SRSD develops planning, composing, and revising skills along with student motivation and writing self-efficacy. All three programs are designed to promote mastery and then fluency. Together with early reading skill development and in the broader context of a PBS model, early writing instruction has the potential to improve the communication skills of students with BD in the primary grades.

CHAPTER 8

Management of Instructional Situations

We detailed the behavioral, demographic, and functional characteristics of students with BD in Chapter 1. As we described, the challenges faced by students with BD are frequently compounded by significant academic deficits. Thus, there remains little question that one of the greatest challenges facing teachers of students with BD is the management of these students' disruptive behaviors, which undermine their learning abilities. Addressing this challenge requires teachers to implement effective classroom and instructional management procedures. Classroom management strategies provide structure and have the substantial, indirect effect of facilitating appropriate student behavior during instructional situations (Martella et al., 2003). The first few weeks of school are extremely important in terms of classroom and instructional management; good classroom and instructional managers devote a significant amount of time to teaching routines and expectations. Classroom and instructional management consists of routines for behaviors such as entering the classroom in the morning and responding to, or asking, a question. Classroom and instructional management is predicated upon behavioral expectations that are necessary for teaching and learning to occur.

This chapter focuses on the intersection between management and instruction. In addition to the use of effective teacher presentation techniques (discussed in Chapter 2) and scientifically based assessment and instructional practices (discussed in Chapters 3–7), this chapter assumes that teachers have developed and taught general expectations and routines and established group management procedures for all students—including individualized procedures for students with BD. These teacher behaviors and activities are essential to ensuring that all students with BD are attentive and ready to participate in, and benefit from, instruction. We begin by describing the placement of students with BD during instructional situations. This description is followed by a discussion of teacher awareness, interpersonal interaction, and self-control skills critical to managing instructional situations. Next, we detail self-management procedures that can be used to improve student performance. We then describe an instructional management procedure (Teacher–Student Learning Game) teachers can use to decrease the relative levels of disruptive behavior and improve on-task student behavior that occur during instructional situations. Finally, we conclude the chapter by summarizing its major points.

PLACEMENT OF STUDENTS WITH BD DURING INSTRUCTIONAL SITUATIONS

Where teachers place students with BD during instructional situations can have a dramatic effect on students' relative levels of disruptive versus on-task behaviors. Evidence shows that location impacts student behavior—especially the behavior of students with academic difficulties (Doyle, 1986). There are essentially two zones in which teachers can choose to place students: action and public. The *action zone* is front and center relative to the focus of instruction; the *public zone* is, essentially, all other areas (e.g., middle, side, and back of the room).

Based on our experience, two rules must be followed when planning where to position students with BD in the classroom. First, *always position students with BD in the action zone* (when given a choice, these students tend to sit in the public zone). This arrangement enables teachers to maintain instructional control because the students will be better able to remain focused throughout the instructional situation. This arrangement also enables teachers to provide students with higher rates of social reinforcement and to respond sooner to their disruptive behavior. Second, *avoid placing students with BD next to each other*; these students often subtly encourage one another's disruptive behavior. Students with BD should be placed in the action zone and should be surrounded by model students. We encourage the reader to study the potential placement of students with BD in the action zone in Figure 8.1 for a whole-group instructional situation. Small-group instructional situations are comprised only of an action zone.

TEACHER AWARENESS SKILLS

Managing instructional situations requires teachers to be aware of all areas and events occurring in the classroom. Kounin and his colleagues (Kounin, 1970; Kounin & Gump, 1974) introduced a number of important instructional situation management concepts that are relevant for contemporary elementary (Evertson, Emmer, & Worsham, 2000) and secondary classrooms (Emmer, Evertson, &

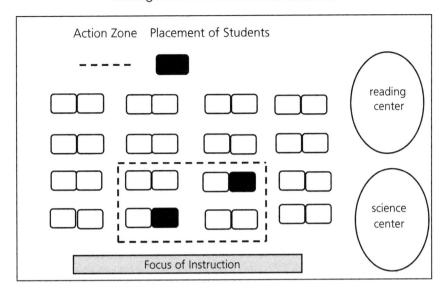

FIGURE 8.1. Positioning students with BD in the action zone.

Worsham, 2000). These concepts can be categorized into those teachers use to: (1) prevent disruptive behavior; (2) manage movement; and (3) maintain group focus.

Preventing Disruptive Behavior

The ability to be observant of, and attentive to, what is going on in the classroom has been termed "withitness." Withitness and overlapping behaviors are both critical to reducing the impact of external interruptions and student disruptive behavior on the flow of instructional situations (Everstson et al., 2000; Emmer et al., 2000). *Withitness behaviors* are those by which teachers communicate to students that they know what is going on (effective monitoring) and identify and correct disruptive behavior promptly. "With it" teachers have fewer discipline problems and higher rates of on-task behavior (Emmer et al., 2000; Everston et al., 2000).

Overlapping behavior is the ability to attend to two or more simultaneous events at the same time without becoming so immersed in one that the other is neglected—an important instructional management skill. For example, a student gets up from his seat, without permission, to sharpen his pencil during a small-group instructional situation while the teacher is instructing a lesson. The teacher with good overlapping skills will deal with this (e.g., "Jim, take your seat—you can use this pencil") and continue teaching without stopping the lesson. Overlapping, when combined with withitness, produces managerial success during instructional situations. Teachers are able to protect instructional situations from external interruptions or disruptive student behavior. Additionally, reacting early to disruptive behavior enables teachers to use less intrusive responses, such as eye contact, redirection, or quiet reprimands, which interfere little with the lesson or distract other students.

Managing Movement

Managing movement includes appropriate curriculum pacing, lesson pacing, and transition management. *Curriculum pacing* refers to the rate at which students progress through the curriculum. The rate of movement across a curriculum area should be based on students' mastery of the content (see mastery instruction and progress monitoring practices in Chapters 2 and 3, respectively). However, there is a direct relationship between the amount of curriculum content covered and the amount of student learning. Thus, it is important for teachers to ensure mastery of material by individual students while also moving through the curriculum content in a timely fashion. This balance is achieved through the use of effective teacher presentation methods and scientifically based instructional practices and programs.

Lesson pacing is influenced by teachers' momentum and smoothness within instructional situations. *Momentum* refers to planning lessons to avoid slowdowns and using a brisk pace during instructional situations. Teachers avoid disruptions to momentum by not dwelling on parts of lessons or including too many parts in a lesson. *Smoothness* refers to staying on track with the lesson and avoiding digressions. We encourage readers to study some of the common problems that disrupt lesson pacing presented in Table 8.1.

Transitions between instructional situations provide the context for much disruptive behavior. Teachers often underestimate the time students need to adjust to transitions, such as moving from group to individual instructional situations, or vice versa. Thus, it is important to plan for transitions and facilitate them by providing students with some intermediate steps. Teachers might use something like the following to facilitate transitions:

> "It's time to transition. Remember how we move in our classroom from one area to another? We move without noise, we maintain our personal space, and we move in number order on my signal, starting with number 1, then number 2, and so on. Get ready to transition. Begin! Everyone: Great job of moving without noise, maintaining your personal space, and moving on my signal. Eyes on me! Before we begin, are there any questions about the activity you are about to begin? Independent workers, remember my expectations: No noise, stay in your seat, finish work neatly and completely, and ask questions during transition. You may begin your work!"

Additionally, it is important to establish expectations during instructional sessions and signals to facilitate transitions. The following guidelines should be used to plan for transitions.

1. Be sure that there are clear avenues for students to move to the designated instructional area.
2. Develop a signal to indicate an impending transition.

TABLE 8.1. Common Problems That Disrupt Lesson Pacing

Problem	Definition	Example
Dangle	Teacher leaves a topic or activity "dangling" to do something else or to insert some new material.	"All right, please take out your math books. Turn to page . . . oops, I forgot to send this form to the office. Raise your hand if you ride the bus. All right, where were we?"
Flip-flop	Like a dangle, except the topic inserted is left over from an earlier activity.	"OK, let's leave vocabulary now. We'll pick up on the discussion tomorrow. Please move your chairs into your writing groups. Take only your pencils and a blank piece of paper. (*Students move into their groups and the teacher begins to give instructions for the writing activity.*) All right, now, does everyone understand what I want you to do? Oh, and did everyone remember to write down your vocabulary workbook assignment? I put it on the board, pages 235–242. OK, go ahead and start."
Thrust	Teacher inserts some information at a point when students are involved in another activity, and it seems irrelevant to them.	Students are working quietly on a standardized test. The teacher has been circulating and offering help; otherwise, there is scarcely a sound in the room. The teacher looks up and comments quietly, "When you're done, bring your test booklets to the front table and put your answer sheets in this box." Students continue to work quietly. When they begin completing their tests, the teacher must explain to each one individually where to put the test booklet and answer sheet.
Stimulus-bound	Teacher is distracted by some irrelevant stimulus and draws the class's attention to it and away from the lesson.	Students are taking turns reading their writing out loud. Each student's reading is followed by comments from the rest of the class. During one such discussion, the teacher notices a student reading a paperback. "What are you reading, Alice?" She asks. "Have you read anything else by that writer?"

Note. From Evertson, Emmer, and Worsham (2000). Published by Allyn and Bacon. Copyright 2000 by Pearson Education. Reprinted with permission from the publisher.

3. Secure students' attention and remind them of expectations regarding noise level, travel direction, and personal space issues.
4. Secure students' attention to end a transition and designate the beginning of the next activity.

Maintaining Group Focus

Helping students maintain focus is critical to increasing student engagement during instructional situations. Teachers who maintain a group focus are more successful at promoting student achievement and goal-directed behavior and preventing disruptive behavior than those who do not. The process of maintaining group focus requires teachers to keep all members of the group actively involved, alert, and accountable for their performance. *Group focus behaviors* are those behaviors teachers use to maintain a focus on the group, rather than on an individual student.

Accountability and group alerting are used to maintain group focus. *Accountability* refers to the extent to which the teacher holds students accountable and responsible for their task performances throughout a lesson. Teachers use unison responding to achieve accountability during large- and small-group instruction. *Unison responding* requires all students to respond to teacher-initiated prompts upon a signal. For example, during sight-word instruction, teachers would say, "What sight word?", provide wait time (also called "think time"), and drop their hand (signal). All students would then provide (say or write) the sight word. *Group alerting* refers to the extent to which the teacher involves nonreciting students (i.e., maintains their attention and keeps them "on their toes"). Teachers call on individual students during both large- and small-group instruction to achieve group alerting. This possibility requires all students to think about the response. For example, during individual turns (when probing students' mastery of sight words taught), teachers might announce, "Individual turns: What sight word?", provide wait time, and then call on an individual student.

INTERPERSONAL INTERACTION SKILLS

Interpersonal interaction skills provide the foundation upon which to achieve effective management of instructional situations. There are three specific factors that enhance interpersonal interactions: (1) noncontingent interactions; (2) clear communication; and (3) prompts versus corrections.

Noncontingent Interactions

Noncontingent teacher–student interactions are those in which teachers engage in positive social interactions with a student independent of any kind of behavior or request from a student. Such interactions provide the basis for effective contingent interactions during instructional situations. Providing noncontingent interactions to students with BD is especially important because they are 30 times less likely to have positive exchanges with teachers (Martella et al., 2003). By increasing the frequency of positive social interactions with students, teachers raise the density of reinforcement in the classroom—which makes them natural reinforcers and provides the basis for contingent interactions (e.g., compliance, response to teacher questions) during instructional situations.

Clear Communication

Clear communication practices can improve the relative rates of disruptive and on-task student behavior during instructional situations. Teachers commonly use communication practices that increase the risk of teacher–student power struggles or noninstructional interactions (Nelson & Roberts, 2000). For example, it is common for teachers to ask students what they need to be doing when students are violating an expectation during an instructional situation. Response to this type of query opens the door for a teacher–student power struggle or, at best, a prolonged noninstructional discussion. The following is an example of poor communication between a teacher and student during an instructional situation. The student is out of his seat and is disturbing two other students during independent seatwork.

TEACHER: Ben, what do you need to do?

BEN: Sharpen my pencil.

TEACHER: You don't have a pencil.

BEN: I was going to borrow one from Jorge.

TEACHER: What is the rule about leaving your seat?

BEN: I have to put my hand up.

TEACHER: Well, go back to your seat and put your hand up.

What would have been a more appropriate teacher response? In this case, the teacher should have told Ben to return to his seat and indicate that he would receive help momentarily.

Clear communication practices during instructional situations require teachers to know what they want from students and to communicate those expectations directly. Language should be kept as simple and direct as possible. The basic rule is that the more language teachers use during instruction, the less likelihood of securing and maintaining student attention. Avoid the following pitfalls:

1. Open-ended questions (e.g., "Would you like to . . . ?" or "What do you need to be doing?")
2. Extra words (e.g., "I would be pleased if everyone . . . ")
3. Gaps in directions for activities (e.g., "Who knows the answer to question 3?" Teacher fails to precede this question with "Open your book to page 24")

Prompts versus Corrections

Utilizing prompts with students, rather than corrections, is critical to effective communication and management of instructional situations. Teachers often misunderstand the difference between prompts and corrections. Prompts occur *before* behavior and result in a correct behavior, such as, "Open your math book to page 72." Corrections occur *after* an incorrect behavior, such as this response to a student who gets up out of her seat to visit with a friend: "Julie, you need to go back to your desk and work on problems 1–10."

The different types of prompts include: (1) verbal statements (questions or comments); (2) gestures; (3) modeling; and (4) guiding prompts. In short, always use a level of prompting that elicits the correct or expected response. A verbal question is used to encourage a student to give a correct response (e.g., "What do you need to be doing?"), whereas a verbal statement tells students what the correct response is (e.g., "Ben, take your seat"). A gesture prompt uses a physical signal to indicate what the student should be doing (e.g., placing index finger against the lips to indicate that the student should stop talking). A model prompt involves demonstrating the desired behavior for the student (e.g., the teacher places a math book on the desk in front of her to encourage the student to take out his or her math book). A guiding prompt occurs when the teacher helps the student enact the correct response (e.g., the teacher places the student's math book on his or her desk).

The different types of prompting can be combined to increase the likelihood of eliciting correct or expected responses. For example, teachers might combine a verbal prompt (e.g., "Teacher asks the questions") with a model prompt (e.g., the teacher holds index finger against his or her mouth). In addition, appropriate corrections require that a higher level of prompting be used when the student fails to respond successfully. For example, if a student fails to take out his or her book after a verbal prompt (statement), teachers could simply proceed to a guiding prompt (take the book out for the student). Of course, if teachers are continually correcting a student, they should assess what level of prompting is required to elicit the correct response and enable the student to be more successful. We recommend that the reader study the descriptions of the different types of prompting provided in Table 8.2.

TABLE 8.2. Types of Prompting

Type (least to most intrusive)	Description
Verbal— question	A question used to direct students' attention to the task (e.g., "What problems do you need to be working on?").
Verbal— statement	A few simple words used to let the student know what to do (e.g., "Ben, take your seat," when Ben is out of his seat sharpening his pencil).
Gesture	Movement used to let students know what to do (e.g., pointing at the problems they should be working on).
Model	Demonstration to show students what to do (e.g., showing students how to solve a math problem).
Guiding	Guiding a student through an activity (e.g., watching and monitoring a student while he or she performs the problem or activity).

TEACHER SELF-CONTROL SKILLS

Teachers must maintain self-control when working with students during instructional situations. Of course, this is easier said than done. Nearly every teacher has experienced the frustration of working with disruptive students. Nevertheless, it is important for teachers to learn to control themselves if they are to work effectively with all students. Disruptive students tend to key in on subtleties of teachers' voice inflection and body language when they are being disruptive. Maintaining self-control when students are disruptive centers around two primary areas: paraverbal and nonverbal communication skills.

Paraverbal Communication

Paraverbal communication includes voice inflection and volume. The inflection and volume of teachers' voices are critical when responding to students' disruptive behavior. A majority of the message teachers deliver to disruptive students is interpreted from sources other than their words (e.g., inflection and volume). Teachers only need to alter their voice inflection or volume to convey a completely different message to students than that transmitted by their words. An even cadence and somewhat flat affect will increase the likelihood that students will respond to early attempts to stop disruptive behavior. All communication should be even and matter-of-fact, with little or no affect. Communications should avoid inflections of impatience, condescension, or inattention; the volume should be appropriate to the distance and situation; and the delivery should have an even cadence or rhythm. The best way for teachers to monitor their communications with students around disruptive behavior is to focus on how the students respond to teachers' communications. Teachers should not merely assume that students have heard their words.

Nonverbal Communication

Nonverbal communication involves personal space and body language. Personal space is the first element of nonverbal communication. Because personal space is dependent upon the context or situation, teachers should be careful about encroaching into the students' personal space when they are demonstrating disruptive behavior. The personal space of a student who is being disruptive is likely to extend farther than personal space under normal conditions (typically 2–3 feet). Even though teachers may believe that they will be more effective by moving very close to disruptive students, this may not be the case for some students—especially those with BD.

Body language is the second important facet of nonverbal communication. A face-to-face, shoulder-to-shoulder (i.e., challenge) position also increases the likelihood that students will not respond positively to teachers' attempts to stop disruptive behavior. Teachers may be speaking to students with a calm, reassuring voice, but their body language may communicate a direct challenge to the students. Students' failure to comply with teachers' early attempts to stop disruptive behavior may be due to teachers' invasion of students' personal space or teachers taking a challenge position.

SELF-MANAGEMENT PROCEDURES

A range of self-management procedures has been used effectively to improve the social behavior and academic performance of students with BD. These include goal setting, self-recording, and self-evaluation (Jenson, Rhode, Reavis, & 2000; Lane & Beebe-Frankenberger, 2004; Mooney et al., 2005). These self-management procedures make explicit the implicit skills necessary for self-regulated performance. The assumption underlying goal setting, self-recording, and self-evaluation is that the most successful students develop an implicit repertoire of self-regulated skills that they can apply across varied contexts. The explicit and associated implicit processes for goal setting, self-recording, and self-evaluation are presented in Table 8.3. Self-management procedures can be used to target academic performance or social behavior during instructional situations, and they can be applied alone as well as in tandem with one another, depending upon the situation. Further, self-management procedures require the active involvement of the student in the development and implementation of the intervention.

Although the student is actively involved in the development of self-management procedures, it is critical to teach students how to use them. Teaching students to use a self-management procedure is similar to teaching an academic skill. The first step is to provide students with a rationale for using the self-management procedure. For example, in the case of self-recording, the teacher introduces the proposition that it is important for students to learn how to keep track of their own behavior as it relates to achieving a specified goal or outcome. This understanding helps

TABLE 8.3. Explicit and Implicit Processes Underlying Self-Management Procedures

Procedure	Explicit process	Implicit process
Goal setting	Student sets performance goal	Student monitors and evaluates performance relative to the performance goal
Self-monitoring	Student monitors performance	Student evaluates performance relative to a performance goal
Self-evaluation	Student evaluates performance	Student monitors and compares performance relative to performance goal

students to become more aware of their own behavior by recording a specified target behavior. The second step is to directly teach students how to use the self-management procedure. Teachers can use the mastery instruction procedures described in Chapter 2 to teach students the self-management procedure and to give students an opportunity to ask questions to clarify any misunderstandings they may have about its purpose and use. Further, teachers give students immediate and corrective feedback when they first start to use the self-management procedures. The goal is to ensure that students fully understand how to use the self-management procedure. A brief description of the steps for developing goal setting, self-recording, and self-evaluation procedures follow. (See Table 8.4 for an outline of the development steps; also see Jenson et al., 2000; Lane & Beebe-Frankenberger, 2004, for detailed descriptions of these self-management procedures).

Goal Setting

Goal setting involves identifying and establishing how to achieve a specific academic or social goal. Developing a goal-setting procedure includes the seven steps outlined in Table 8.4. The first step is to arrange a goal-setting conference with the student and other relevant individuals. The goal of this conference is to

TABLE 8.4. Steps for Developing Goal-Setting, Self-Recording, and Self-Evaluation Procedures

Procedure/steps	Description
Goal setting	
1	Arrange a conference.
2	Identify a goal.
3	Clarify discrepancies.
4	Identify a solution.
5	Identify positive consequences for meeting the goal.
6	Develop monitoring plan.
7	Write a simple goal contract.
Self-recording	
1	Identify a target behavior.
2	Develop a recording form.
3	Identify consequences for correct monitoring and performance.
4	Establish follow-up procedures.
Self-evaluation	
1	Identify target behavior and self-evaluation standard.
2	Choose an accuracy-matching procedure.
3	Develop a self-evaluation form.
4	Identify consequences for accurate monitoring and performance.
5	Establish follow-up procedures.

fully engage the student in all aspects of the development and implementation of the goal-setting procedure. The second step is to identify a goal for the student. Identifying a goal includes identification of the problem (current level of performance) and specification of the desired outcome (expected level of performance). The third step is to clarify the discrepancy between the current and expected levels of performance for the student. The discussion of the discrepancy should be factual, positive, and matter-of-fact. Supporting baseline information should be shared with students to help them understand the extent to which their current performance is discrepant from what is expected. The fourth step is to identify a solution to solve the problem, using a problem-solving approach. This approach includes: (1) brainstorming two to four solutions or different things the student and/or teacher could do to solve the problem; (2) assessing the relative advantages and disadvantages of the potential solutions; and (3) picking one of the solutions to implement. The fifth step is to identify the consequences for meeting the goal. Student motivation to achieve the goal is enhanced by specifying a contingent reinforcer for meeting the goal. Of course, teachers should capitalize on naturally occurring reinforcers (e.g., improvement in grades) whenever possible. The sixth step is to develop a monitoring plan, which can be formal (e.g., self-recording) or informal (e.g., regular student and teacher meeting). The final step is to formulate a goal-setting contract. The contract should specify the goal, the solution, specific aspects of the solution, monitoring and evaluation procedures, review date, and signatures of all responsible parties. An example of a goal-setting contract is provided in Figure 8.2.

Name: _Claire_____   Date: _____

Goal: _Correctly complete 90% or more of independent math assignment problems_____

Solution: Pay attention and work practice problems_____

Specific things I need to do:

       1. Follow along and write down the steps for solving problems.

       2. Work practice problems with the teacher and rest of the class.

       3. Write down the page number and problem numbers to be completed.

       4. Write out each problem, following the steps for solving problems.

How will I know I am meeting my goal?

       1. I will complete all of the assigned math problems.

       2. I will get 90% or more of them correct.

Review date: _Start of each math period_____

Student signature: _____

Teacher signature: _____

FIGURE 8.2. Example of goal-setting contract.

Self-Recording

Self-recording requires students to observe and record their own behavior to improve academic or social performance. In the academic domain, two forms of self-recording procedures are used to improve academic productivity. In the first form students self-record their on-task behavior or attention during instruction. Self-recording of on-task behavior or attention increases academic productivity indirectly because improvements are likely to have a consequent effect on academic productivity. In the second form of self-recording, students self-record their academic productivity directly (e.g., number of correct math problems). Examples of self-recording forms in which the target is on-task behavior during independent math seatwork and the number of correct math problems are depicted in Figure 8.3.

Developing a self-recording procedure includes the four steps outlined in Table 8.4. The first step is to identify the target behavior. The target behavior may emerge from a formal goal-setting procedure such as the one described previously, or it can be identified informally through a discussion with students. The second

Name: _Claire_ _____   Date: _____

Target: _On-task behavior during independent math seatwork_ _____

Check whether you were on task or off task during each of the time periods.

Time	On task	Off task
10:00	✓	___
10:10	✓	___
10:15	___	✓
10:20	✓	___

I get 1 minute of computer time for every check.

Name: _Claire_ _____   Date: _____

Target: _Number of math problems completed correctly_ _____

Record the number of problems that you answered correctly during the session.

Time	On task
Monday	7
Tuesday	14
Wednesday	12
Thursday	4
Friday	10

I get 1 minute of computer time for every five correct problems.

FIGURE 8.3. Example of self-recording forms for on-task behavior and number of correct mathematics problems.

step is to develop a form to record the target behavior. This step can be done independently or with students. The self-recording form should be simple and easy to use; it must reflect not only the needs of the learner but also the context(s) in which it will be used. The third step is to identify any consequences for self-recording the target behavior. Consequences can be linked to self-recording to ensure that students learn how to observe and record their own behavior, and, if applicable, linked to students' performance of the target behavior. The final step is to establish follow-up procedures to allow the teacher and student to discuss the student's progress and, if appropriate, decreasing the self-monitoring procedure.

Self-Evaluation

The focus of both goal setting and self-recording is to establish a performance goal and to observe and record the behavior necessary to achieve the goal. In essence, self-evaluation involves the comparison of a target behavior being self-observed (and self-recorded, if necessary) and a performance goal. Self-evaluation is important during instructional situations because it is often difficult for teachers to provide immediate feedback to students. Self-evaluation procedures reduce the probability that students will practice incorrect or inappropriate behavior during instruction. For example, it is not uncommon for students to make errors when learning a new skill. Self-evaluation immediately after a student performs the new skill can prevent him or her from practicing errors. Self-evaluation also may serve as a prompt to students to independently self-correct by requesting instruction or help from peers. Additionally, two primary procedures are used to ensure accurate self-evaluations by students. The first and most common procedure is to compare students' self-evaluations with those of teachers. The second procedure is to compare students' self-evaluations with those of peers. Regardless of the procedure, the extent to which students are able to match teachers' or peers' evaluation of the target behavior determines the accuracy of students' self-evaluations.

Developing a self-evaluation procedure includes the five steps outlined in Table 8.4. The first step is to identify the target behavior and self-evaluation standard. The target behavior can be identified through an informal goal-setting process or directly determined by teachers. The second step is to determine the matching procedure (i.e., teacher, peer) used to check the accuracy of students' self-evaluation. The matching procedure should be individualized to meet students' needs. For example, a rating scale comprised of a happy face, a straight face, and a sad face may be more appropriate for younger students than a numerical rating scale. The third step is to develop the form students' use to self-evaluate their performance. The form can be created with students or independently by teachers. Further, it may be necessary to embed a self-recording procedure into the self-evaluation form to allow the student to observe and record the target behavior, if necessary. A sample self-evaluation form for on-task behavior during instruction is provided in Figure 8.4. The fourth step is to identify consequences linked to students' self-evaluations. Consequences can be linked to the accuracy of the self-

Name: _Claire_   Date: _____

Target: _On-task behavior during math class_

Rate the extent to which you were on task during math class.

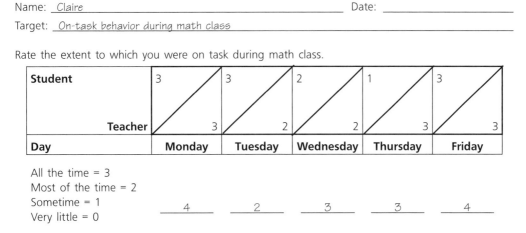

Student	3	3	2	1	3
Teacher	3	2	2	3	3
Day	**Monday**	**Tuesday**	**Wednesday**	**Thursday**	**Friday**

All the time = 3
Most of the time = 2
Sometime = 1   ___4___   ___2___   ___3___   ___3___   ___4___
Very little = 0

I get 1 minute of computer time for every teacher rating that matches mine.

FIGURE 8.4. Example of self-recording forms for on-task behavior and number of correct mathematics problems.

evaluations to ensure that students learn how to accurately evaluate their own behavior, and, if applicable, linked to students' performance of the target behavior. The final step is to establish a follow-up procedure to allow the teacher and student to discuss the student's progress and, if appropriate, decrease the self-evaluation procedure.

TEACHER–STUDENT LEARNING GAME

The Teacher–Student Learning Game, which we describe in this section, is used as an instructional management procedure and can be applied effectively with students who have BD. This Teacher–Student Learning Game can be used by teachers in conjunction with any individual behavioral management systems used by students, such as self-monitoring, behavioral contracts, etc. The Teacher–Student Learning Game stems from behavioral theory and is based on the Good Behavior Game, which has been validated in a number of field trials (e.g., Barrish, Saunders, & Wolf, 1969; Dolan et al., 1993).

Description

The Teacher–Student Learning Game is a competition-based behavioral management strategy between the teacher and students that is used in instructional situations. The game is user-friendly and can be implemented in a range of settings, including large and small groups within the core curriculum, support classrooms (e.g., special education), and individually. Clear implementation procedures allow for the use of the Teacher–Student Learning Game by a wide array of educators, including classroom teachers, resource teachers, and paraeducators. The only materials needed to implement the game are a small white board and a marker.

The goals of the Teacher–Student Learning Game are to increase on-task, and reduce disruptive, behavior during instructional situations. The game is especially useful for students with BD because it encourages them to manage their own and their peers' behavior through a process of group reinforcement and mutual self-interest. Further, the game helps teachers avoid coercive teacher–student interactions (i.e., power struggles) over disruptive behavior during instructional situations by redirecting students at such times. Avoiding coercive teacher–student interactions is especially important in the case of students with BD. These students are likely to initiate such interactions over instructional demands (Nelson & Roberts, 2000; Patterson, 1995).

The game implementation procedures are straightforward. Teachers develop and use a set of positive and observable expectations to guide student behavior during instructional situations. The expectations are developed prior to the first day of school and are taught and reviewed with students when the instructional situations occur naturally in classrooms during the first 3 days of school. Teachers use an easily accessible small white board (e.g., placed in their lap or on a table in front of them) or flip chart to make hash marks (representing points) under a T-chart. One half of the T-chart is labeled *Teacher,* and the other is labeled *Students* (see Figure 8.5). The teacher makes five hash marks (facilitating the totaling of the

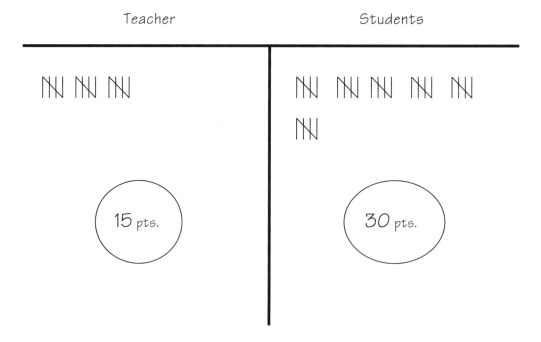

FIGURE 8.5. Example of Teacher–Student Learning Game T-chart.

number of points earned) under the student side of the T-chart when the teacher observes students demonstrating the expected behavior or having success on lesson tasks. Conversely, the teacher makes five hash marks under the teacher side of the T-chart when he or she observes disruptive student behavior. Marking the teacher side of the T-chart redirects students toward expected behavior without initiating coercive teacher–student interactions or power struggles over disruptive behavior during instructional situations. Each hash mark represents a point.

The teacher tallies the points the students and he or she earned at the end of the instructional situation and provides students with social recognition or administers the appropriate prize, privilege, or special activity for winning the game. If the teacher wins, he or she points out the areas in which students need to work during the next instructional opportunity. Teachers review the things on which students need to focus at the start of the next lesson.

The Teacher–Student Learning Game is not used during every instructional situation. Teachers use the game when it is clearly needed (i.e., students are not demonstrating the expected behavior) or randomly throughout the year. Intermittent use of the Teacher–Student Learning Game not only makes it more fun and exciting for students, but serves to develop students' self-control. Teachers should aim to use the game less frequently during the course of a school year.

The following two considerations are important in implementing the Teacher–Student Learning Game. First, teachers establish expectations for each instructional situation (e.g., small group, large group, independent) that are clear, concise, and explicit, so that students understand them and know how to behave in order to follow them. The expectations should be worded positively and relatively few in number (i.e., ≤ 5). The expectations should be taught systematically to students in ways that help them understand how to demonstrate them. Additionally, the expectations should be taught and reviewed the first 3 days of school during instructional situations. The expectations are then reviewed with students on an ongoing basis during the school year, whenever teachers win the Teacher–Student Learning Game. Second, the Teacher–Student Learning Game should be implemented to acknowledge and reinforce students for meeting the expectations or redirect them when they exhibit disruptive behavior. Next, we describe these three steps more fully and address common questions that arise when the Teacher–Student Learning Game is implemented.

Implementation Steps

Establishing Expectations

The first step in implementing the Teacher–Student Learning Game is for teachers, prior to the first day of school, to operationally define a small number of positively stated expectations to guide student behavior during each instructional situation used in their classroom. Defining the expectations in operational terms is critical to communicating and teaching the expectations to students. Further, operational definitions maintain objectivity and consistency across time. Consistency in the expectations ensures that teachers and students become familiar with their respective roles during each of the instructional situations. Operationally defined expectations for a range of instructional situations are described below. These expectations are specific to instructional situations and rely on more general classroom expectations, such as how to follow directions. Expectations for each instructional situation are stated positively and are four to five in number. Of course, these can be adjusted to meet the specific needs of teachers and instructional situations that occur in their classroom.

Large- and Small-Group Instruction

1. *Demonstrate learner position*: Students' backs are against the back of the chair, feet are on the floor in front of the chair, and hands are together on desk/lap.
2. *Look at the focus of instruction*: Students' eyes are on the instructional materials, teacher, or a peer.
3. *Answer on signal*: Students start and stop on teacher signal (group and individual).
4. *Respond to teacher-initiated queries and focus on subject*: Students' responses are only teacher-initiated and subject focused.
5. *Use classroom voice*: Students use "6-inch voices" (i.e., use a conversational tone—speaking in a voice that would be considered appropriate in a classroom—not too loud).

Structured Independent Instruction

1. *Stay in seat*: Students' backs are against the back of the chair, feet are on the floor in front of the chair, and hands are busy working.
2. *Maintain complete silence*: Students do not talk or make sounds.
3. *Finish work neatly and completely*: Students complete their work and use their best handwriting or coloring.
4. *Ask questions correctly*: Students ask questions by raising hands, and they ask questions only during transitions when the teacher is working with other students.

Less Structured Independent Instruction

1. *Listen carefully*: Students sit still, do not talk or make sounds, and focus on the speaker when necessary.
2. *Communicate nicely*: Students use nice words and 6-inch voices.
3. *Stay subject focused*: Students' work and interaction with peers is focused on the subject.
4. *Ask questions correctly*: Students ask questions by raising hands and they ask questions only during transitions when the teacher is working with other students.

Individual Instruction

1. *Demonstrate learner position*: Student's back is against the back of the chair, feet are on the floor in front of the chair, and hands are together on desk/lap.
2. *Look at the focus of instruction*: Student's eyes are on the instructional materials, teacher, or a peer.
3. *Answer on signal*: Student starts and stops on teacher signal.
4. *Use classroom voice*: Student uses 6-inch voice.

Teaching Expectations

The second step in implementing the Teacher–Student Learning Game is for teachers to systematically teach and review with students the expectations for each instructional situation during the first 3 days of school. Additionally, teachers review the expectations whenever they win the game. A three-step approach is used to teach students the expectations for the instructional situations.

1. *Discuss the need for the expectations.* Students need to understand why the expectations are important. Begin by having students identify problems they experienced during large, small, independent, or individual instructional situations. Then point out that most of these problems occur because students are unaware of what they are supposed to do during instructional situations. Students also have different ideas about what they need to be doing during instructional situations. Share with students that teachers have different ideas about what students should do and that even teachers themselves sometimes are unsure what they want students to do during instructional situations. Next, talk with students about the expectations for an instructional situation. A laminated poster of the expectations should be posted in a visible location. Point out that the primary goal of the expectations is to ensure everyone's success. Communicate that it is important for all students to manage their own behavior and support their peers during instructional situations.

2. *Teach the expectations.* It is critical that teachers teach the expectations to students in a thorough manner. The goal is to identify exactly what students need to do and say in order to demonstrate the expectations. When teaching expectations, it is best to focus on one instructional situation at a time. In other words, do not teach the expectations for all of the possible instructional situations that can occur in the classroom at one time. Instead, teach the expectations for each instructional situation as it naturally occurs throughout the first few days of schools. The Looks Like, Sounds Like T-chart in Figure 8.6 is used to teach students the expectations. Teachers can create a transparency of the T-chart to use on the overhead projector, flip chart, or white board, then begin by writing the particular expectation in the box at the top of the T-chart. Teachers discuss and model what students should do (Looks Like) and say (Sounds Like) when they demonstrate the expectation that is being taught. It is important that teachers discuss and model for students both

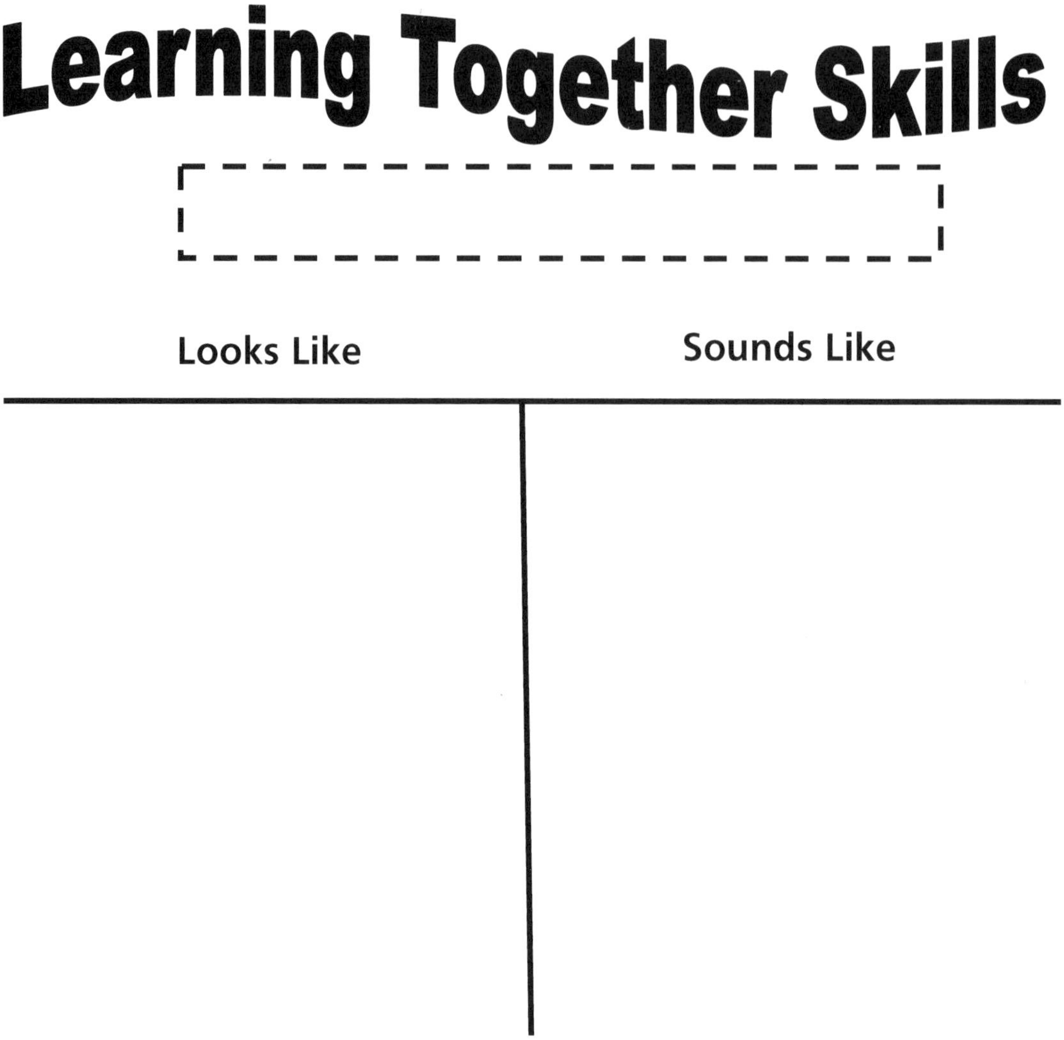

Learning Together Skills

Looks Like   Sounds Like

FIGURE 8.6. Looks Like, Sounds Like T-chart for teaching expectations.

examples and nonexamples of the expectation. This process should be highly interactive. Teachers may call on students to model examples of the expectations, but they should avoid doing so in the case of nonexamples.

3. *Practice the expectations.* After teaching what the expectations look and sound like, give students an immediate opportunity to practice them. The best way to do this is to plan an actual lesson that enables students to practice the skills. The content of the lesson should be simple and straightforward so that students can focus primarily on the expectations during the lesson. During the lesson, use the Teacher–Student

Learning Game (further described below) to give students immediate feedback on the extent to which they are demonstrating the expectations. It is useful to focus on both the group and individual students who are doing a good job meeting the expectations. Refer to the posted Looks Like, Sounds Like T-Chart (see Figure 8.6) in those cases in which students are not demonstrating a particular expectation correctly. At the end of the activity, reflect on how well students demonstrated the expectations. Take a few minutes to brainstorm with the students all the good behaviors that were observed and the problem responses that need more practice.

Implementing the Teacher–Student Learning Game

On the first day of school, the teacher announces that he or she is going to use the Teacher–Student Learning Game during all instructional situations the first 3 days of school to help students remember the expectations. The teacher indicates that, like all games, the Teacher–Student Learning Game has rules and scoring procedures. The teacher explains how the game is played; the explanation should include the following points.

1. *Why do we need to play the Teacher–Student Learning Game?* The goals of the game are to help students learn as much as they can and to manage their own behavior and support each other.
2. *When is the Teacher–Student Learning Game played?* The game can be played during all instructional situations used in the classroom (e.g., large and small groups, individual, structured and unstructured independent learning). Teachers might use the game at the start of, or during, an instructional situation in which they want to redirect students toward the expected behavior without initiating coercive teacher–student interactions or power struggles over disruptive behavior. The teacher decides when the game is played; however, the game is played in every instructional situation, during the first 3 days of school, to help students learn the appropriate expectations and how to play the game. Teachers then use the game when it is clearly needed (i.e., when students are not demonstrating expected behavior) as well as randomly throughout the year. The intermittent use of the Teacher–Student Learning Game makes it more fun to play and serves to help students develop self-control skills.
3. *How do students and teachers score points?* Students score 5 points each time the teacher notices students demonstrating the expectations during an instructional situation or when students are having success on lesson tasks. Teachers score 5 points each time they notice students exhibiting behavior that is disruptive to learning. Teachers do not point out who is disrupting the lesson, and only teachers decide when points are awarded.
4. *How do teachers keep track of the points?* Teachers use a T-chart, as shown in Figure 8.5 and described earlier.
5. *What happens when the game is over?* See the discussion and the goals of the Teacher–Student Learning Game on pp. 160–161.

Common Questions and Answers

We address common questions that arise when using the Teacher–Student Learning Game in this section.

Question: For how long should the teacher play the Teacher–Student Learning Game?

Answer: The game should be played during distinct instructional situations. For example, during a 90-minute literacy block, the teacher may elect to play the Teacher–Student Learning Game during the initial whole-group instruction or small-group differentiated instruction portion of the literacy block.

Question: How does the teacher begin the Teacher–Student Learning Game at the start of an instructional situation?

Answer: Teachers begin the Teacher–Student Learning Game by getting the students' attention (e.g., "Everyone, learner position and eyes on me") and telling them "We're going to be playing the Teacher–Student Learning Game today during. . . . " Immediately make five hash marks on the T-chart under the student side when most, if not all, of the students demonstrate the learner position and are looking at the teacher (and say, "Students score 5 points for learner position and eyes on me"). Although the teacher may have to start the game by making five hash marks on the T-chart under the teacher side in those cases in which some students do not demonstrate the learner position or are not looking at him or her, attempt to start the game by having students score the initial points. Avoid singling out the offending student(s). Simply state, "Teacher scores 5 points; some students did not demonstrate learner position and eyes were not on me," and then start the lesson.

Question: How does the teacher start the Teacher–Student Learning Game during an instructional session?

Answer: Teachers may elect to start the game at some point in a lesson to redirect students who are exhibiting disruptive behavior. Teachers do not call attention to the students. Rather, they simply pause, gain the attention of all the students (e.g., "Everyone: learner position and eyes on me"), and tell them "We're going to be playing the Teacher–Student Learning Game for the remainder of the. . . . " Immediately make five hash marks on the T-chart under the student side when most, if not all, of the students demonstrate the learner position and are looking at the teacher, and say, "Students score 5 points for learner position and eyes on me." Although the teacher may have to start the game by making five hash marks on the T-chart under the teacher side in those cases in which those students who were exhibiting disruptive behavior continue to do so, avoid singling out the offending students. Simply score the points and start teaching the lesson. If students continue to exhibit disruptive behavior, the teacher should implement classroom or individual disciplinary procedures.

Question: How often does the teacher record scores during the instructional situation?

Answer: Teachers record scores approximately four to eight times during the instructional situation to minimize disruption to the lesson: They record scores for students when students are demonstrating the expectations and at times that are least disruptive to the lesson, and they record scores for themselves when students are exhibiting behavior that is disruptive to the lesson.

Question: What ratio of teacher-to-student wins is appropriate?

Answer: Teachers focus on catching students demonstrating the expectations or having success on lessons rather than on their disruptive behavior. A general rule of thumb is that students should win approximately 80% of the games.

Question: Can the teacher single out individual students during the Teacher–Student Learning Game?

Answer: Teachers can single out individual students who are demonstrating the expectations. This recognition is especially useful for those students who frequently exhibit disruptive behavior, have limited learning success, or are not well accepted by the group. Singling out these students for demonstrating the expectations or learning success (e.g., "I noticed that John is doing a great job of . . . ") is a nice way of validating them and possibly improving their standing among their peers. Avoid singling out individual students for exhibiting disruptive behaviors. The Teacher–Student Learning Game should be used as a redirect procedure in these cases.

Question: What should the teacher do in those cases in which a student who is exhibiting disruptive behavior does not respond to the redirect in the Teacher–Student Learning Game?

Answer: Teachers simply initiate their standard disciplinary procedures in these cases.

Question: How does the teacher use the Teacher–Student Learning Game during those times in which he or she is using two or more instructional situations at a time?

Answer: Teachers commonly use two or more instructional situations during a given time. For example, teachers may have a majority of students working in an independent instruction situation while they are conducting a small-group differentiated instruction lesson or assessing individual students. Teachers can elect to use the Teacher–Student Learning Game in any one of the instructional situations. In the above example, teachers could use the game to encourage students working in the independent instructional situation to demonstrate the expected behaviors. Teachers simply initiate the game at the start of the independent instructional situation and play it with the students while continuing to conduct the small-group differentiated instructional lesson.

CONCLUSIONS

The overall purpose of this chapter was to describe some areas that are critical to the management of instructional situations. These areas focus on the intersection between management and instruction. We provided information on the placement of students with BD within instructional situations to improve their relative levels of disruptive versus on-task behavior. Placing students in the action zone and ensuring that they are surrounded by model students can have a dramatic, positive effect on behavior. Furthermore, teachers must place students with BD in the action zone because they are likely to avoid it if given the choice.

We also discussed teacher awareness, interpersonal interaction, and self-control skills. Teachers' awareness skills include those they use to prevent disruptive behavior, manage movement, and maintain group focus. Classrooms are complex settings. Many events that are potentially disruptive to instructional situations occur on a regular but often unpredictable basis. Teachers who are "with it" and demonstrate overlapping skills prevent disruptive behavior by: (1) protecting instructional situations from external interruptions; and (2) attending to two or more simultaneous events. Whereas withitness and overlapping skills concern teachers' ability to ensure that external events and disruptive behavior do not intrude into the flow of the lesson, movement management is accomplished by avoiding teacher-caused delays during the lesson. Movement management skill involves the ability to maintain instructional momentum through the use of appropriate curriculum pacing, lesson pacing, and transition management. The presence of instructional momentum means that students are moving through the curriculum at an appropriate pace, with high levels of success, which, in turn, has a positive effect on students' relative rates of disruptive and on-task behaviors.

Interpersonal and self-control skills involve personal attributes of teachers that increase their ability to effectively teach students with BD. Teachers who provide students with high rates of noncontingent interactions, communicate clearly with students, and use prompts rather than corrections will experience greater success than those who do not. High rates of noncontingent interactions will increase the probability that students will respond to contingent requests made by teachers. Clear communication practices during instructional situations center on teachers knowing what they want from students and using simple and direct language to communicate their expectations to students. Further, teachers who use prompts with students rather than corrections will be more effective in their communication. It is much more effective to provide a level of prompting that produces the desired response from students than to correct them continually. Teachers' ability to communicate effectively with students who have BD is enhanced when they exhibit good paraverbal and nonverbal self-control skills. The ability to be matter-of-fact and unemotional and use appropriate personal space and body language during teacher–student interactions regarding disruptive behavior increases the likelihood of a positive outcome.

Goal-setting, self-recording, and self-evaluation procedures make explicit the implicit skills necessary for self-regulated performance. The assumption underlying these self-management procedures is that successful students develop and apply an implicit repertoire of self-regulated skills across varied contexts. Self-management skills are flexible in that they can be applied across a range of academic and social behaviors. These procedures are user-friendly in that they can be easily integrated into a range of instructional situations to augment teachers' effective instruction.

Finally, we described the Teacher–Student Learning Game, a competition-based behavioral management strategy for instructional situations. The game can be used flexibly by teachers across the full range of instructional situations that they use in their classroom. The goals of the game are to increase on-task, and reduce disruptive, behaviors during instructional situations. The Teacher–Student Learning Game encourages students to manage their own and peers' behaviors and is used to redirect students when they demonstrate disruptive behavior.

References

Abikoff, H. B., Jensen, P. S., Arnold, L. L. E., Hoza, B., Hechtman, L., Pollack, S., et al. (2002). Observed classroom behavior of children with ADHD: Relationship to gender and comorbidity. *Journal of Abnormal Child Psychology, 30*, 349–359.

Achenbach, T. M. (2001). *Manual for the child behavior checklist/4–18 and 2001 profile.* Burlington: University of Vermont, Department of Psychiatry.

Adams, M. J. (1998). *Beginning to read: Thinking and learning about print.* Cambridge, MA: MIT Press.

Al Otaiba, S., & Fuchs, D. (2002). Characteristics of children who are unresponsive to early literacy intervention. *Remedial and Special Education, 23*, 300–316.

American Psychiatric Association. (2000). *Diagnostic and statistical manual of mental disorders* (4th ed., text rev.). Washington, DC: Author.

Anderson, J. A., Kutash, K., & Duchnowski, A. J. (2001). A comparison of the academic progress of students with EBD and students with LD. *Journal of Emotional and Behavioral Disorders, 9*, 106–115.

Anderson, R. C., Hiebert, E. H., Scott, J. A., & Wilkinson, I. A. G. (1985). *Becoming a nation of readers: The report of the Commission on Reading.* Washington, DC: National Institute of Education.

Baker, L., & Cantwell, D. P. (1987). Factors associated with the development of psychiatric illness in children with early speech/language problems. *Journal of Autism and Developmental Disorders, 17*, 499–510.

Barriga, A. Q., Doran, J. W., Newell, S. B., Morrison, E. M., Barbetti, V., & Robbins, B. D. (2002). Relationships between problem behaviors and academic achievement in adolescents: The unique role of attention problems. *Journal of Emotional and Behavioral Disorders, 10*, 233–240.

Barrish, H. H., Saunders, M., & Wolf, M. M. (1969). Good Behavior Game: Effects of individual contingencies for group consequences on disruptive behavior in a classroom. *Journal of Applied Behavior Analysis, 2,* 119–124.

Barton-Arwood, S. M., Wehby, J. H., & Falk, K. B. (2005). Reading instruction for elementary-age students with emotional and behavioral disorders: Academic and behavioral outcomes. *Exceptional Children, 72,* 7–27.

Batche, G., Elliott, J., Graden, J. L., Grimes, J., Kovaleski, J. F., Prasse, D., et al. (2005). *Response to Intervention: Policy considerations and implementation.* Alexandria, VA: National Association of State Directors of Special Education.

Beitchman, J. H., Wilson, B., Johnson, C. J., Atkinson, L., Young, A., Adlaf, E., et al. (2001). Fourteen-year follow-up of speech/language-impaired and control children: Psychiatric outcome. *Journal of the American Academy of Child and Adolescent Psychiatry, 40,* 75–82.

Bereiter, C., & Scardamalia, M. (1987). *The psychology of written composition.* Hillsdale, NJ: Erlbaum.

Brier, N. (1995). Predicting antisocial behavior in youngsters displaying poor academic achievement: A review of risk factors. *Developmental and Behavioral Pediatrics, 16,* 271–276.

Brophy, J., & Good, T. (1986). Teacher-effects results. In M. C. Wittrock (Ed.), *Handbook of research on teaching* (3rd ed., pp. 328–375). New York: Macmillan.

Bushell, D., & Baer, D. M. (1994). Measurably superior instruction means close, continual contact with the relevant outcome data. Revolutionary! In R. Gardner, D. M. Sainato, J. O. Cooper, T. E. Herron, W. L. Heward, J. Eshleman, et al. (Eds.), *Behavior analysis in education: Focus on measurably superior instruction* (pp. 3–10). Belmont, CA: Wadsworth.

Carnine, D. W., Silbert, J., Kame'enui, E. J., & Tarver, S. G. (2004). *Direct instruction reading* (4th ed.). Upper Saddle River, NJ: Pearson Education.

Carr, S. C., & Punzo, R. P. (1993). The effects of self-monitoring of academic accuracy and productivity on the performance of students with behavioral disorders. *Behavioral Disorders, 18,* 241–250.

Catts, H. W., Fey, M. E., Xuyang, Z., & Tomblin, J. B. (1999). Language basis of reading and reading disabilities: Evidence from a longitudinal investigation. *Scientific Studies of Reading, 3,* 331–362.

Choate, J. S. (1987). Synthesizing assessment and programming. In J. S. Choate, T. Z. Bennett, B. E. Enright, L. S. Miller, J. A. Poteet, & T. A. Rakes (Eds.), *Assessment and programming basic curriculum skills* (pp. 231–238). Boston: Allyn & Bacon.

Clarke, B., & Shinn, M. R. (2002). *Test of Early Numeracy (TEN): Administration and scoring of AIMSweb early numeracy measures.* Eden Prairie, MN: Edformation. Retrieved from *www.aimsweb.com.*

Coalition for Evidence-Based Policy. (2002). *Bringing evidence-driven progress to education: A recommended strategy for the U.S. Department of Education, 2002.* Washington, DC: U.S. Department of Education.

Cohen, N., Davine, M., Horodezsky, N., Lipsett, L., & Isaacson, L. (1993). Unsuspected language impairment in psychiatrically disturbed children: Prevalence and language and behavioral characteristics. *Journal of the American Academy of Child and Adolescent Psychiatry, 32,* 595–603.

Comprehensive School Reform Program Office, Office of Elementary and Secondary Education, U.S. Department of Education. (2002). *Scientifically based research and the Comprehensive School Reform (CSR) program.* Washington, DC: U.S. Department of Education.

Coutinho, M. J. (1986). Reading achievement of students identified as behaviorally disordered at the secondary level. *Behavioral Disorders, 11,* 200–207.

Dawson, L., Venn, M. L., & Gunter, P. L. (2000). The effects of teacher versus computer reading models. *Behavioral Disorders, 25,* 105–113.

Deno, S. L. (1985). Curriculum-based measurement: The emerging alternative. *Exceptional Children, 52,* 219–232.

Deno, S. L. (2003). Curriculum-based measures: Development and perspectives. *Assessment for Effective Intervention, 28*(3 & 4), 3–12.

Deno, S. (2005). Problem-solving assessment. In R. Brown-Chidsey (Ed.), *Assessment for intervention: A problem-solving approach* (pp. 10–42). New York: Guilford Press.

Deno, S. L., Mirkin, P. K., & Wesson, C. (1984). How to write effective data-based IEPs. *Teaching Exceptional Children, 16,* 99–104.

Dixon, R. C., Isaacson, S., & Stein, M. (2007). Effective strategies for teaching writing. In M.D. Coyne, E. J. Kame'enui, & D. W. Carnine (Eds.), *Effective teaching strategies that accommodate diverse learners* (3rd ed., pp. 111–138). Upper Saddle River, NJ: Pearson Education.

Dolan, L. J., Kellam, S. G., Brown, C. H., Werthamer-Larsson, L., Rebok, G. W., Mayer, L. S., et al. (1993). The short-term impact of two classroom-based preventive interventions on aggressive and shy behaviors and poor achievement. *Journal of Applied Developmental Psychology, 14,* 317–345.

Donahue, M., Cole, D., & Hartas, D. (1994). Links between language and emotional/behavioral disorders. *Education and Treatment of Children, 17,* 244–254.

Doyle, W. (1986). Classroom organization and management. In M. C. Wittrock (Ed.), *Handbook of research on teaching* (3rd ed., pp. 392–431). New York: Macmillan.

Ehri, L. C. (1999). Phases of development in learning to read words. In J. V. Oakhill & R. Beard (Eds.), *Reading development and the teaching of reading: A psychological perspective* (pp. 79–108). Oxford, UK: Blackwell.

Ehri, L. C. (2005). Learning to read words: Theory, findings, and issues. *Scientific Studies of Reading, 9,* 167–188.

Ehri, L. C., & McCormick, S. (1998). Phases of word learning: Implications for instruction with delayed and disabled readers. *Reading and Writing Quarterly, 14,* 135–163.

Emmer, E. T., Evertson, C. M., & Worsham, M. E. (2000). *Classroom management for secondary teachers* (5th ed). Boston: Allyn & Bacon.

Epstein, M. H., & Cullinan, D. (1983). Academic performance of behaviorally disordered and learning-disabled pupils. *Journal of Special Education, 17,* 303–307.

Epstein, M. H., Kinder, D., & Bursuck, B. (1989). The academic status of adolescents with behavioral disorders. *Behavioral Disorders, 14,* 157–165.

Epstein, M. H., Nelson, J. R., Trout, A. L., & Mooney, P. (2005). Achievement and emotional disturbance: Academic status and intervention research. In M. H. Epstein, K. Kutash, & A. J. Duchnowski (Eds.), *Outcomes for children and youth with emotional and behavioral disorders and their families: Programs and evaluation best practices* (2nd ed., pp. 451–477). Austin, TX: PRO-ED.

Evertson, C. M., Emmer, E. T., & Worsham, M. E. (2000). *Classroom management for elementary teachers* (5th ed.). Boston: Allyn & Bacon.

Fink-Chorzempa, B., Graham, S., & Harris, K. R. (2005). What can I do to help young children who struggle with writing? *Teaching Exceptional Children, 37*(5), 64–66.

Franca, V. M., Kerr, M. M., Reitz, A. L., & Lambert, D. (1990). Peer tutoring among behaviorally disordered students: Academic and social benefits to tutor and tutee. *Education and Treatment of Children, 13,* 109–128.

Frank, A. R., & Brown, D. (1992). Self-monitoring strategies in arithmetic. *Teaching Exceptional Children, 24*(2), 52–53.

Fuchs, D., & Fuchs, L. S. (2006). Introduction to Response to Intervention: What, why, and how valid is it? *Reading Research Quarterly, 41,* 93–99.

Fuchs, D., Fuchs, L. S., Bahr, M. W., Fernstrom, P., & Stecker, P.M. (1990). Prereferral intervention: A prescriptive approach. *Exceptional Children, 56,* 493–513.

Fuchs, D., Fuchs, L. S., Thompson, A., Svenson, E., Yen, L., Otaiba, S. A., et al. (2001). Peer-assisted learning strategies in reading: Extensions for kindergarten, first grade, and high school. *Remedial and Special Education, 22,* 15–21.

Fuchs, D., Mock, D., Morgan, P. L., & Young, C. L. (2003). Responsiveness-to-Interventions: Definitions, evidence, and implications for the learning disabilities construct. *Learning Disabilities: Research and Practice, 18,* 157–171.

Fuchs, L. S. (2004). The past, present, and future of curriculum-based measurement research. *School Psychology Review, 33,* 188–192.

Fuchs, L. S., & Fuchs, D. (1986). Effects of systematic formative evaluation: A meta-analysis. *Exceptional Children, 53,* 199–208.

Fujiki, M., Brinton, B., Morgan, M., & Hart, C. H. (1999). Withdrawn and sociable behavior of children with language impairment. *Language, Speech, and Hearing Services in the Schools, 30,* 183–195.

Gajar, A. (1979). Educable mentally retarded, learning disabled, emotionally disturbed: Similarities and differences. *Exceptional Children, 45,* 470–472.

Gallagher, T. M. (1999). Interrelationships among children's language, behavior, and emotional problems. *Topics in Language Disorders, 19,* 1–15.

Gaskins, I. W. (2004). Word detectives. *Educational Leadership, 61*(6), 70–73.

Gaskins, I. W., Ehri, L. C., Cress, C., O'Hara, C., & Donnelly, K. (1996–1997). Procedures for word learning: Making discoveries about words. *The Reading Teacher, 50,* 312–327.

Geary, D. C., Bow-Thomas, C. C., & Yao, Y. (1992). Counting knowledge and skill in cognitive addition: A comparison of normal and mathematically disabled children. *Journal of Experimental Child Psychology, 54,* 372–391.

Gersten, R., & Chard, D. (1999). Number sense: Rethinking arithmetic instruction for students with mathematical disabilities. *Journal of Special Education, 33*(1), 18–28.

Good, R. H., & Kaminski, R. A. (Eds.). (2002). *Dynamic Indicators of Basic Early Literacy Skills* (6th ed.). Eugene, OR: Institute for the Development of Educational Achievement. Retrieved from *www.dibels.uoregon.edu.*

Graham, S. (1983). Effective spelling instruction. *Elementary School Journal, 83,* 560–567.

Graham, S. (2006). Writing. In P. A. Alexander & P. H. Winne (Eds.), *Handbook of educational psychology* (2nd ed., pp. 457–478). Mahwah, NJ: Erlbaum.

Graham, S., & Harris, K. R. (2002). Prevention and intervention for struggling writers. In M. Shinn, H. Walker, & G. Stoner (Eds.), *Interventions for academic and behavior problems: II. Preventive and remedial techniques* (pp. 589–610). Washington, DC: National Association of School Psychologists.

Graham, S., & Harris, K. R. (2003). Students with learning disabilities and the process of writing: A meta-analysis of SRSD studies. In L. Swanson, K. R. Harris, & S. Graham (Eds.), *Handbook of research on learning disabilities* (3rd ed., pp. 383–402). New York: Guilford Press.

Graham, S., & Harris, K. R. (2006). Preventing writing difficulties: Providing additional handwriting and spelling instruction to at-risk children in first grade. *Teaching Exceptional Children, 38*(5), 64–66.

Graham, S., Harris, K. R., & Fink, B. (2000). Extra handwriting instruction: Preventing writing difficulties right from the start. *Teaching Exceptional Children, 33*(2), 88–91.

Graham, S., Harris, K. R., & Fink-Chorzempa, B. (2002). Contribution of spelling instruction to the spelling, writing, and reading of poor spellers. *Journal of Educational Psychology, 94*, 669–686.

Graham, S., Harris, K. R., & Fink-Chorzempa, B. (2003). Extra spelling instruction: Promoting better spelling, writing, and reading performance right from the start. *Teaching Exceptional Children, 35*(6), 66–68.

Graham, S., Harris, K. R., & Loynachan, C. (1993). The basic spelling vocabulary list. *Journal of Educational Research, 86*, 363–368.

Greenbaum, P. E., Dedrick, R. F., Friedman, R. M., Kutash, K., Brown, E. C., Lardieri, S. P., et al. (1996). National Adolescent and Child Treatment Study (NACTS): Outcomes for children with serious emotional and behavioral disturbance. *Journal of Emotional and Behavioral Disorders, 3*, 130–146.

Greenberg, M., Lengua, L., Cole, J., & Pinderhughes, E. (1999). Predicting developmental outcomes at school entry using a multiple-risk model: Four American communities. *Developmental Psychology, 35*, 403–417.

Gresham, F. M. (2003). *Responsiveness to Intervention: An alternative approach to the identification of learning disabilities.* Riverside: University of California.

Gresham, F. M., MacMillan, D. L., & Bocian, K. (1996). Behavioral earthquakes: Low frequency, salient behavior events that differentiate students at-risk for behavioral disorders. *Behavioral Disorders, 21*(4), 277–292.

Gunter, P. L., Callicott, K., Denny, R. K., & Gerber, B. L. (2003). Finding a place for data collection in classrooms for students with emotional/behavioral disorders. *Preventing School Failure, 48*(1), 4–8.

Gunter, P. L., Hummel, J., Denny, R. K., & Mooney, P. (2006, February). *Simplifying performance assessment measures.* Paper presented at the annual Midwest Symposium for Leadership in Behavior Disorders, Kansas City, MO.

Harris, K. R., & Graham, S. (1996). *Making the writing process work: Strategies for composition and self-regulation.* Cambridge, MA: Brookline Books.

Harry, B. (1994). *The disproportionate representation of minority students in special education: Theories and recommendations.* Alexandria, VA: Project FORUM, National Association of State Directors of Special Education.

Hart, B., & Risley, T. R. (1995). *Meaningful differences in the everyday experience of young American children.* Baltimore: Brookes.

Hayes, J., & Flower, L. (1980). Identifying the organization of writing processes. In L. Gregg & E. Steinberg (Eds.), *Cognitive processes in writing* (pp. 3–30). Hillsdale, NJ: Erlbaum.

Horowitz, S. M., Bility, K. M., Plichta, S. B., Leaf, P. J., & Haynes, N. (1998). Teacher's assessments of behavioral disorders. *American Journal of Orthopsychiatry, 68*, 350–361.

Huffman, L. C., Mehlinger, S. L., & Kerivan, A. S. (2000). *Risk factors for academic and behavioral problems at the beginning of school.* Retrieved from *www.ce-credit.com/articles/riskfactorsacademic.pdf*

Jenkins, J. R., & O'Connor, R. (2002). Early identification and intervention for young children with reading/learning disabilities. In R. Bradley, L. Danielson, & D. P. Hallahan

(Eds.), *Identification of learning disabilities: Research to practice* (pp. 99–151). Mahwah, NJ: Erlbaum.

Jenson, W. R., Rhode, G., & Reavis, K. H. (2000). The tough kid toolbox book. Longmont, CO: Sopris West.

Kaufman, J. M. (2006). *Characteristics of children's behavior disorders* (7th ed.). Columbus, OH: Merrill.

Klein, D., Braams, B. J., Parker, T., Quirk, W., Schmid, W., Wilson, W. S., et al. (2005). *The state of state math standards 2005*. Washington, DC: Thomas B. Fordham Foundation.

Knitzer, J. (1996). The role of education in systems care. In B. A. Stroul (Ed.), *Children's mental health: Creating systems of care in a changing society* (pp. 197–213). Baltimore: Brookes.

Kounin, J. S. (1970). *Discipline and group management in classrooms*. New York: Holt, Rinehart & Winston.

Kounin, J. S., & Gump, P. (1974). Signal systems of lesson settings and the task-related behavior of preschool children. *Journal of educational Psychology, 66*, 554–562.

Lane, K. L., & Beebe-Frankenberger, M. (2004). *School-based interventions: Tools you need to succeed*. Boston: Pearson.

Lane, K. L., Graham, S., Harris, K. R., & Weisenbach, J. L. (2006). Teaching writing strategies to young students struggling with writing and at risk for behavioral disorders: Self-regulated strategy development. *Teaching Exceptional Children, 39*(1), 60–64.

Lardierh, S. P., & Pugh, A. M. (1996). National Adolescent and Child Treatment Study (NACTS): Outcomes for children with serious emotional and behavioral disturbance. *Journal of Emotional and Behavioral Disorders, 4*, 130–146.

Lee, Y. Y., Sugai, C., & Horner, R. H. (1999). Using an instructional intervention to reduce problem and off-task behaviors. *Journal of Positive Behavior Interventions, 1*(4), 195–204.

Levendoski, L. S., & Cartledge, G. (2000). Self-monitoring for elementary school children with serious emotional disturbances: Classroom applications for increased academic responding. *Behavioral Disorders, 25*, 211–224.

Lewit, E. M., Terman, D. L., & Behrman, R. E. (1997). Children and poverty: Analysis and recommendations. *Future of Children, 7*, 4–24.

Logan, G. D. (1992). Attention and preattention in theories of automaticity. *American Journal of Psychology, 105*, 317–339.

Marchand-Martella, N. E., Martella, R. C., Nelson, J. R., Waterbury, L., Shelly, S. A., Cleanthous, C., et al. (2002). Implementation of the sound partners reading program. *Journal of Behavioral Education, 11*, 117–130.

Marchand-Martella, N. E., Slocum, T. A., & Martella, R. (2004). *Introduction to direct instruction*. Boston: Pearson Education.

Martella, R. C., Nelson, J. R., & Marchand-Martella, N. E. (1999). *Research methods: Learning to become a critical research consumer*. Boston: Allyn & Bacon.

Martella, R. C., Nelson, J. R., & Marchand-Martella, N. E. (2003). *Managing disruptive behaviors in the schools: A schoolwide, classroom, and individualized social learning approach*. Boston: Allyn & Bacon.

Maslen, B. L., & Maslen, J. R. (2006). *Bob books set 5—Long vowels*. New York: Scholastic.

Mathes, P. G., Torgesen, J. K., Allen, S. H., & Allor, J. H. (2001). *First-grade PALS: Peer-Assisted Literacy Strategies*. Longmont, CO: Sopris West.

Mattison, R. E., Hooper, S. R., & Glassberg, L. A. (2002). Three-year course of learning disorders in special education students classified as behavioral disorder. *Journal of the American Academy of Child & Adolescent Psychiatry, 41*, 1454–1461.

Mattison, R. E., Spitznagel, E. L., & Felix, B. C. (1998). Enrollment predictors of the special education outcome for students with SED. *Behavioral Disorders, 23,* 243–256.

McConaughy, S. H., & Skiba, R. J. (1994). Comorbidity of externalizing and interalizing problems. *School Psychology Review, 22,* 421–436.

McDougall, D., & Brady, M. P. (1995). Using audio-cued self-monitoring for students with severe behavior disorders. *Journal of Educational Research, 88,* 309–317.

McEvoy, A., & Welker, R. (2000). Antisocial behavior, academic behavior, and school climate: A critical review. *Journal of Emotional and Behavioral Disorders, 8,* 130–140.

Meadows, N. B., Neel, R. S., Scott, C. M., & Parker, G. (1994). Academic performance, social competence, and mainstream accommodations: A look at mainstreamed and non-mainstreamed students with serious behavioral disorders. *Behavioral Disorders, 19,* 170–180.

Mercer, C. D., & Mercer, A. R. (2005). *Teaching students with learning problems* (7th ed.). Upper Saddle River, NJ: Pearson.

Meyer, M. S., & Felton, R. H. (1999). Repeated reading to enhance fluency: Old approaches and new directions. *Annals of Dyslexia, 49,* 283–306.

Mooney, P., Epstein, M. H., Reid, R., & Nelson, J. R. (2003). Status and trends of academic intervention research for students with emotional disturbance. *Remedial and Special Education, 24,* 273–287.

Mooney, P., Ryan, J. B., Uhing, B. M., Reid, R., & Epstein, M. H. (2005). A review of self-management interventions targeting academic outcomes for students with emotional and behavioral disorders. *Journal of Behavioral Education, 14,* 203–221.

Moses, R. P., & Cobb, C. E. (2001). *Radical equations: Math literacy and civil rights.* Boston: Beacon.

National Academy of Sciences. (1998). *Preventing reading difficulties in young children.* Washington, DC: National Academy Press.

National Center on Student Progress Monitoring. (2007). *What is progress monitoring?* Retrieved January 15, 2007, from *www.studentprogressmonitoring.org.*

National Council of Teachers of Mathematics. (2006). *Principles and standards for school mathematics.* Reston, VA: National Council of Teachers of Mathematics.

National Reading Panel. (2000). *Teaching children to read: An evidence-based assessment of the scientific research literature on reading and its implications for reading instruction.* Bethesda, MD: National Institute of Child Health and Human Development, National Institutes of Health.

National Research Council. (2001). *Adding it up: Helping children learn mathematics* (J. Kilpatrick, J. Swafford, & B. Findell, Eds.). Mathematics Learning Study Committee, Center for Education, Division of Behavioral and Social Sciences and Education. Washington, DC: National Academies Press.

National Research Council. (2002). *Scientific research in education* (R. J. Shavelson & L. Towne, Eds.). Committee on Scientific Principles for Educational Research. Washington, DC: National Academies Press.

National Research Council. (2004). *Learning and instruction: A SERP research agenda. Panel on learning and instruction* (M. S. Donovan & J. W. Pellegrino, Eds.). Division of Behavioral and Social Sciences and Education. Washington, DC: National Academies Press.

National Research Council. (2005). *How students learn: History, mathematics, and science in the classroom. Committee on How People Learn, a targeted report for teachers* (M. S. Donovan &

J. D. Bransford, Eds.). Division of Behavioral and Social Sciences and Education. Washington, DC: National Academies Press.

Nelson, J. R., Benner, G. H., & Cheney, D. A. (2005). An investigation of the language skills of students with emotional disturbance served in public school settings. *Journal of Special Education, 39,* 97–105.

Nelson, J. R., Benner, G. H., & Gonzalez, J. E. (2005). An investigation of the effects of a prereading intervention on the early literacy skills of children at risk of emotional disturbance and reading problems. *Journal of Emotional and Behavioral Disorders, 13,* 3–12.

Nelson, J. R., Benner, G. H., Lane, K., & Smith, B. (2004). Academic skills of K–12 students with emotional and behavioral disorders. *Exceptional Children, 71,* 59–73.

Nelson, J. R., Benner, G. H., Neil, S., & Stage, S. (2006). The interrelationships among language skills, externalizing behavior, and academic fluency and their impact on the academic skills of students with emotional disturbance. *Journal of Emotional and Behavioral Disorders, 14,* 209–216.

Nelson, J. R., & Roberts, M. L. (2000). Ongoing reciprocal teacher–student interactions involving disruptive behaviors in general education classrooms. *Journal of Emotional and Behavioral Disorders, 8,* 27–38.

Nelson, J. R., Stage, S. A., Duppong-Hurley, K., Synhorst, L., & Epstein, M. H. (2007). Risk factors predictive of the problem behavior of children at risk for emotional and behavioral disorders. *Exceptional Children, 73,* 367–379.

Nelson, J. R., Stage, S. A., Epstein, M. H., & Pierce, C. D. (2005). Effects of a prereading intervention on the literacy and social skills of children. *Exceptional Children, 72,* 29–45.

O'Shaughnessy, T. E., Lane, K. L., Gresham, F. M., & Beebe-Frankenberger, M. E. (2003). Children placed at risk for learning and behavioral difficulties: Implementing a schoolwide system of early identification and intervention. *Remedial and Special Education, 24,* 27–35.

Owens, R. E. (2001). *Language development: An introduction* (5th ed.). Needham Heights, MA: Simon & Schuster.

Patterson, G. (1995). Coercion as a basis for early age of onset for arrest. In J. McCord (Ed.), *Coercion and punishment in long-term perspectives* (pp. 81–105). New York: Cambridge University Press.

Penno, D. A., Frank, A. R., & Wacker, D. P. (2000). Instructional accommodations for adolescent students with severe emotional or behavioral disorders. *Behavioral Disorders, 25,* 325–343.

Perie, M., Grigg, W., & Dion, G. (2005). *The nation's report card: Mathematics 2005 (NCES2006-453).* U.S. Department of Education, National Center for Education Statistics. Washington, DC: U.S. Government Printing Office.

Pierce, C. D., Reid, R., & Epstein, M. H. (2004). Teacher mediated interventions for children with emotional and behavioral disorders and their academic outcomes: A review. *Remedial and Special Education, 25,* 175–188.

Powell-Smith, K. A., & Shinn, M. R. (2004). *Administration and scoring of written expression curriculum-based measurement (WE-CBM) for use in general outcome measurement.* Eden Prairie, MN: Edformation. Retrieved from *www.aimsweb.com.*

Pressley, M., Burkell, J., Cariglia-Bull, T., Lysynchuk, L., McGoldrick, J. A., Schneider, B., et al. (1995). *Cognitive strategy instruction* (2nd ed.). Cambridge, MA: Brookline Books.

Raudenbush, S. (2002). *Scientifically-based research": U.S. Department of Education seminar on scientifically-based research.* Washington, DC: U.S. Department of Education.

Reid, R., & Lienemann, T. O. (2006). *Strategy instruction for students with learning disabilities.* New York: Guilford Press.

Rosenshine, B. V., & Stevens, R. (1986). Teaching functions. In M. C. Wittrock (Ed.), *Handbook of research on teaching* (3rd ed., pp. 376–391). New York: Macmillan.

Ruhl, K. L., Hughes, C. A., & Camarata, S. M. (1992). Analysis of the expressive and receptive language characteristics of emotionally handicapped students served in public school settings. *Journal of Childhood Communication Disorders, 14,* 165–176.

Ryan, J. B., Reid, R., & Epstein, M. H. (2004). A review of peer-mediated intervention studies on academic achievement for students with emotional and behavioral disorders. *Remedial and Special Education, 25,* 330–341.

Salvia, J., Ysseldyke, J., & Bolt, S. (2007). *Assessment in special and inclusive education* (10th ed.). Boston: Houghton Mifflin.

Santangelo, T., Harris, K. R., & Graham, S. (2007). Self-regulated strategy development: A validated model to support students who struggle with writing. *Learning Disabilities: A Contemporary Journal, 5*(1), 1–20.

Scruggs, T. E., & Mastropieri, M. A. (1986). Academic characteristics of behaviorally disordered and learning disabled students. *Behavioral Disorders, 11,* 184–190.

Scruggs, T. E., Mastropieri, M. A., & Tolfa-Veit, D. (1986). The effects of coaching on standardized test performance of learning disabled and behaviorally disordered students. *Remedial and Special Education, 7,* 37–41.

Shapiro, E. S., & Kratochwill, T. R. (Eds.). (2000). *Conducting school-based assessments of child and adolescent behavior.* New York: Guilford Press.

Shinn, M. R. (1989). *Curriculum-based measurement: Assessing special children.* New York: Guilford Press.

Shinn, M. R. (2004). *Administration and scoring of mathematics computation curriculum-based measurement (M-CBM) and math fact probes for use with AIMSweb.* Eden Prairie, MN: Edformation. Retrieved from *www.aimsweb.com.*

Shinn, M. R., & Shinn, M. M. (2002). *Administration and scoring of spelling curriculum-based measurement (S-CBM) for use in general outcome measurement.* Eden Prairie, MN: Edformation. Retrieved from *www.aimsweb.com.*

Silbert, J., Carnine, D., & Stein, M. (1981). *Direct instruction mathematics.* Columbus, OH: Merrill.

Skinner, C. H., Bamberg, H. W., Smith, E. S., & Powell, S. S. (1993). Cognitive cover, copy, and compare: Subvocal responding to increase rates of accurate division responding. *Remedial and Special Education, 14,* 49–56.

Skinner, C. H., Ford, J. M., & Yunker, B. D. (1991). A comparison of instructional response requirements on the multiplication performance of behaviorally disordered students. *Behavioral Disorders, 17,* 56–65.

Skinner, C. H., Turco, T. L., Beatty, K. L., & Rasavage, C. (1989). Cover, copy, and compare: A method for increasing multiplication performance. *School Psychology Review, 18,* 412–420.

Smith, D. D., & Lovitt, T. C. (1982). *The computational arithmetic program.* Austin, TX: PRO-ED.

Snider, V. E., & Crawford, D. (2004). Mathematics. In N. E. Marchand-Martella, T. A. Slocum, & R. C. Martella (Eds.), *Introduction to direct instruction* (pp. 206–245). Boston: Pearson Education.

Social Security Administration. (2006). *Benefits for children with disabilities.* Retrieved November, 2006, from *www.socialsecurity.gov.*

Stein, S., & Merrell, K. W. (1992). Differential perceptions of multidisciplinary team members: Seriously emotionally disturbed vs. socially maladjusted. *Psychology in the Schools, 29,* 320–330.

Sugai, G., Sprague, J. R., Horner, R. H., & Walker, H. M. (2000). Preventing school violence: The use of office discipline referrals to assess and monitor school-wide discipline inter-ventions. *Journal of Emotional and Behavioral Disorders, 8,* 94–101.

Sullivan, E. B. (1927). Age, intelligence, and educational achievement of boys entering Whittier State School. *Journal of Delinquency, 11,* 23–38.

Swartz, S. L., Mosley, W. J., & Koenig-Jerz, G. (1987). *Diagnosing behavior disorders: An analy-sis of state definitions, eligibility criteria and recommended procedures.* Chicago: Council for Exceptional Children.

Toppelberg, C. O., & Shapiro, T. (2000). Language disorders: A 10–year research update review. *Journal of the American Academy of Child and Adolescent Psychiatry, 39,* 143–152.

Trout, A. L., Epstein, M. H., Mickelson, W. T., Nelson, J. R., & Lewis, L. M. (2003). Effects of a reading intervention for kindergarten students at-risk of emotional disturbance and reading deficits. *Behavioral Disorders, 28,* 313–326.

U.S. Department of Education. (2002). *Twenty-fourth annual report to Congress on the imple-mentation of the education of the handicapped act.* Washington, DC: U.S. Government Print-ing Office.

U.S. Department of Education. (2004). *Individuals with Disabilities Education Act.* Washington, DC: Author.

U.S. Department of Education, Office of the Under Secretary. (2002). *No child left behind: A desktop reference.* Washington, DC: Author.

U.S. Department of Health and Human Services. (1999). *A report of the Surgeon General.* Rockville, MD: U.S. Public Health Service.

Vaughn, S., Levy, S., Coleman, M., & Bos, C. S. (2002). Reading instruction for students with LD and EBD: A synthesis of observation studies. *Journal of Special Education, 36,* 2–13.

Vaughn, S., & Linan-Thompson, S. (2004). *Research-based methods of reading instruction: Grades K–3.* Alexandria, VA: Association for Supervision and Curriculum Development.

Wagner, M. M. (1995). Outcomes for youths with serious emotional disturbance in second-ary school and early adulthood. *The Future of Children: Critical Issues for Children and Youths, 5,* 90–112.

Wagner, M. M., Kutash, K., Duchnowski, A. J., Epstein, M. H., & Sumi C. (2005). The chil-dren and youth we serve: A national picture of the characteristics of students with emotional disturbances receiving special education. *Journal of Emotional and Behavioral Disorders, 13,* 79–96.

Walker, H. M., Colvin, G., & Ramsey, E. (1995). Antisocial behavior in school: Strategies and best practices. Pacific Grove, CA: Brooks/Cole.

Walker, H. M., & Severson, H. (1990). *Systematic Screening for Behavior Disorders* (SSBD). Longmont, CO: Sopris West.

Walker, H. M., & Severson, H. H. (1992). *Systematic Screening for Behavior Disorders: Technical manual.* Longmont, CO: Sopris West.

Warr-Leeper, G., Wright, N. A., & Mack, A. (1994). Language disabilities of antisocial boys in residential treatment. *Behavior Disorders, 19,* 159–169.

Wehby, J. H., Falk, K. B., Barton-Arwood, S., Lane, K. L., & Cooley, C. (2003). The impact of comprehensive reading instruction on the academic and social behavior of students with emotional and behavioral disorders. *Journal of Emotional and Behavioral Disorders, 11,* 225–238.

Wehby, J. H., Symons, F. J., & Hollo, A. (1997). Promote appropriate assessment. *Journal of Emotional and Behavioral Disorders, 5,* 45–54.

Wilson, L., Cone, T., Bradley, C., & Reese, J. (1986). The characteristics of learning disabled and other handicapped students referred for evaluation in the state of Iowa. *Journal of Learning Disabilities, 19,* 553–557.

Wright Group/McGroup. (1999). *Corrective reading decoding A: Presentation manual.* New York: McGraw-Hill.

Wright Group/McGraw-Hill. (2003). *Reading mastery I, 2002 classic edition: Teacher presentation book C.* New York: McGraw-Hill.

Yell, M. L., & Stecker, P. M. (2003). Developing legally correct and educationally meaningful IEPs using curriculum-based measurement. *Assessment for Effective Instruction, 28,* 73–88.

Ysseldyke, J. E., & Algozzine, B. (1995). *Special education: A practical approach for teachers* (3rd ed.). Boston: Houghton Mifflin.

Zimmerman, B., & Risemberg, R. (1997). Becoming a self-regulated writer: A social–cognitive perspective. *Contemporary Educational Psychology, 22,* 73–101.

Index

"f" following a page number indicates a figure;
"t" following a page number indicates a table.